SOCIAL PSYCHOLOGY AND WORLD PEACE:
A PRIMER

Social Psychology and World Peace: A Primer

Editors:
Halford H. Fairchild, Ph.D.
and
Heather Feigá Fairchild, Esq.

Foreword By:
Theresa Bonpane and Blase Bonpane

Indo American Books
2261, Ground Floor, Hudson Line,
Kingsway Camp, Delhi-110 009 (INDIA)
E-mail: sales@iabooks.com, www.iabooks.com

Book Team
President : Vijay Sharma
Sr. Vice President : Puneet Singh (London)
Vice President : Kanika Sharma (London)
Pre-Press : P. K. Mishra
Vice-President Marketing : Agnel Henry
Editorial : Sunil Dutt

I S B N : 93-82661-56-5

Digitally Printed & Published in India by
Indo American Books
2261, Ground Floor, Hudson Line, Kingsway Camp
Delhi 110009, INDIA. Ph.: 91-011-42870094
Email: sales@iabooks.com
Website: www.iabooks.com

Dedication

For future generations:

May you live in Peace.

Halford H. Fairchild, Ph.D.

Heather Feigá Fairchild, Esq.

Culver City, CA

March, 2018

Let us not deceive ourselves;

We must elect world peace or world destruction.

~ Bernard Baruch

We believe in peace.

We believe in the way of love.

~ Congressman John Robert Lewis

Table of Contents

Foreword

The Greatest International Crime is War

THERESA BONPANE AND BLASE BONPANE

OFFICE OF THE AMERICAS

For over a half a century, our lives have been dedicated to ending our nation's role as the world's most virulent killing machine. Some thirty million people have been killed by our government since the end of World War II.

We visited legislators, demonstrated, practiced civil disobedience and were arrested many times. We have lived in solidarity with the oppressed people of Latin America. We have spoken out on every form of independent media and, at times, on commercial media.

The response of the U.S. government can be translated as: "We don't care what you and your kind want. We want perpetual war." During the Cold War, many called us communists. Today, we are even labelled as *terrorists*, in spite of the fact that our methods are non-violent.

The war system and its weapons of nuclear biocide can be abolished. We must repent of the war system as Germany repented of Nazism. What is required is a *new internationalism*.

We live on a tiny planet with a single system of breathable air, one interconnected ocean and a shared environmental future. No one on Earth can live in isolation from environmental disaster.

We must end war to save the natural environment. Militaries, even during times of peace, are the greatest polluters on the planet.

Militaries at war and life on this planet are simply incompatible.

The U.S. and others have deployed nuclear weapons every year since the 1945 obliterations of Hiroshima and Nagasaki. Thousands of nuclear bombs circle the Earth in the U.S.'s "nuclear triad" — land, sea and air. They are used the same way bank thieves rob a bank without pulling the trigger. It is a miracle that we have not yet experienced a nuclear catastrophe.

We can look at violence from its most basic level (interpersonal and family relationships). We can look at it from the top, including the imminent danger of nuclear biocide. We can look at it from our national behavior and the religion of "American Exceptionalism."

Our focus has been ending or reducing government violence, yet those who focus on personal and interpersonal peace are completely justified. We diverge for different reasons, nevertheless our objective of peaceful coexistence is the same.

Violence begets violence. The Crusaders massacred the inhabitants of Mosul in 1098 AD. The Muslim leader Saladin took Aleppo from the Crusaders in 1185 AD and proclaimed jihad against the Crusader States. The U.S.'s wanton bombing of Laos and Cambodia gave rise to the fanatic governance of Pol Pot. So, too, the U.S.'s unrestrained bombing in Afghanistan and Iraq led to the birth of ISIS, which is reminiscent of the 11th Century "Crusader States" in the Levant.[1]

The *Bible's* Old Testament is replete with killing in the name of religion. "God's" people are permitted to kill "Infidels." Time and time again, religious justifications have cloaked malice and promoted violence.

Manipulating God for political purposes should be abhorrent to any moral person. The idea that "God is on our side" to justify killing others is a charade that must be exposed and rejected.

Violence comes in many forms. Institutional violence is often part of political systems. A lack of distributive justice is an act of violence. A lack of livable wages is violence. Police brutality is institutional violence. A vindictive, punitive prison system in the United States holds more than 25% of the globe's prisoners, mostly poor people of color. It is *carceral violence.*

---

[1] Levant is a geographical/historical term referring to a large area in the Eastern Mediterranean. Described by some as the "crossroads of Western Asia, the Eastern Mediterranean and Northeast Africa," today, Levant is employed to refer to modern events in, and the people of, Cyprus, Egypt, Iraq, Israel, Jordan, Lebanon, Palestine, Syria and Turkey.

False patriotism glorifies war, which our founders called the last refuge of scoundrels. Aggressive war makers do not communicate and do not practice diplomacy.

In 1991, I (Blase) was part of a delegation to Baghdad and spent five hours talking to Yasser Arafat. Yet our government forbade the U.S. Ambassador to the United Nations to speak to Arafat – the one person who could have mediated peace in Iraq. Massive bombing of the people of Iraq followed within days of our visit.

Taxation without representation remains as much of a problem today as it was in 1776. As citizens, we have literally no say on how our tax dollars are spent. The average member of Congress pays no attention to the majority of his or her constituents. We, and millions of others, are opposed to spending trillions of dollars to "modernize" nuclear warfare. We, and most Americans, do not approve of perpetual war in the Middle East or anywhere else.

NATO, created to circumvent the United Nations, has become an international threat to peace. The byproducts of our war system are the one million homeless people living on our streets, a flawed system of medical and mental health care, and the costs of higher education are out of the reach for the average family.

The greatest international crime is aggressive war. Yet war is normalized by the billions of public relations dollars spent to influence public opinion. This propaganda, and the war itself, is paid for by the American taxpayer.

We are living in a time of clear and present danger. We are also witnessing a great awakening of our people. The 2016 U.S. presidential campaign of Senator Bernie Sanders was one of the greatest expressions of people power in U.S. history. The movement ignited by that campaign is just beginning. Violence will diminish as we practice the democratic socialism advocated by this historic campaign.

This is the beginning of an era of activism in which no one can afford to be a mere spectator. The threats we face are the most severe in human history. Guided by the legacy of Dr. Martin Luther King, Jr., we must apply the power of non-violent disobedience, massive demonstrations, boycotts, divestments and sanctions. Those who are socially conscious must enter electoral politics.

Movements for peace are forming all around. We must band together with like-minded people to move our world toward peace and non-violence.

Theresa and Blase Bonpane
Founders, Office of the Americas
www.officeoftheamericas.org

Editors' Biographical Notes:
Who are Blase and Theresa Bonpane?

Blase Bonpane, considered by many the vanguard of liberation theology, and Theresa Bonpane have dedicated their lives to protecting human rights of the oppressed and promoting world peace.

The seeds of peace were sown during Blase's youth and led him to the seminary, where he was ordained a Maryknoll[1] priest. His activism blossomed while working as a missionary in Guatemala, in the midst of a violent revolution. While advocating for the rights of indigenous people on issues of health, education and literacy, and labor organization; Blase became an outspoken critic of the human rights abuses he witnessed, including U.S. funded military's genocide of the indigenous Mayan population. That unflinchingly honest and frank commentary earned him the reputation of subversive and agitator, resulting in his expulsion from Guatemala in 1967. The Maryknoll Fathers of the Catholic Church also censured Blase with a gag-order, preventing him from voicing public disagreement and criticisms of U.S. involvement in the Guatemalan civil war.

Blase, knowing his conscience would not allow him to abandon the people of Guatemala or be silent about the atrocities he witnessed, defied the Church's order and contacted the media. He met with journalists from the *Washington Post* and released material he gathered about the U.S. military's involvement in Guatemala[2]–leading to his separation from the Maryknoll Fathers.

Undaunted, Blase continued to pursue social justice efforts throughout Latin America. Meanwhile in 1969, he accepted a teaching position at California State University, Los Angeles. It was there that he met former Maryknoll Sister, Theresa Killeen, who had recently returned from a mission in Talcahuano, Chile, where she served as a high school principal. Theresa shared his passion for social justice and commitment to a life of peace activism. They married in 1970 and were blessed with two children, Colleen Marie and Blase Martin.

---

[1]. Maryknollers, also known as "Marines of the Catholic Church," are missionaries devoted to social justice and advancing peace for all. They often live and work side-by-side with indigenous populations of impoverished countries to combat poverty, provide healthcare and education and uplift communities.

[2]. Washington Post, February 4, 1968, "A Priest in Guatemala."

Yet even with the rigors or raising a family, Blase and Theresa's commitment to human rights and improving the lives of indigenous people all over the world never wavered or diminished. They have worked on the ground for international peace initiatives in Mexico, Guatemala, El Salvador, Nicaragua, Costa Rica, Honduras, Panama, Colombia, Ecuador, Cuba, Japan and Iraq.

In 1983, Blase and Theresa founded the Office of the Americas, a non-profit organization dedicated to furthering the cause of international social justice and peace through broad-based educational programs including lectures, press conferences and radio and television commentary. The Office of the Americas' mission is to end the long-standing international culture of militarism. To that end, the Office of the Americas endeavors to educate the public and religious and social justice organizations about human rights issues, specifically by exposing those who commit crimes against humanity and holding them accountable – which necessarily includes identifying the illegal and immoral aspects of United States' domestic and foreign policy.

The Office of the Americas disseminates its message and scholarship via mainstream and independent media (including press conferences, television and radio commentary and lectures). It also publishes "Blase Bonpane Reports" and produces *World Focus* for the Pacifica Radio Network, which is broadcast on KPFK, Los Angeles (90.7 FM).

The Office of Americas created *World Focus* with the goal of shedding light on critical issues generally ignored by commercial media. In each episode, Blase interviews some of the brightest intellectuals and activists of our time and offers a fresh, critical perspective of U.S. foreign policy and its role in the many 'unnecessary' wars since the end of World War II. While regular guests include internationally renowned social critics like Noam Chomsky, Chris Hedges, Oliver Stone and Seymour Hersh; *World Focus* also features local activists discussing their current work. Written transcripts and audio versions of each episode are available for free at www.OfficeoftheAmericas.org.

Today, Blase and Theresa continue to work tirelessly for social justice and promote peace.

Notes

Blase Bonpane received his Ph.D. in Social Science from University of California, Irvine in 1984. He has served on the faculties of the University of California, Los Angeles; California State University, Northridge; and California State University, Los Angeles.

Theresa Killeen Bonpane earned her bachelor of education degree from Mary Rogers College at Maryknoll, New York. She pursued her postgraduate studies at California State University, Los Angeles; the University of California, Los Angeles; and the University of California, Santa Barbara.

Preface

On the Origins and Purposes of This Book

HALFORD H. FAIRCHILD, PH.D.

AND HEATHER FEIGÁ FAIRCHILD, ESQ.

It is not enough to say, "we must not wage war." It is necessary to love peace and sacrifice for it. We must concentrate not merely on the negative expulsion of war, but on the positive affirmation of peace.

~ Martin Luther King, Jr.

This book presents strategies for World Peace derived from the research, theory, and practice of social psychology.

In the teaching of Social Psychology at Pitzer College in Spring 2016, Halford tasked his students with applying concepts and ideas from the text, *Principles of Social Psychology – 1st International Edition* (Jhangiani & Tarry, 2014), to the problem of World Peace.

Students considered World Peace on many levels – from intra-individual to international and global – so their efforts reflect a wide range of concerns.

This preface describes the inspirations that beget this book: intellectual traditions in African American studies; Paulo Freire's *Pedagogy of the Oppressed*; and the horrific cases of violence that permeated the news for the past several years.

Geneses

This book is the product of many influences. On some levels, it is built upon the activist philosophy and research of W.E.B. DuBois (*Souls of*

Black Folk) and Carter G. Woodson (*Miseducation of the Negro*). The seminal works of these African American scholars influenced our thinking long after they had died.

Paulo Freire's *Pedagogy of the Oppressed* challenged educators to make students more *producers* of knowledge than *consumers*.

Halford's years as a professor at predominantly White institutions – teaching psychology and African American Studies – taught him that much of conventional orthodoxy in higher education is flawed and should be challenged and discarded.

In the Fall of 2015, Halford was approaching his last year of teaching before early retirement. Heavy on his heart was the senseless slaughter of 20 children and 6 teachers at Sandy Hook Elementary School; the 9 African American parishioners murdered during *Bible* study on June 17, 2015 at Emanuel African Methodist Episcopal Church in Charleston, South Carolina; and recurrent cases of gun violence, terrorism and war. He challenged his Seminar in Social Psychology to research and produce *(Re)Solving Violence in America* (Fairchild, 2016a).

It was a transformative experience for all involved.

The project imbued our writing a sense of *purpose*. Classroom sessions were writing workshops. We read and critiqued each other's drafts. The book project gave us a *mission*, a desire to make a difference in the world.

In Halford's final semester of teaching (he retired from Pitzer College on June 30, 2016), he decided to replicate the success of *(Re)Solving Violence*. He came to the conclusion that this was the *correct* purpose of higher education: to challenge students to be *producers* of knowledge; to provide them with the requisite tools and methods; and to then give them the feedback, help and support to become *effective* writers.

In Spring 2016, Halford taught two classes: Introduction to African American Psychology and Social Psychology. The former class produced *Black Lives Matter: Lifespan Perspectives* (Fairchild, 2017a), the latter class produced *Social Psychology and World Peace: A Primer*.

During the final editing of this book, Donald J. Trump was inaugurated the 45th President of the United States. This event added a sense of *urgency* to our project as President Trump embodies many of values, attitudes and policies that are antithetical to our pursuit of World Peace.

A World at War

This book was inspired by our angst at the violence and war that has become commonplace throughout the world. *(Re)Solving Violence in America* (Fairchild, 2016a) was also motivated by this concern, and concluded that the resolution of violence in America required the cessation of America's propagation of violence abroad (Fairchild, 2016b).

Dozens of wars are being waged in virtually every corner of the globe. Most of the lives lost in these wars were by weapons made in the U.S.A. The United States has the greatest arsenal of weapons of mass destruction and maintains an omni-present threat of nuclear annihilation over the entire planet.

Worldwide, violence claims more than 1.6 million lives every year – 4,400 lives a day, nearly 200 lives every hour. Terrorism is nearly a daily occurrence, threatens everyone on Earth, and is taking new forms.

On July 14, 2016, a terrorist drove a 19 ton cargo truck through a Bastille Day crowd gathered to watch fireworks in Nice, France. Eighty-six people were killed and hundreds were injured. Six months later, on December 19, 2016, another "truck driving terrorist" plowed through a bustling holiday market in Berlin, Germany, killing twelve and injuring dozens of others.

In November, 2015, a coordinated series of attacks took 137 lives (including 7 of the attackers) in Paris: a bomb at a rock concert, a shooting of patrons at an outdoor restaurant and bar, and suicide bombers at a sports stadium. Six months later, on June 12, 2016, a gunman killed 49 people at a nightclub in Orlando, Florida. Six months after that, a gunman killed 39 people in a nightclub in Istanbul on January 1, 2017.

Unfortunately, these new forms of terrorism cannot be prevented and are easy to imitate.

As much as we abhor the terrorist acts described above (and many others), they pale in comparison to the state-sponsored violence perpetrated by the United States and its allies.

In 2016, the U.S. dropped more than 26,000 bombs against targets in Iraq, Afghanistan, Syria, Yemen, Pakistan, Libya and Somalia (Benjamin, 2017). According to Oakford (2016), the U.S. also exports its weapons of individual and mass destruction. In 2014, U.S. arms sales – to nearly 100 countries – was $36.2 billion dollars (an increase from $26.7 billion the previous year). The U.S. accounts for more than a third of the arms sales worldwide, followed by the Soviet Union. Many members of the European Union – England, France, Sweden, Germany – also sell armaments to war-torn regions of the world.

On "Objectivity"

Most academic disciplines claim to advance theory and research "objectively," without imposing personal or group values or aims on the conduct of academic discourse.

Objectivity requires that the researcher and theorist seek knowledge in a "value-free" manner. But as discussed herein and our companion books, "Anything that is value free is valueless" (Fairchild, 1995).

Many branches of psychology – particularly those representing discriminated against populations (especially ethnic and sexual minorities and women) eschew notions of "objectivity" or the idea that "value-free" is even possible. Instead, non-mainstream approaches recognize that academic pursuits are embedded in value systems that – when unacknowledged – produce flawed outcomes in research, theory and practice.

The entirety of Western academia – its theories, methods and findings – is the product of history. Academia flourished in Europe during the Age of Enlightenment (15th – 18th Centuries) and matured in the New World as the nascent United States expanded to the Pacific Ocean.

Throughout this history, European countries explored and conquered Africa, the Americas, Asia, and the Pacific. During this time, indigenous people were conquered, killed and enslaved.

The acts of inhumanity perpetrated by European and American imperialists required intellectual justifications that were provided in the halls of academe. It is our view that the traditional academic disciplines – social sciences, natural sciences and the humanities – are tainted by these biases.

Objectivity is a myth.

Our Values and Biases

Rather that pretend that this work is "objective," we proclaim our values and biases (at least those within our awareness) so that readers can be informed about how they may have influenced the production of this text.

Our World View

Much of our world view has been articulated above: we understand the present socio-economic order is the product of conquest. That conquest involved clashes of people, cultures, civilizations and races. As noted throughout this text, we view the United States as the prime mover in instigating and perpetuating armed conflicts throughout the world. It is therefore incumbent upon the United States to take a leadership role in transforming its war making policies to the pursuit of World Peace.

Our Values

This book is an affirmation of our willingness to challenge the perspectives and biases of traditional academic disciplines (Fairchild, 2017b). We value American ideals of freedom and equality for all; however, we also recognize that those values have been violated from this nation's founding, in the present, and into the foreseeable future.

Our orientation to scholarship is that it should be consciously pursued in order to solve pressing social problems. We urged the student-contributors to this volume to search for *solutions* to the problems that they identified.

We value life and reject lethal violence as a means to resolve conflict.

Our Biases

The storehouse of knowledge in Euro/American academia is flawed by its embrace of ideologies of White Supremacy, Male Supremacy and Manifest Destiny. These ideologies are deeply implicated in the perpetuation of war.

The social sciences have been notably absent from challenging the *status quo* of structured inequality. Indeed, they have often been *complicit* in creating and maintaining inequality.

Scholarship should produce *improvements* in social relationships. We seek egalitarian gender relationships in all world cultures. We pursue the debunking of White Supremacy and the affirmation of racial equality. We believe that the redistribution of wealth is necessary to ensure the wellbeing of every human being.

We believe that wars are fought to further corporate and financial interests, and, therefore, are never morally justified.

Our Purpose

We strive for a world where all of its people can share the Earth's bounty equally and peacefully co-exist.

An Overview of This Textbook

This book is organized in thirteen parts. The first 12 parts correspond to the organization of a typical social psychology textbook and cover the main topic areas of the field. *Principles of Social Psychology, 1st International Edition* (Jhangiani & Tarry (2014) was selected because of its open access status (free). The first 12 part overviews in the current text parallel the chapter organization of Jhangiani and Tarry (2014) and were written by Halford.

Halford tasked students to write a paper for each of the 12 parts (revised early in the semester to every other part), that could be included in this volume. They were urged to do their best to "make a statement" that would in some way promote World Peace. Students adhered to the *"Fairchild Method for Writing a Review of Literature"* – a step-by-step process for asking a specific question, finding the relevant evidence, and synthesizing it into a coherent paper (Fairchild, 2017c).

Part 13 is a selection of invited papers and two speeches by U.S. President Barack Obama that are especially pertinent to our subject matter.

Sprinkled through the text are several "interludes." These are song lyrics by peace activists in Southern California.

Each chapter concludes with one or more discussion questions. These allow readers to think more deeply about the point of view presented in the chapter. These questions may serve as take-home essay assignments and/or as stimuli for in-class discussion.

References

Benjamin, M. (2017). America dropped 26,171 bombs in 2016. What a bloody end to Obama's reign. *The Guardian* (January 9, 2017). https://www.theguardian.com/commentisfree/2017/jan/09/america-dropped-26171-bombs-2016-obama-legacy

Fairchild, H.H. (1995). Placing Blacks at center of psychology. *Los Angeles Times*, July 31, 1995 (City Times Section, page 12).

Fairchild, H.H. (Ed.). (2016a). *(Re)Solving violence in America*. Delhi: Indo American Books.

Fairchild, H.H. (2016b). (Re)Solving violence in America. Chapter 11 (pp. 87-100) in H.H. Fairchild (Ed.), *(Re)Solving violence in America*. Delhi: Indo American Books.

Fairchild, H.H. (2017a). *Black Lives Matter: Lifespan Perspectives*. Delhi: Indo American Books.

Fairchild, H.H. (2017b). Redefining excellence in higher education. Chapter 5 (pp. 26-29) in H.H. Fairchild (Ed.), *Black Lives Matter: Lifespan Perspectives*. Delhi: Indo American Books.

Fairchild, H.H. (2017c). On the origins of this book. Preface (pp. xxxii – xlii) in H.H. Fairchild (Ed.), *Black Lives Matter: Lifespan Perspectives*. Delhi: Indo American Books.

Jhangiani, R., & Tarry, H. (2014). *Principles of social psychology – 1st international edition*. Licensed under a Creative Commons Attribution-NonCommerical-ShareAlike 4.0 International License.

Oakford, S. (2016). The US is selling weapons to nearly half the countries in the world. *Vice News* (February 22). https://news.vice.com/article/the-us-is-selling-weapons-to-nearly-half-the-countries-in-the-world

First Interlude

Ode to Peace

DENNIS DAVIS

From the pulpit a general raised his hand
Preaching violence against Islam
While his Christian soldiers marched on and on
Through his killing field in the name of his God
But, "Thou Shall Not Kill"

Let the war be done, let the peace be won
Let the war be done, let the peace be won...Now!

Mothers, daughters and children flee
His advancing army of liberty
His sword so swift with death's indifference
In his torture prisons shackled innocents
But the souls of those he's trampled upon
Won't rest until his bloody crown
Of hate and fear lie buried in the ground

Heal the victims of this war
The mother's loss of the child she bore
Heal the father's sorrow and restlessness
A sister's longing, heal her emptiness
Heal the weeping widow veiled in black
She knows her man won't be coming back
Heal the broken hearted wipe away the tears
Heal the soldier's wounds and the children's fear
Heal the shattered lives and tattered family ties
Let the wars be done, let the peace be won now
Let the wars be done ...live in peace as one...Now!

Part 1
The ABCs of Social Psychology Definition, History and Methods

Defining Social Psychology

Social psychology locates behavior within its social context. Jhangiani and Tarry (2014) defined social psychology as "...the scientific study of how we feel about, think about, and behave toward the people around us; and how our feelings, thoughts, and behaviors are influenced by those people" (p. 13). Social psychology is the scientific study of reciprocal social influences.

Social psychologists generally contemplate social influences in terms of the "ABCs": Affects (emotions), Behaviors (or behavioral intentions) and Cognitions (thoughts and attitudes).

The History of Social Psychology

Many historians of social psychology point to Triplett's early study (1898) on social influence: when people performed simple tasks, such as reeling in the line on a fishing rod, their performance was more energetic when they were observed by others.

One noted social psychologist (Aronson, 1999), suggested that Aristotle was the world's "first" published social psychologist by virtue of his alleged writings:

> "More than 300 years b.c., Aristotle, the world's first published social psychologist, wrote: 'We believe good men more fully and more readily than others...'" (Aronson, 1999, The Social Animal (8th Ed), p. 74.)[1]

Much of the early empirical work in social psychology was in the area of attitudes: what they are, how they are measured, how they might be

---

[1] This attribution is an instance of cultural appropriation (James, 1954/1992). At least two thousand years before Aristotle, Egyptian scholars wrote elaborate stories and philosophies that explored social relationships.

changed? Emory Bogardus (1925) was among the first to develop a scale to measure the "social distance" that people felt toward other national or racial groups. This early concern with inter-group attitudes and relations was a hallmark of American social psychology.

Social psychology's embrace of taking positions on controversial social issues was concretized in the formation of the Society for the Psychological Study of Social Issues (SPSSI) in 1936 (www.spssi.org.) Since its founding, SPSSI has devoted its attention to the problems of war and peace, racial prejudice and discrimination, gender inequalities, sexuality, environmental issues, and social justice.

Evolutionary Influences

Unfortunately, evolutionary perspectives have been increasingly influential in all areas of psychology. Evolutionary psychology figures prominently in Jhangiani and Tarry (2014), and suffers the problems that derive from irrefutable theorizing and teleological reasoning. Buss (2014), for example, argued that jealousy in men was evolutionarily adaptive because it enhanced their reproductive success. Jhangiani and Tarry (2014) suggested that these evolutionary pressures led to hostility and violence as being the norm in human affairs. Similarly, Bloom and Dess (2003) devoted an entire text to evolutionary explanations for homicide, rape and other acts of interpersonal violence.

A full critique of the evolutionary perspective is beyond the scope of this volume. However, due to its increasing prominence in the social sciences, it deserves close scrutiny for the following reasons:

1. As noted above, evolutionary thinking invokes irrefutable theorizing. One of the most hallowed principles of scientific methods is that hypotheses and theories be testable. When theories or hypotheses are testable, they may be proven or disproven. Evolutionary thinking is irrefutable because its theorizing is inherently *expost facto*. The evolutionary "explanation" is one in which the *theory always fit the data*.

2. Evolutionary thinking is teleological, wherein the end results are viewed as purposively driven. In this sense, evolutionary explanations "explain everything" because all extant behaviors have "survival value." (If they did not have survival value, those behaviors would have been extinguished through natural selection.) By this way of thinking, *everything* is due to evolution. Hindsight is 100%.

3. Evolutionary theories are untestable. Evolutionary processes occur over tens of thousands of years; we have no methodological tools – or patience – to assess the veracity of evolutionary theory.

4. Evolutionary theory embraces a decidedly *naturist perspective*. The long-standing *nature vs. nurture* debate has been solved: contemporary psychologists overwhelmingly agree that human behavior is the product of the *interaction* of nature *and* nurture. Evolutionary theory relies too heavily on the naturist point of view that attributes human behavior to genetically determined proclivities passed down the generations through the process of natural selection.

5. The *naturist perspective* gives evolutionary thinking a sense of *inevitability*. Human beings are mere puppets, in a sense, of their DNA inheritance.

6. The sense of inevitability robs us of our sense of *human agency*. If we are violent or aggressive because of the battle of the genes, then we are necessarily challenged to control these inborn instincts.

7. The idea that DNA seeks its replication imbues these molecules with motivation and intentionality. At its heart, evolutionary thinking embraces anthropomorphic reasoning: attributing human motivations to molecules of DNA.

8. Evolutionary theory relies heavily on *magical thinking*. For example, it is said that one reason people mate with attractive partners is because it gives their DNA the best chance to procreate. (Attractive people are presumed to be healthier and, therefore, more likely to successfully reproduce.) Exactly how do DNA molecules detect these reproductive probabilities? How does DNA communicate with the rest of the sense systems – eyes, ears, etc. – in making these mating choices?

9. Evolutionary thinking and scientific racism are constant bedfellows. The idea of "survival of the fittest" has been used to justify the racial caste system that has characterized the world's social order for hundreds, if not thousands, of years. One of the more odious examples of this thinking was articulated in *The Bell Curve* (Herrnstein & Murray, 1994).

10. The concept of *survival of the fittest* often serves as a justification for inter-group conflict, violence and war.

Evolutionary explanations pervade every chapter of Jhangiani and Tarry (2014). Evolutionary perspectives appear to be ascendant in the social sciences, with several journals devoted to the topic. A PsychInfo search of "evolutionary psychology" conducted on January 5, 2017 yielded 7,091 citations. The first of these was Herbert Spencer's textbook published in 1872. Table 1 shows the number of articles relevant to evolutionary psychology from 1872 to the end of 2016.

Table 1

Articles in Evolutionary Psychology from 1872 to 2016

Time Period	# of Citations
1872 – 1980	249
1980 – 1989	239
1990 – 1999	405
2000 – 2009	2,901
2010 – 2016	3,274
Total	7,068

Although we do not doubt the veracity of Darwinian theory when applied to the evolution of species; its application to explain differences in outcomes for human beings is problematic. Indeed, the *survival of the fittest* idea is deeply implicated in justifications for inequality and war. As such, the debunking of Social Darwinism is a recurrent theme in the current text.

Situational Influences

From its inception, social psychology has recognized the interaction between the person and the situation. Kurt Lewin, one of the pioneers in the field, distilled this idea with the equation, "Behavior $= f$ (person, social situation)" (Jhangiani & Tarry, 2014, p. 17).

Conducting Research in Social Psychology

Research in social psychology utilizes a variety of methods and, throughout this text, we imagine ways that research might be applied to the problems that serve as obstacles to World Peace.

Archival studies explore research questions by tapping into an existing – that is, archived – dataset. These datasets exist for virtually every research topic imaginable. By their nature, archival studies are most suitable to correlational analyses.

Observational studies in social psychology are often conducted in schools or other institutional settings where observers make unobtrusive recordings of interactions of interest.

Case studies report on a specific incident, such as a case of suicide or the background and circumstances of a mass shooting.

Survey research involves the collection of questionnaire data from a sample, randomly chosen, to represent a larger population (for example, a sample of voters). Survey research is also *correlational*, in that researchers can only assess how variables co-vary.

Experimental research enables the researcher to reach *cause and effect* conclusions because an *independent variable* is manipulated to produced changes in some outcome variable, also known as the *dependent variable*.

The Myth of Objectivity

All research and theory is conducted within a certain socio-political context. Researchers occupy different positions within the social order and therefore have a number of inescapable biases in the conduct of their work. This book is no exception. However, rather than adhere to a myth of objectivity, we affirmed each author's subjective point of view. We urged contributors to proclaim their values and to be solution-oriented in our quest for World Peace.

This issue is explored in more detail in the Preface, which also presents the subjectivities of the editors. To summarize, we view the problem of global violence as emanating from the nation-state. In particular, Western power has been consolidated in the United States; and the U.S. is the greatest purveyor of violence in the world. As such, it is incumbent on the U.S. to exercise its moral authority and economic power to cease the practice of war and lead other countries in the quest for World Peace.

We anticipate that our point of view may be at odds with many readers. Some may perceive our position as anti-American or treasonous. Yet it is love for our country and humanity that motivates our critique of American militarism and foreign policy.

Chapter Overviews

In the following chapters, contributors explore a number of applications of social psychology's history and methods to achieve World Peace.

Chapter 1 (*Evolutionary Psychology and World Peace* by Nick Abreu) critiques evolutionary approaches to understanding conflict. Abreu argues that these pessimistic approaches deny free will and human agency.

Chapter 2 (*Peace in Dorm Life* by Earl M. Schultz) explores the social challenges of dorm life in residential colleges. Shultz suggests that collectivism may promote peaceful interpersonal relationships.

Chapter 3 (*Seeking World Peace Through Global Citizenship* by Samuel Martin) compares and contrasts individualism and collectivism. To achieve World Peace, Martin encourages us to develop our identity as a global citizen.

Chapter 4 (*Collectivism Preserves Peace* by Sasha Forbath) makes a connection between competition and violence. Forbath decries the epidemic of gun violence and recommends establishing new norms for the non-violent resolution of conflict.

Chapter 5 (*A Research Program for World Peace* by Halford H. Fairchild, Ph.D.) describes how various methodologies (case studies, surveys and experiments) may be applied to the pursuit of World Peace. Fairchild calls for a comprehensive research program for World Peace.

References

Aronson, E. (1999). *The social animal* (8th Edition). NY: Worth Publishers.

Bloom, R.W., & Dess, N. (Eds.). (2003). *Evolutionary psychology and violence.* Westport, CT and London: Praeger.

Bogardus, E. S. (1926). Social Distance in the City. *Proceedings and Publications of the American Sociological Society. 20*, 40–46.

Buss, D.M. (2014). Comment: Evolutionary criteria for considering an emotion 'basic': Jealousy as an illustration. *Emotion Review, 6*(4), 313-315.

Herrnstein, R., & Murray, C. (1994). *The bell curve: Intelligence and class structure in American life.* NY: Free Press.

Jhangiani, R., & Tarry, H. (2014). *Principles of social psychology – 1st international edition.* Licensed under a Creative Commons Attribution-NonCommerical-ShareAlike 4.0 International License.

Spencer, H. (1872). *The principles of psychology, Volume 2, Second Edition.* London: Williams and Norgate.

Triplett, N. (1898). The dynamogenic factors in pace-making and competition. *American Journal of Psychology, 9*(4), 507–533.

Editors' Discussion Questions

1. Elliott Aronson (1999) presented the Greek philosopher, Aristotle, as the "first" published social psychologist. What is wrong with this assertion? Why does it matter?

2. Do you agree or disagree with the editors' critique of evolutionary theory? Why or why not?

3. What is "objectivity"? Is it possible? Why or why not?

Chapter 1

Evolutionary Psychology and World Peace

NICK ABREU

Abstract: Evolutionary psychology asserts that behavior is "hard wired" and a product of natural selection. This approach is critiqued because it denies *free will* and human agency.

Evolutionary psychologists focus on many concepts to explain human behavior and cognition as a function of evolutionary processes.

One key argument advanced by evolutionary psychologists is that "the cognitive programs of the human brain are adaptations. These adaptations exist because they produced behavior in our ancestors that enabled them to survive and reproduce" (Barkow, Cosmides & Tooby, 1992).

Violent acts – such as murder and rape – occur daily. Individuals of color experience discrimination. Urban gangs battle over territory. Bullying is a problem that confronts children of all ages. Are these problems an inherent part of human nature?

Evolutionary psychology views violence as a product of natural selection, wherein violent acts are used to ensure one's survival (as war assures a country's survival). But evolutionary explanations for human behavior ignore the concept of *free will*.

Humans with normal cognitive processes are able to make their own decisions. Most people would agree that a world without violence is preferred to a world at war.

When further investigating solutions to widespread violence, the ideas of evolutionary psychology limit humans' potential to make change. Evolutionary psychology suggests that the only solution to violence is millions of years down the road – when humans have somehow evolved into more altruistic beings.

As an alternative to the constraints of natural selection, we must embrace *free will* and actively pursue a social evolution that celebrates peace over war.

References

Barkow, J.H., Cosmides,, L., & Tooby, J. (editors) (1992). *The Adapted Mind: Evolutionary Psychology and the Generation of Culture.* Oxford & New York: Oxford University Press.

Editors' Discussion Questions

1. Is violence in our DNA? Why or why not?
2. How can we exercise free will – as individuals or societies – to usher in World Peace?

Chapter 2

Peace in Dorm Life

EARL M. SCHULTZ

Abstract: Life in a residential college dormitory involves many challenges. Social influence and norms can determine whether one's dorm life experience is positive or negative. Encouraging and embracing collectivism can promote social harmony and the formation of peaceful interpersonal relationships.

Students attending a residential college inevitably encounter roommate challenges. The college dorm room is an intimate social situation that establishes new social norms and often exposes cultural differences. The dorm room serves as the student's temporary home, a place that should foster peaceful feelings, thoughts and behaviors. Social psychology (the scientific study of how we feel about, think about, and behave toward the people around us – and how our feelings, thoughts, and behaviors are influenced by those people) provides a useful framework for understanding how to attain peace within one's college living environment.

Social psychology identifies three essential elements that influence whether one has a peaceful college dorm life: social influence, social norms, and collectivism.

Social influence describes how people affect our thoughts, feelings, and behaviors; and how we affect theirs. To cultivate positive experiences, roommates should develop an awareness of cultural differences that might influence their interactions.

Social norms are the ways of thinking, feeling, or behaving that are shared by group members and perceived by them as appropriate. College roommates should establish norms that promote peace of mind and body by establishing healthy habits in terms of sleeping, eating, studying and exercising (Asch, 1955; Cialdini, 1993).

The concept of collectivism emphasizes our connectedness with others and interdependence. Roommates practicing collectivism enjoy improved physical and mental well-being because they know they can depend on each other. The trust formed through collectivism often increases cooperation and fosters more harmonious living.

Students living together in a college dormitory can exercise specific precautions and use approaches from social psychology to create interpersonal relationships that encourage and ensure peace within their living environment.

References

Asch, S. (1955). Opinions and social pressure. *Scientific American, 11*, 32.

Cialdini, R. B. (1993). *Influence: Science and practice* (3rd ed.). New York, NY: HarperCollins College Publishers.

Editors' Discussion Questions

1. What are the challenges of dorm life? Of living with a roommate?

2. The author argues that collectivism enhances interpersonal relationships. Is this true in an individualistic society? Why or why not?

3. How does a culture of individualism affect interpersonal relationships?

Chapter 3

Seeking World Peace
Through Global Citizenship

SAMUEL MARTIN

Abstract: Individualism and collectivism are compared and contrasted. Collectivism is more amenable to the development of an identity as a *global citizen*, which is a pathway towards World Peace.

Individualism, a set of cultural norms common in Western societies, emphasizes self-enhancement and independence. This concept is especially popular in the United States, where ideas like *individual freedoms* and *private property* are held sacred and protected by a powerful government.

American youth are encouraged to develop individuality and value their own unique sense of *self*. However, the emphasis on *self* can blind us to global issues. For example, *the American Dream* prioritizes personal success above all else, which often comes at the expense of society and the world at large.

Unlike individualism, collectivism embraces our 'connectedness' and is oriented more towards interdependence. It emphasizes positive social relationships to benefit a group and often arises in the context of close or familial relationships.

A strong sense of *global collectivism*, where individuals extend their concerns to include the welfare of the world, has yet to develop.

World Peace requires that each of us considers him or herself a *global citizen*, one who relishes the opportunity to learn from others and values the global good above the individual (and national) self-interest.

Editors' Discussion Questions

1. How does *individualism* contribute to conflict? Is *collectivism* the remedy?

2. What constitutes "the global good"?

Chapter 4

Collectivism Promotes Peace

Sasha Forbath

Abstract: Concern for others is necessary for World Peace. Individualism, the prevailing ideology in the West, contributes to competition and violence. The U.S. is suffering from an epidemic of gun violence. To reduce gun violence and encourage peaceful interactions, we must embrace and promote norms for the non-violent resolution of conflict.

World Peace is impossible until concern for others becomes widespread. If individuals are focused primarily on their personal well-being, they will not be motivated to eliminate violence in other places. For humanity to eradicate violence and live in harmony, people must shift their self-concern to empathy and concern for others.

Western culture is grounded in individualism, wherein people are taught to be independent and act in a way that benefits themselves. Individualist societies do not encourage people to act in a way that benefits the collective. Instead, members of individualist societies often engage in destructive behavior to further their own agenda. As a result of individuals following personal agendas, the Western world faces increasing levels of violence.

Currently, the U.S. faces an unprecedented gun shooting epidemic, one that has been described as "contagious" (Gupta, 2015). Yet gun violence is preventable. If Western society restructures itself to emphasize collectivism rather than individualism; then violent behavior should decrease, as interpersonal violence is antithetical to those who value interconnectedness.

East Asian cultures embrace collectivism, and understand the importance of interdependence and concern for others. In collectivist societies, empathy and compassion are ingrained in children from a young age; and its members are taught to act in a manner that prioritizes the entire group, rather than simply acting out of self-interest.

In collectivist societies, gun violence is far less common which can be attributed to cultures that emphasize interdependence on others rather than independence.

Ultimately, world peace can only be achieved if societies restructure their ideals so that violent behavior is no longer an accepted social norm.

References

http://www.cnn.com/2015/10/05/health/gupta-stopping-violence/

https://www.theobjectivestandard.com/issues/2012-spring/individualism-collectivism/

Editors' Discussion Questions

1. How does violence in our society affect you?

2. How can we restructure norms to make violence less acceptable?

Chapter 5

A Research Program for World Peace

HALFORD H. FAIRCHILD, PH.D.

Abstract: Research on World Peace may be conducted with a variety of methodologies: case studies, surveys and experiments. A comprehensive research program is needed to identify the individual, cultural and institutional interventions that may lead to World Peace.

Social scientists use a variety of research methodologies. This chapter suggests a program of research in the pursuit of World Peace.

Case Studies

Case studies are the intensive investigations of a single person or event. Unfortunately, case studies of World Peace are not easy to find. Of the hundreds of nations on Earth, only 11 have been reported to be relatively free of violent conflict (Switzerland, Japan, Qatar, Mauritius, Uruguay, Chile, Botswana, Costa Rica, Vietnam, Panama and Brazil).[1]

According to the Global Peace Index[2], the ten most peaceful countries were Ireland, Denmark, Austria, New Zealand, Switzerland, Finland, Canada, Japan, Australia and the Czech Republic. The United States ranked 50th on this list of 162 countries, with the most non-peaceful

---

[1] http://www.independent.co.uk/news/world/politics/world-peace-these-are-the-only-11-countries-in-the-world-that-are-actually-free-from-conflict-9669623.html

[2] https://en.wikipedia.org/wiki/Global_Peace_Index

countries being Syria, Iraq, Afghanistan, the Central African Republic, Somalia and Sudan.[3]

Research on World Peace might include case studies of the most peaceful countries and societies. Some of this research could be done through historical and even archeological lenses.

Cultural historians may find long periods of *Peace* among comparatively isolated populations in the world. Descriptions of *Peaceful* living might be historically reconstructed among Native Peoples in the Americas, the Pacific, Asia and elsewhere.

These case studies, whether current or historical, may provide formulas for harmonious social living. Less helpful are those studies that rely on evolutionary explanations (e.g., Böhm, Rusch & Gürerk, 2015).

Survey Research

Survey research is a useful tool for capturing social attitudes and values. Many studies on the attitudes toward war and peace have already been conducted (e.g., Bizumic, Stubager, Mellon, Van der Linden, Iyer & Jones, 2013; Grussendorf, McAlister, Sandström, Udd, & Morrison, 2002), including those to assess veterans' reactions to war and their adjustment to non-combat roles in society (e.g., Znakov, 1989).

Inasmuch as the public's attitudes influence a nation's entrance and/ or exit from war, a need exists for on-going surveys of international populations to assess global attitudes toward war and peace. Such data collections would enable social scientists to answer questions such as: How do attitudes change in the face of significant world events such as terrorist attacks? How might attitudes change in response to public service announcements that promote World Peace?

Experimental Studies

Researchers interested in World Peace might employ experimental methods in a variety of ways: (1) to explore the effects of intervention programs designed to affect attitudes and/or behaviors; (2) to measure the media's influence on attitude change in different segments of the population; and (3) to test hypotheses about the factors that affect inter-nation conflict.

---

[3] The editors opine that the United States should be ranked as first on this list due to its nuclear "triad" (the constant threat of nuclear annihilation by land, sea and/or air), its annual military expenditures that exceed the total of the next eight countries combined, its export of military weaponry to war-torn countries as a form of "foreign aid," and its engagement in conflicts that have killed millions of innocent civilians in dozens of countries in just the past twenty years.

Experimental methods may be invoked in a variety of program evaluations. Fairchild (2016) proposed "human relation retreats" to be attended by representatives of opposing or warring factions (for example, all of the social studies teachers in Israel and Palestine). These retreats would be designed to facilitate inter-group dialogue and foster friendship. Such retreats may lay the groundwork for eventual Peace in the Middle East. The success of these programs could be evaluated with experimental or quasi-experimental methodologies.

Peace studies that employed experimental methods include the following:

- Bjerstedt (1987) considered the efficacy of a variety of peace activities among school children.

- Geva and Hanson (1999) examined the public's support for the use of force based on "democratic peace" (avoiding violence against other democratic countries).

- Johnson, McDermott, Cowden & Tingley (2012) evaluated individuals' level of aggression in a series of simulated international crises (e.g., a hostage crisis, a counter-insurgency campaign, and a coup). They reported that aggressive responses were predicted by political party affiliation, liberalism/conservatism, and preference for U.S. military action in the Middle East.

- Li, Li, Huang and Chiu (2015) explored the tenets of the contact hypothesis as it related to the attitudes of Singaporeans towards the Japanese during World War II.

- Will, van Lier, Crone and Güroðlu (2015) used the tools of social neuroscience to identify brain mechanisms associated with feelings of inclusion/exclusion in an intergroup relations context.

References

Bizumic, B., Stubager, R., Mellon, S., Van der Linden, N., Iyer, R., & Jones, B. M. (2013). On the (in)compatibility of attitudes toward peace and war. *Political Psychology, 34*(5), 673-693.

Bjerstedt, Å. (1987). Approaching a 'preparedness for peace': Notes on a research and development project. *Educational & Psychological Interactions, 90*13.

Böhm, R., Rusch, H., & Gürerk, Ö. (2015). What makes people go to war? Defensive intentions motivate retaliatory and preemptive intergroup aggression. *Evolution And Human Behavior*, doi:10.1016/j.evolhumbehav.2015.06.005

Fairchild, H.H. (Ed.). (2016). *(Re)Solving violence in America.* Indo American Books.

Geva, N., & Hanson, D. C. (1999). Cultural similarity, foreign policy actions, and regime perception: An experimental study of international cues and democratic peace. *Political Psychology, 20*(4), 803-827. doi:10.1111/0162-895X.00168

Grussendorf, J., McAlister, A., Sandström, P., Udd, L., & Morrison, T. C. (2002). Resisting moral disengagement in support for war: Use of the 'Peace Test' Scale among student groups in 21 nations. *Peace And Conflict: Journal Of Peace Psychology, 8*(1), 73-84. doi:10.1207/S15327949PAC0801_7

Johnson, D. P., McDermott, R., Cowden, J., & Tingley, D. (2012). Dead certain: Confidence and conservatism predict aggression in simulated international crisis decision-making. *Human Nature, 23*(1), 98-126. doi:10.1007/s12110-012-9134-z

Li, C., Li, D., Huang, Z., & Chiu, C. (2015). Peace and War: Rewarding Intergroup Contacts Make Past Intergroup Aggression Unforgivable. *Peace and Conflict: Journal of Peace Psychology,* doi:10.1037/pac0000140

Will, G., van Lier, P. C., Crone, E. A., & Güroðlu, B. (2015). Chronic childhood peer rejection is associated with heightened neural responses to social exclusion during adolescence. *Journal of Abnormal Child Psychology,* doi:10.1007/s10802-015-9983-0

Znakov, V. V. (1989). Understanding of the situations of violence and humiliation of human dignity by the participants in the war in Afghanistan. *Psikologicheski-Zhurnal, 10*(4), 113-124.

Editors' Discussion Questions

1. Describe how each of the research methods – case studies, surveys and experiments – might be used in a program for achieving World Peace.

2. The machinery of war is profitable. Companies that manufacture the weapons of war do so for financial gain. How might it be possible to make Peace profitable?

Part 2
Social Cognition

It is the cultivation of love and compassion, our ability to enter into and to share another's suffering, that are the preconditions for the continued survival of our species... To understand the suffering of others.... Means to possess true empathy... The feeling of community with all living creatures can be attained only if we recognize that we are all basically united and dependent on one another.

~ Dalai Lama

Social cognition is concerned with how we think about our social worlds. Unfortunately, much of this thinking is error prone. These errors lead to interpersonal conflicts on the micro level, and international conflicts at the macro level.

Sources of Social Knowledge

Social knowledge, like all knowledge, is learned and occurs in a variety of ways (Jhangiani & Tarry, 2014).

Similar to Pavlov's conditioning of dogs to salivate at the sound of a bell, social knowledge and attitudes may be acquired by the association of events in our social worlds. Social hierarchies produce experiences that create the attitudinal climate that justifies those hierarchies. For example, Jim Crow laws in the U.S. mandated segregated public facilities and thereby reinforced the idea of Black inferiority/White supremacy (e.g., African Americans were remanded to the "back of the bus" and forced to use substandard public facilities). For generations, millions of White children experienced African Americans only as servants. This form of learning is known as *classical conditioning* or *associational learning*.

Social attitudes form through a process of rewards and punishments (known as *operant* or *respondent conditioning*). For example, whether a child is praised or punished for forming a cross-racial friendship affects the likelihood of such friendships recurring.

Social attitudes are also acquired via exposure to mass media – a form of observational learning first described by Albert Bandura (Bandura, Ross & Ross, 1961; 1963). Taken together, our social knowledge – of a person or group – forms what social psychologists call a *schema*, the "...knowledge representations that include information about a person, group, or situation" (Jhangiani & Tarry, 2014, p. 59).

Creating schemas (mental representations) of the enemy in order to justify war is a major obstacle to achieving World Peace (Rieber, 1991). These schemas are difficult to counter-act, as new information is assimilated in order to produce a *confirmation bias*: interpretations support the existing belief system.

Schemas also may create a *self-fulfilling prophecy*, wherein the holder of the belief interacts with social targets in a way that produces the very behaviors that the person prophesized. An example would be a teacher who treats minority children as if they are incapable of learning and, therefore, does not challenge them, reward them or nurture them; and the children respond by under-performing.

The Power of Expectations

The self-fulfilling prophecy demonstrates the power of expectations. These expectations – our stores of social knowledge or schemas – are influenced by a number of factors. The *salience* of an attitude object is the extent to which it is easily noticeable. Racial minority status, for example, is typically more *salient* than religious status. Schemas may also vary in their *cognitive accessibility* – the readiness with which they come to mind. In the U.S., schemas for African Americans might be more accessible than those for Native Americans (who have been more "out of sight and out of mind" in contemporary American ethno-cultural politics).

Unfortunately, social knowledge is susceptible to error and bias. In addition to the *confirmation bias* noted earlier, people are prone to believe that their opinion is more likely to be shared by the majority, a problem known as the *false consensus bias* (Jhangiani & Tarry, 2014). This error in thinking has also been known as *pluralistic ignorance* (Breed & Ktsanes,1961), and is sometimes subject to conformity pressures or the unique decision-making processes that occurs in groups known as *groupthink* (Janis, 2007). A related problem is the *overconfidence bias*, "...a tendency to be overconfident in our own skills, abilities, and judgments" (Jhangiani & Tarry, p. 78). In fact, we are biased about our biases, something that Jhangiani and Tarry (2014) refer to as "The Bias Blind Spot."

Social Cognition and Affect

Our thoughts and feelings influence each other. People in a good mood have more positive thoughts about themselves and others. Our moods and feelings shape our thoughts in ways that are consistent with those feelings.

According to Jhangiani and Tarry (2014), every stimulus evokes an affective evaluation; and the *affective heuristic* suggests that we use those feelings as a short cut to our thoughts about that stimulus. For example, the term "radical Jihadist terrorist" evokes strong emotions that have a number of negative cognitions (beliefs) tied to those emotions.

Given that "affective states can directly influence our social judgments" (Jhangiani & Tarry, 2014, p. 92), it could be that the general public's support for war is due, in part, to the celebration of heroism in mass marketed motion pictures.

People with positive thoughts or expectations about the future (what Jhangiani & Tarry, 2014, refer to as an *optimistic explanatory style*), tend to live longer, healthier and happier lives. When coupled with a sense of *self efficacy* (the belief that we have the ability to produce the outcomes we seek), individuals have the capacity to shape utopian futures.

Chapter Overviews

Chapter 6 (*Learning to Live in Harmony: A Step Toward World Peace* by Yiran "Krystal" Li and Halford H. Fairchild, Ph.D.) explores the effects of confirmation bias and the self-fulfilling prophecy on interpersonal relationships. Li and Fairchild propose that negative expectations should be avoided in order to promote harmonious relationships.

Chapter 7 (*Domestic Terrorism and Islamophobia: Shattering Misconceptions* by Sasha Forbath) suggests that anti-Muslim sentiments were fueled by the U.S. government following the terrorist attacks on September 11, 2001. Forbath urges the eradication of Islamophobia as a prerequisite to World Peace.

Chapter 8 (*Learning Prejudice Through Associational Learning* by Austin Caviness) posits that prejudices are acquired by exposure to negative media images. Caviness illustrates this problem with several examples: the shooting of Black men, doll preference research, and attitudes towards Muslims following September 11, 2001.

Chapter 9 (*SAT's 'Halo Effect' Casts a Long Shadow* by Halford H. Fairchild, Ph.D.) questions the value of the SAT as a criterion for admission to colleges and universities. Fairchild asserts that the billions spent on testing should be re-directed to providing more seats in colleges and universities.

Chapter 10 (*Can Attribution Theory Bring Peace to the Middle East?* by Halford H. Fairchild, Ph.D.) suggests that taking the enemy's perspective may lead to an understanding of the U.S.'s culpability in fomenting war in the Middle East. Fairchild concludes that the U.S. is responsible for bringing peace to the Middle East.

Editors' Discussion Questions

1. How did you form your racial attitudes? What were the major influences in forming these attitudes? Have your racial attitudes changed over time? Describe.

2. What "schemas" or "mental representations" do we have for atheists? For Christians? For Muslims? For Jews? For Buddhists? Where do these ideas originate? How accessible are these ideas – and are they more accessible for one group than another?

3. Is a conflict-free world possible? If yes, what steps are required and how long will it take to achieve World Peace? If no, how should we live in the midst of perpetual conflict?

References

Bandura, A., Ross, D., & Ross, S. A. (1961). Transmission of aggression through imitation of aggressive models. *Journal of Abnormal and Social Psychology*, *63*, 575-582.

Bandura, A., Ross, D., & Ross, S. A. (1963). Imitation of film-mediated aggressive models. *Journal of Abnormal and Social Psychology*, *66*, 3-11.

Breed, W., & Ktsanes, T. (1961). Pluralistic ignorance in the process of opinion formation. *Public Opinion Quarterly*, *25*(3), 382-392. doi:10.1086/267034

Janis, I. L. (2007). Groupthink. In R. P. Vecchio, R. P. Vecchio (Eds.). *Leadership: Understanding the dynamics of power and influence in organizations (2nd ed.)* (pp. 157-169). Notre Dame, IN, US: University of Notre Dame Press.

Jhangiani, R., & Tarry, H. (2014). *Principles of social psychology – 1st international edition.* Licensed under a Creative Commons Attribution-NonCommerical-ShareAlike 4.0 International License.

Rieber, Robert W. (1991). *The psychology of war and peace: The image of the enemy.* NY: Plenum Press.

Chapter 6

Living to Live in Harmony:
A Step Toward World Peace

Yiran "Krystal" Li

and Halford H. Fairchild, Ph.D.

Abstract: World Peace requires harmony in all relationships, from interpersonal to the international. How people relate to others is based on past experiences and subject to "confirmation bias." Negative expectations may create a "self-fulfilling prophecy." Such expectations must be avoided in order to create more harmonious relationships.

Achieving "World Peace" should start with improving our interpersonal relationships.

Relationships are challenged when we adapt to new environments, which happens all of the time: enrolling in college, moving to a new neighborhood, changing jobs or careers, and meeting new people.

How we encounter others for the first time is largely influenced by our past experiences, and how we have learned to adjust to people from different backgrounds or personalities. The aforementioned may be the result of *associational learning,* wherein a group is generally perceived with positive or negative attributes based upon specific past experiences (Jhangiani & Tarry, 2014).

Creating new relationships with positive or negative expectations may produce the very outcomes we expect, which social psychologists commonly refer to as *confirmation bias.*

Negative expectations or images of others – as necessarily happens in combat or war (Rieber, 1991) – influence our perceptions and create a self-fulfilling prophecy.

The solution is to avoid the cycle of negative expectations in our social relationships. Maintaining harmonious and positive social relationships is a necessary step in achieving and sustaining peace around the globe.

References

Jhangiani, R., & Tarry, H. (2014). *Principles of social psychology – 1st international edition*. Licensed under a Creative Commons Attribution-NonCommercial-ShareAlike 4.0 International License.

Rieber, Robert W. (1991). *The psychology of war and peace: The image of the enemy*. NY: Plenum Press.

Editors' Discussion Questions

1. How do expectations affect how we interact with people from different backgrounds? In what circumstances are your expectations of others positive? Negative?

2. Where do stereotypes and other attitudes originate? Do sources differ for the learning of positive versus negative attitudes?

Chapter 7

Domestic Terrorism and Islamophobia: Shattering Misconceptions

Sasha Forbath

Abstract: Following the terrorist attacks of September 11, 2001, the U.S. government waged a campaign that fueled Islamophobia and anti-Muslim sentiments. Confirmation bias and reconstructive memory bias contribute to anti-Muslim prejudice. Stereotyped thinking, particularly Islamophobia, must be eradicated if World Peace is to be achieved.

Stereotypes shape our world. Derived from the media and broader society, stereotypes lead individuals to judge others based on group affiliations. These judgements become problematic when people fear for their livelihood and safety because of *perceived* threats from others.

Following the terrorist attacks of September 11, 2001, the U.S. government inflamed Islamophobia and anti-Muslim sentiments by creating racist policies and fueling a "war on terror." This resulted in the erroneous labeling of many Muslims as terrorists.

According to a survey conducted by Gallup in 2010, the Muslim community was 17% more likely to experience racial or religious discrimination than any other religious community. A staggering 48% of Muslims reported experiencing either racially or religiously motivated discrimination.

After 9/11, any terrorist act organized by Muslims provided a *confirmation bias* that Muslims were to blame for terrorism. The 2013 *U.S. News and World Report* found that non-Muslims carried out more than 90% of all terrorist attacks in America. This begs the question: Why does society reinforce the Muslim terrorist stereotype when they are statistically less likely to participate in terrorist activities than other demographic groups?

Reconstructive memory bias, the tendency to "remember things that match our current beliefs," is a possible explanation for the persisting stereotype of Muslim terrorists (Hilsabeck, Gouvier & Bolter, 1998). Following the 9/11 attacks, the media used any terrorist actions organized by Muslims to support this stereotype, ignoring the fact that Muslims do not commit the majority of terrorist activities in the United States.

The reinforcement of prejudices and stereotypes lead individuals to dangerous assumptions. Islamophobia is one of the many forms of prejudices that must be addressed and eliminated before all nations can be at peace. Until institutionalized racism and racial profiling are eradicated, it will be impossible to achieve World Peace.

References

Hilsabeck, R. C., Gouvier, W. D., & Bolter, J. F. (1998). Reconstructive memory bias in recall of neuropsychological symptomatology. *Journal of Clinical and Experimental Neuropsychology (Neuropsychology, Development and Cognition: Section A), 20*(3), 328-338.

Jhangiani, R., & Tarry, H. (2014). *Principles of social psychology – 1ˢᵗ international edition.* Licensed under a Creative Commons Attribution-NonCommerical-ShareAlike 4.0 International License.

http://www.soundvision.com/article/islamophobia-statistics-usa-2011

http://www.gallup.com/poll/157082/islamophobia-understanding-anti-muslim-sentiment-west.aspx

http://www.globalresearch.ca/non-muslims-carried-out-more-than-90-of-all-terrorist-attacks-in-america/5333619

Editors' Discussion Questions

1. What are prevailing stereotypes about Muslims? Where do they originate?

2. How are prejudices and stereotypes reinforced in society?

Chapter 8

Learning Prejudice Through Associational Learning

AUSTIN CAVINESS

Abstract: Entertainment media shapes social attitudes by presenting stereotyped images of some groups. Through associational learning, Black people and other minorities are devalued. This is evinced by the commonplace shootings of unarmed Black men, and the doll preference studies of Kenneth and Mamie Clark. Another example is in the attitudes towards Muslims following the terrorist attack of September 11, 2001. People should be valued on their own qualities and merits, not on the basis of media portrayals.

> *"Change the way you look at things and the things you look at change."*
> ~ Wayne W. Dyer

From birth, we are programmed to think and process things in a particular way. Through children's books, stories, television and movies, individuals learn "what is good or bad." It is through these associations that we develop prejudices about people, places and things.

The media shapes, and oft times manipulates, public opinion.

Like a Disney movie, media and news outlets manipulate stories to elicit certain emotions. Disney's *The Lion King* portrayed the villain, Scar, as dark; whereas the protagonist was blonde. Similarly, local and national news focus on events in minority communities that reinforce negative stereotypes.

In recent instances of unarmed Black men murdered by White police or vigilantes – Trayvon Martin, Michael Brown and Philando Castile immediately come to mind (Fairchild, 2016) – the victims were portrayed in the most unappealing images, despite the fact that graduation photographs and

27

other more positive images were readily available. These portrayals, through the process of "associational learning" (Jhangiani & Tarry, 2014), create an unsympathetic disposition among at least some members of the audience.

In the 1940s, Kenneth and Mamie Clark performed the famous "Doll Test" which assessed children's preference for light and dark skin tones (Clark, 1939). Their findings were influential in the 1954 *Brown vs. Board of Education* decision that desegregated the nation's schools. This study was a powerful demonstration of *associational learning*: the repeated association of white things with good and black things with bad translates into an attitudinal climate that falsely elevates the egos of Whites, while devaluing those of Blacks.

Associational learning also occurred in the wake of the terrorist attacks on September 11, 2001. Media coverage of the attacks and their aftermath included images of people associated with Al Qaeda, many of whom belonged to the Islamic religion. Soon afterwards, many Muslims (followers of Islam) were victimized by hate crimes that targeted their religion.

Through new technologies, the increasingly intimate connections of people around the globe make it more imperative that mass media act responsibly and avoid distorted or stereotyped portrayals. We must learn to value individuals uniquely for who they are and how they move through and contribute to the world – not on false associations absorbed from the media.

References

Clark, M. (1939). *The development of consciousness of self in Negro preschool children.* Unpublished master's thesis, Howard University, Washington, DC.

Fairchild, H. H. (Ed.). (2016). *(Re)Solving Violence in America.* Delhi: Indo American Books.

Fiske, S. T., & Neuberg, S. L. (1990). A continuum of impression formation, from category based to individuating processes: Influences of information and motivation on attention and interpretation. In M. P. Zanna (Ed.), *Advances in experimental social psychology* (Vol. 23, pp.1–74). New York, NY: Academic.

Jhangiani, R., & Tarry, H. (2014). *Principles of social psychology – 1st international edition.* Licensed under a Creative Commons Attribution-NonCommerical-ShareAlike 4.0 International License.

http://www.naacpldf.org/brown-at-60-the-doll-test

Editors' Discussion Questions

1. List some examples of negative media portrayals of a particular group. List examples of those that are positive. How do they compare?

2. How do positive and negative media representations differ for different groups?

3. How should media and related industries be regulated to avoid negative stereotyping?

Chapter 9

SAT's 'Halo Effect' Casts a Long Shadow[1]

HALFORD H. FAIRCHILD, PH.D.

Abstract: The value of the SAT as a criterion for admission to colleges and universities is challenged. The SAT reflects and recreates class and racial biases and is a weak predictor of college success. These problems are duplicated in the standardized tests that are required for admission to graduate and professional schools. Instead of spending billions on testing that excludes students, those funds ought to be re-directed to providing more seats in colleges and universities.

In the Fall of 2001, the University of California (UC) began to question the relevance of the SAT in college admissions. This was an invigorating move for American higher education, long overdue.

The SAT is ideally viewed as a yardstick of merit (academic aptitude or achievement); it has been used for decades as a key criterion for admission to four-year colleges and universities. In reality, the SAT is a poorly defined test that reflects racial and economic privileges. It reproduces sex, race and class inequalities in access to the nation's educational resources that produce wealth and power.

The SAT affords an all-too-easy sorting of students' applications into the categories of 'admit,' 'maybe admit' or 'do not admit.' The problem is that many students in the 'do not admit' category could succeed with flying colors if they were given the opportunity.

The SAT creates a halo effect that colors the more holistic evaluation of applicants' statements of purpose and letters of recommendation. It fosters

---

[1] This Chapter was revised from a previously published essay in the *Los Angeles Times*, Opinion Section, February 26, 2001. Other "standardized" admissions tests, such as the ACT, suffer from the same problems as the SAT.

a mind-set that is tough to overcome for students who do not have the "test-wiseness" to correctly fill in the answer bubbles to questions about obscure vocabulary or reasoning that is embedded in White cultural trivia. Students might be expected to know Shakespeare or Voltaire, but they are safe if they are ignorant of Wheatley or Nkrumah. After more than 40 years of college teaching, I have learned that the single most important criterion for a student's success is his or her motivation and effort – attributes that are *not* reflected in SAT scores.

I have witnessed students with abysmal SAT scores excel and those with stellar scores flounder. For millions of aspiring college students, the SAT tests students on material that they have not been taught. In the context of known racial inequalities in educational opportunity, the use of an inflexible yardstick such as the SAT is inherently racist.

The SAT II, a subject-matter test, is not an improvement. Students are advised to take the verbal and math sections of the SAT II (and a subject area of their choosing), which recreate the same biases as the original SAT. *Standardized tests cannot assess merit in the context of non-standardized educational experiences.* The comparison of students with wholly different secondary school experiences on the same inflexible yardstick is especially unfair to modest income and minority students, and renders the scores uninterpretable. This is also true for the tests that act as gatekeepers to the professions: the MCAT (for medicine), the LSAT (for law) and the GRE (for social sciences and humanities).

The under-representation of minorities who face discrimination in undergraduate programs dramatically worsens in graduate schools. Much is at stake for Atkinson's proposal and the multi-billion dollar testing and test-preparation industries. Students waste valuable time and money preparing for exams that are irrelevant to their success or failure in higher education. Students take the tests several times in hopes of improving their scores – a cost that is prohibitive to all but the most affluent families.

SAT scores are weak predictors of first-year college success, explaining only 10% of the variance in grades, and have virtually no bearing on subsequent success or failure. Other measures of presumed merit, such as grade-point averages, are also problematic. GPAs are inflated by advanced placement courses that may produce GPAs above 4.0. Students in predominantly African American and Latino schools have less access to honors and advanced placement (AP) courses, just as they have less access to books and experienced teachers.

In a perverse irony, African American and Latino communities support public institutions from which they do not benefit in proportion to their tax dollars. Admission procedures must eschew criteria that have known biases and incorporate those that allow students' drive and determination to manifest. They should emphasize the importance of critical thinking, intercultural awareness and a healthy skepticism of the so-called knowledge items contained in the SAT.

Instead of spending billions of dollars to exclude students, we should redirect those dollars to create more seats in more colleges and universities. At Pitzer College, students, faculty and staff have been engaged in an ongoing dialogue about the merits of the SAT. In a recent opinion study on the matter, the college's constituencies have been nearly evenly divided. Atkinson's bold proposal may nudge us in the right direction. [2]

Editors' Discussion Questions

1. What are your good and bad experiences with standardized tests such as the SAT?

2. What is your opinion about standardized tests as a criterion for college admission or graduate school?

3. How is the issue of standardized testing related to the pursuit of World Peace?

---

[2] In 2001, I proposed to the Pitzer College Council (the governing body of students, staff and faculty) that the SAT be banned. After two years of debate, Pitzer College became one of a handful of liberal arts colleges that made the SAT optional. The SAT is not required for students graduating in the top 10% of their high school classes; and applicants can submit a graded math test and essay in lieu of the SAT. In the ensuing decade, a growing percentage of prospective students opted not to submit SAT scores; and Pitzer received an increasing number of applications, became more selective, and rose in the national ranks of liberal arts colleges.

Chapter 10

Can Attribution Theory Bring Peace to the Middle East?

HALFORD H. FAIRCHILD, PH.D.

Abstract: The fundamental attribution error ignores the situational determinants of others' behavior. By taking the perspective of the other, an empathetic understanding may lead us to understand the U.S.'s culpability in the wars in the Middle East. That understanding is necessary to bring peace to the region.

For individuals and groups, fundamental attribution errors are commonplace. The essence of the error is the failure to appreciate the situational determinants of others' behavior. The behavior of others is too often perceived as emanating from purely internal or dispositional drives; the circumstances confronting the individual is overlooked.

We can bring peace to the Middle East by assuming the perspectives of "the other." If we can better understand each side's perspectives on why it fights, perhaps we can use that insight to end the bloodshed. If we better understand the reasons why we as human beings fight one another – the *true* reasons – perhaps we can end war and search for peaceful solutions to conflicts. Unfortunately, self-serving biases operate among nations states and their armies, as those who kill are loathe to point the fingers at themselves as the cause of the bloodshed. Yet, that is precisely what is needed to end violent conflict and war.

The problem with the Wars in the Middle East is that the U.S. and its allies make the fundamental attribution error that ISIL is evil and seeks to establish a "caliphate" to take over not just the Muslim world, but the entire globe. Further, the fundamental attribution error perceives the motives of ISIL as dispositional – in their hearts and souls. This allows the West to justify the indiscriminate bombing of towns and infrastructure, and murdering thousands of innocents.

But what are some of the *situational determinants* that motivate ISIL to fight the West?

The Middle East was plunged into turmoil when the U.S. invaded Iraq in March 2003. From the perspective of the Arab fighter – in Iraq, Iran or Syria – the U.S. was an occupying force that destroyed cities, towns and ways of life. Tens of thousands of innocent Arab and Muslim lives were lost to the U.S. invasion. Thousands of men were arrested, jailed, tortured and killed over a dozen years.

The ISIL fighters seek retribution for the crimes against humanity committed by the U.S. and its allies, and want a return of their sovereign lands and resources.

By considering the perspective of "the other," the U.S. and its allies may come to realize that ISIL's fight is not entirely without justification. The U.S. – the self-proclaimed leader of the "free world" – has a responsibility to end the slaughter – because we started it in the first place.

I have seen the enemy, and he is us![1]

When we empathize with "the other" – instead of demonizing them as "the enemy" – we may find ourselves culpable for the conflict and therefore responsible for its solution.

Editors' Discussion Questions

1.   Why is the demonization of the enemy an error in cognition?

2.   In what ways should the U.S. take responsibility for ending war in the Middle East?

---

[1] This phrase is modified from many other sources (see www.google.com).

Second Interlude

Ballad of Don White

ROSS ALTMAN

Abstract: This song lyric is a tribute to Don White, a peace activist who protested U.S. Government intervention in Central America.

The last time I saw Don White
He was standing on a windswept stage
With a bullhorn in one hand, a sign in the other
And a voice that belied his age
He looked the same twenty years ago
Marching for El Salvador
By the way he was gay, he wore a toupee
And a sweatshirt that said, *"No War."*

Chorus:
   Don White presenté
   Long may he live
   Adios compañero
   So much he had to give.

"So how's the revolution going?"
I asked this nonviolent soldier
At a protest to close the School of the Assassins
Outside Ft. Benning, Georgia
The twinkle in his eye
Said all I needed to know
I almost believed in miracles
Cause Don White told me so. (Ch.)

To some he's a snake oil medicine man
Just like the wizard of Oz
Saying *Si! Si! Puedes* – Yes we can –

35

For every hopeless cause
He stood up there and he made the pitch
For every check you wrote
To keep one more left wing, shoe string
Grassroots shipwrecked movement boat afloat. (Ch.)

I guess he ate one too many
Pies at the House of Pies
One too many Fatburgers
And one too many fries
You never mistook Don White
For Ghandi's ascetic self-denial
But who said the revolution
Could not be lived with style – and a smile. (Ch.)

Somewhere up in Heaven
I know Don's looking down
Hoping we'll fill the bucket
As it goes round and round
Put in some twenties and hundreds
Not just ones and fives
Dig deep down in your pockets
Cause some put in their lives. (Final Chorus.)

Editors' Biographical Note About Don White

Don White (1937 – 2008) was a public school teacher and life-long peace activist in Los Angeles. Deeply committed to equity in public education, he experienced an epiphany when he traveled to Guatemala, in 1976, in response to a devastating earthquake (http://www.carecen-la.org/don_white_tribute_page). While in Central America, he witnessed the effects of U.S. intervention that was costing lives in El Salvador and other countries.

An organizer and fund raiser, Don led and participated in peace demonstrations throughout the country and was instrumental in building sanctuaries for Central American refugees in Los Angeles.

Part 3
The Self

Make a career of humanity. Commit yourself to the noble struggle for equal rights. You will make a greater person of yourself, a greater nation of your country, and a finer world to live in.

~ Martin Luther King, Jr.

The Self

Social psychology is concerned with reciprocal social influences: how we are influenced by others and how we, in turn, influence them. At the center of psychological approaches to social influences is the *Self*.

Theory and research on the *Self* have focused on "the cognitive self," or self concept; the "feeling self," or self-esteem; and the "social self," or defining the person within a social context (Jhangiani & Tarry, 2014).

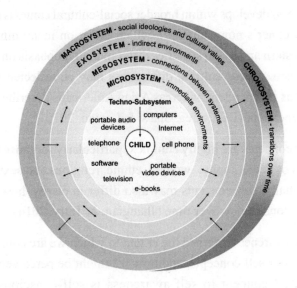

Urie Bronfenbrenner's ***ecological systems theory*** of the *Self* placed the person at the center of ever-broadening sets of social networks (Bronfenbrenner, 1979, 1989).

The above figure, from Johnson & Puplanpu (2008), illustrates the nested social environments that a person inhabits. Johnson and Puplanpu were concerned with the immediate technological influences on children. Our current focus is on the concentric circles surrounding the *Self*: the micro system (immediate household and family environments); the meso-system (neighborhood and regional environments); the exo-system (national and cultural environments); the macrosystem (the ideological values and norms); and the chronosystem (the effects of movement through time).

Bronfenbrenner's ***ecological systems theory*** is a useful heuristic for assessing the causes of war, and for imagining multifaceted strategies for achieving World Peace. We, therefore, refer to it throughout this text.

The Self Concept

The self concept is what we think about ourselves: our personalities, our motivations and our roles and associated responsibilities. We develop and/ or learn our self-concepts through our life experiences – positive and negative – that shape our personalities and social identities.

The *Self* develops within broader social-cultural contexts (the *exosystem* in Bronfenbrenner's nomenclature), which differ on many dimensions. For example, Western and Asian societies differ in their emphasis on individualism vs. collectivism. These cultural differences may be reflected in Americans' self concept as independent, whereas Asian Americans describe themselves as more interdependent (DeAndrea, Shaw & Levine, 2010).

Self concepts are highly complex, particularly for those residing at the intersections of demography: women, ethnic, religious and sexual minorities, etc. Additionally, self concepts may also differ in clarity, how well they are defined, and consistency over time (Jhangiani & Tarry, 2014).

Self awareness refers to the extent to which we are consciously aware of ourselves, our self concepts, and how we might be perceived by others. A closely related concept to self-awareness is self-consciousness. When individuals are induced to be self-aware, they are more likely to engage in morally correct behavior (Jhangiani & Tarry, 2014).

By contrast, in states of de-individuation – wherein the person's sense of self is diminished (as in the case of large groups, or the taking of specific roles) – people often display disinhibited behavior. De-individuation is necessary to justify the killing of innocents in war.

The Self Esteem

Generally, how we *think* about ourselves is related to how we *feel* about ourselves. Positive thoughts lead to positive self esteem; negative thoughts to its opposite. People sometimes go to extraordinary lengths – even to the point of self-delusion – to maintain or enhance a positive feeling about themselves.

Although positive self-esteem is associated with positive mental health, too much of a good thing can be problematic. The narcissistic personality is "…characterized by overly high self-esteem, self-admiration, and self-centeredness" (Jhangiani & Tarry, p. 128). One can readily imagine how these personality dynamics – when aggregated at the national and global levels – might lead individuals to violence and nations to war.

The Social Self

The *Self* is multi-faceted, developing in the nested social networks described earlier. The "micro-system" factors (i.e., home and family) are most important early in life; while in adolescence and early adulthood, the developing *Self* moves through and develops in broader and more mature social networks.

The social environment often applies *labels* to individuals that may affect their interactions and their self-concepts. A label such as "hyperactive" may produce self-fulfilling behaviors, especially when internalized.

Labels may also create, for better or worse, a "halo effect." For example, when someone is labeled as "beautiful," he or she is also perceived as "good," "competent," "successful," etc.

An individual's self-concept may be affected by upward or downward social comparison. If we compare our circumstances with those of someone in a superior position (upward social comparison), our self-esteem is bound to suffer. So too, downward social comparisons might be expected to elevate our sense of *Self*.

Finally, the *Self* is a product of the groups that provide us with a social identity. Most people belong to multiple groups, with diverse and complex social identities. These group memberships and social identities often shift over the course of a lifespan.

Chapter Overviews

Chapter 11 (*Gaining Equality for Women: The Adverse Effects of Media Conditioning* by Alicia Breyer) decries the socialization of gender inequality in Disney movies. Breyer calls for gender equality as a prerequisite for World Peace.

Chapter 12 (*Social Media Creates a False Consensus* by Brandon O'Neal) explains that news and information are filtered to confirm our attitudes and values. O'Neal suggests that being cognizant of these biases may help understand the point of view of others.

Chapter 13 (*Finding Internal Peace to Acquire World Peace* by Max Davis) asserts that World Peace can only be achieved after individuals find inner peace. Davis argues that social media promotes de-individuation and may threaten the self concept.

Chapter 14 (*Meditation, Mindfulness and Peace* by Sasha Forbath) describes Buddhism as a meditative practice that enhances inner peace. Forbath encourages meditative and mindfulness practices to promote wellbeing and World Peace.

Chapter 15 (*Cyberbullying, De-individuation and World Peace* by Brandon O'Neal) discusses cyberbullying as a product of the anonymity of the internet. O'Neal advocates for education on cyberbullying and the socially responsible use of the internet.

Chapter 16 (*Protect the Protestors* by Earl M. Schultz) identifies the origins of protest in inequality. Schultz urges that laws be obeyed and that the use of force should be proportionate and limited.

References

Bronfenbrenner, U. (1979). *The ecology of human development: Experiments by nature and design*. Cambridge, MA: Harvard University Press.

Bronfenbrenner, U. (1989). Ecological systems theory. *Annals of Child Development, 6*, 187-224.

DeAndrea, D. C., Shaw, A. S., & Levine, T. R. (2010). Online language: The role of culture in self-expression and self-construal on Facebook. *Journal of Language and Social Psychology, 29*(4), 425-442. doi:10.1177/0261927X10377989

Jhangiani, R., & Tarry, H. (2014). *Principles of social psychology – 1st international edition*. Licensed under a Creative Commons Attribution-NonCommerical-ShareAlike 4.0 International License.

Johnson, G.M., & Puplampu, K.P. (2008). Internet use during childhood and the ecological techno-subsystem. *Canadian Journal of Learning and Technology, 34*(1). (http://www.cjlt.ca/index.php/cjlt/article/view/172/168)

Editors' Discussion Questions

1. How have each of Bronfenbrenner's circle of social networks – micro, meso, exo, macro, chronos – affected your sense of self? Which of these has been more prominent in your life? How?

2. How is a nation's collective self-esteem related to war? Describe. Can you think of any examples?

Chapter 11

Gaining Equality for Women: The Adverse Effects of Media Conditioning

ALICIA BREYER

Abstract: Gender inequality begins begins at birth. The entertainment media – in particular, Disney movies – have portrayed female characters as secondary to males. The mass media should portray gender equality, which is a prerequisite for World Peace.

How can we accept other cultures, if half of the population in our own culture is devalued?

The problem of gender inequality begins at a young age: children are conditioned by the media and society to perceive women in stereotypical ways.

Disney studios have had major influences on children's social development. Many classic Disney films portray women who are unmarried and/or not romantically involved with a male as malevolent, vengeful and physically undesirable. For example, in *Snow White*, the villain is a widowed queen obsessed with her fading beauty. *Sleeping Beauty*'s villain is a spurned witch with horns on her head, likening her to the devil. In stark contrast, the *princesses* in these movies are rescued by *men* who protect them. For Disney princesses, endings are happy because they culminate in marriage.

Young girls are taught that they must rely on men to provide them with a good life; but if they try to become too independent or powerful, they will be a villain. This is an example of associative learning (Jhangiani & Tarry, 2014), wherein certain experiences and ideas become linked, e.g., an "independent woman" is a "bad woman."

Although the aforementioned films were made before the women's movement, more contemporary films exhibit the same anachronistic biases. Films made in the 1990s –*The Little Mermaid, The Lion King, Aladdin* – shared similar plot lines of a man rescuing a woman in distress, or vanquishing the evil *queenwitch*.

A recent study suggests that we have recently taken a backwards step in filmmaking. Even in films with female protagonists, male characters do the majority of talking and, "on average…men have three times as many lines as women" (Guo, 2016). Young women are socialized to be docile, accommodating and deferential to men.

More than simply offering a reflection of society, the media can transform it by promoting positive images. Especially for child audiences, the media has a responsibility to portray girls and women as equal to their male counterparts. Images of powerful, independent women must be celebrated, rather than regarded with disdain and scorn.

True equality between men and women is necessary for World Peace.

References

Guo, J. (2016). *Researchers have found a major problem with 'The Little Mermaid' and other Disney movies*. Retrieved January 25, 2016 from www.washingtonpost.com.

Jhangiani, R., & Tarry, H. (2014). *Principles of social psychology – 1st international edition*. Licensed under a Creative Commons Attribution-NonCommerical-ShareAlike 4.0 International License.

Editors' Discussion Questions

1. In what ways is gender inequality manifested today? How does it differ in other societies or cultures?

2. What are some examples of mass media programming (television or motion pictures) that *challenge* gender inequality?

Chapter 12

Social Media Creates a False Consensus

Brandon O'Neal

Abstract: People gravitate towards news and social media that support their existing attitudes. *Confirmation bias* occurs when we filter the news to support our attitudes and values. *False consensus bias* happens when we assume that the majority of people agree with our own opinion. These biases should be recognized and eliminated as we try to better understand the point of view of others.

With such a panoply of online news sources, it is easy to focus on media pertinent to one's own views.

Social media posts are ubiquitous. Nearly everyone uses media such as *Twitter, Instagram, Tumblr* and *Facebook* to express their opinions.

Conservatives tend to rely on conservative media outlets, while liberal counterparts turn to liberal sources. This is commonly known as the *confirmation bias,* wherein people seek information that confirms their beliefs. When people solely seek out information that appeals to them, their views become more extreme and entrenched. Social media has exacerbated deep divisions in the U.S. According to the Pew Research Center (2012), Americans' "values and basic beliefs are more polarized along partisan lines than at any point in the past 25 years."

Also exacerbating the division in America is social media's relationship to the *false consensus bias*. People generally assume that others share views similar to their own, and those with contrary opinions are ridiculed and dismissed. Social media serves to reinforce one's beliefs as friends share posts with similar views.

To evolve and progress as a nation, we must end the intense partisanship and political gridlock that plague our government. We must make a genuine effort to understand the opposing side's points of view.

References

Fischhoff, B. (1982). Debiasing. In D. Kahneman, P. Slovic, & A. Tversky (Eds.), *Judgment under uncertainty: Heuristics and biases* (pp. 422-444). Cambridge, England: Cambridge University Press.

Mitchell, A., Gottfried, J., Kiley, J., & Matsa, K. E. (2014, October 20). *Political Polarization & Media Habits.* Retrieved January 31, 2016, from http://www.journalism.org/2014/10/21/political-polarization-media-habits/

Pew Research Center. (2012). Partisan polarization surges in Bush, Obama years: Trends in American values: 1987-2012. http://www.people-press.org/2012/06/04/partisan-polarization-surges-in-bush-obama-years/

Editors' Discussion Questions

1.   Are news sources biased? How? What are your sources for the news?

2.   Is it true that people watch the news programming that is consistent with their personal beliefs and politics? How have you reacted when you watched news outlets whose viewpoints were opposed to yours?

3.   What is your response to friends on social media who express opinions that differ from yours?

Chapter 13
Finding Internal Peace to Acquire World Peace

MAX DAVIS

Abstract: World Peace can be achieved only after people find peace within themselves. Today, inner peace is threatened by social media which creates a sense of de-individuation. Social media may perpetuate stereotypes and threaten self-concepts. People should reduce their reliance on social media.

To achieve World Peace, we must first find internal peace by developing positive and realistic self-concepts.

Self-concept is "a representation that contains knowledge about us, including our beliefs about our personality traits, physical characteristics, abilities, values, goals, and roles, as well as the knowledge that we exist as individuals" (Jhangiani & Tarry, 2014, p. 107). Today, our self-concepts are significantly influenced by globalization, advertising, and the excessive technological stimuli of the modern world.

With over 2 billion Internet users on Earth, comprising 35% of the population (Kemp, 2015), the human race is more connected than ever.

While social media and information technology have a plethora of benefits; those forces can cause *de-individuation*, which occurs when a "person's sense of self is diminished" (Jhangiani & Tarry, 2014, p. 114).

Social media contributes to de-individuation by virtue of its anonymity and ability to establish group norms. Social media also reinforces negative stereotypes, which can alter a person's self-concept and may even result in a self-fulfilling prophecy.

Those pursuing internal peace should limit their use of social media. We must disconnect from social media so that we can truly connect with our inner selves and our environment. If we rely less on social media to establish our ideas, values and identities; we may become more self-aware, develop a more positive self-concept and achieve true inner peace.

References

Jhangiani, R., & Tarry, H. (2014). *Principles of social psychology – 1ˢᵗ international edition.* Licensed under a Creative Commons Attribution-NonCommerical-ShareAlike 4.0 International License.

Kemp, Simon. (2015). Social, Digital & Mobile Worldwide in 2014 – We Are Social UK. *We Are Social UK.* We Are Social, 9 Jan. 2015. Web. 07 Feb. 2016.

Editors' Discussion Questions

1. Describe your use of social media. Do you agree with the author that it creates a sense of de-individuation? Why or why not?

2. How does your use of social media affect your self-concept?

3. How can social media be used to pursue World Peace?

Chapter 14

Meditation, Mindfulness and Peace

SASHA FORBATH

Abstract: Buddhism is an ancient religion and philosophy and a way of finding inner peace through daily meditative practice. Promulgating meditation and Buddhist mindfulness techniques may improve individual well being and eventually lead to World Peace.

World Peace requires that we each, first, achieve peace within. Meditation helps practitioners heighten self-awareness and solidify their self-concepts.

The collection, *Inner Peace, World Peace: Essays on Buddhism and Nonviolence* (Kraft, 1992), demonstrates the power of meditation practice and mindfulness to promote peace worldwide. While it is unrealistic to expect universal conversion to Buddhism, its meditative practices and moral opposition to violence are stances that can be readily adopted by people of all religious and non-religious backgrounds.

The belief that "a single person who experiences peace of mind, or who lives in a non-violent manner, is contributing to the peace of the world" (Kraft, 1992, p. 2) describes the role each person plays in achieving World Peace.

Meditative practices and mindfulness are effective tools in the ongoing pursuit of inner peace. These *peaceful practices within* may contribute to the possibility of peace worldwide.

Reference

Kraft, Kenneth. (1992). *Inner Peace, World Peace: Essays on Buddhism and Nonviolence*. Albany: State U of New York.

Editors' Discussion Questions

1. How can meditation lead to World Peace?
2. What contributes to the lack of "inner peace" in most individuals? In you?

Chapter 15

Cyberbullying, De-individuation and World Peace

Brandon O'Neal

Abstract: Along with soaring internet usage has come cyberbullying and other forms of online aggression. These problems are made possible by the anonymity of the internet, which provides users with a sense of de-individuation. Cyberbullying can erode the self-esteem of some users and, in some cases, even lead to suicide. Education on cyberbullying is needed to prevent these abuses and promote socially responsible use of the internet.

Internet usage has skyrocketed. Indeed, 46.4% of the world population had internet access as of 2015 (Internet World Stats, 2016).

The internet is a domain where individuals can escape reality and act with anonymity. This anonymity can have unfortunate consequences, including online aggression or cyberbullying.

Cyberbullying describes the harm inflicted through the use of computers and other electronic devices (Patchin & Hinduja, 2006). Bullying may come in the form of injurious messages, derogatory comments, or threats.

Online bullying is more prevalent than traditional physical or verbal bullying, and may have a much more profound effect if the offensive comments or images "go viral" (widely spread across the internet). Interconnectivity and widespread use of the internet means that cyberbullying is not limited by physical distance. The anonymity of the internet diminishes self-awareness and concerns about being observed or judged.

Online bullying is a prime example of deindividuation, "a process where certain social conditions reduce our self-awareness and concern with evaluation by others, thus weakening restraints against the expression of undesirable behavior" (Zimbardo, 1969).

49

Cyberbullying affects people around the globe, with many of its victims reporting lower self-esteem (Patchin & Hinduja, 2010).

To progress towards World Peace, we need confident and compassionate citizens and leaders. Education on cyberbullying and instilling a sense of accountability in the use of the internet are necessary to enhance individual and collective wellbeing.

References

Internet World Stats (2016 February 17). World Internet Users Statistics and 2015 World Population Stats. Retrieved February 11, 2016, from http://www.internetworldstats.com/stats.htm

Patchin, J. W., & Hinduja, S. (2006). *Bullies move beyond the schoolyard: A preliminary look at cyberbullying. Youth Violence and Juvenile Justice, 4,* 148–169.

Patchin, J. W., & Hinduja, S. (2010). Cyberbullying and Self-Esteem. *Journal of School Health, 80* (12), 614-621.

Zimbardo, P. (1969). The human choice: Individuation, reason and order versus deindividuation impulse and chaos. In W. J. Arnold & D. Levine (Eds.), *Nebraska Symposium of Motivation* (Vol. 17). Lincoln, NE: University of Nebraska Press

Zimmerman, Adam G. (2012). *Online Aggression: The Influences of Anonymity and Social Modeling.* UNF Theses and Dissertations. Paper 403. http://digitalcommons.unf.edu/etd/403

Editors' Discussion Questions

1. A feature of modern society is the omnipresence of smartphones and social media. Everywhere you turn, you can observe people engaged with their phones. What are the pros and cons of this phenomenon?

2. How prevalent is cyberbullying? What examples can you describe? Have you ever been victimized by online aggression?

Chapter 16

Protect the Protesters

Earl M. Schultz

Abstract: Racial inequality creates tensions, such as the frequent police killings of unarmed Black men, women and children. Those unjustified killings lead to widespread protests. The protesters must be respected, the use of force should be limited and proportionate, and laws must be obeyed.

"Every man of humane convictions must decide on the protest that best suits his convictions, but we must all protest."
~ Martin Luther King, Jr.

America's inequitable distribution of wealth and social goods has inflamed racial tensions, as evinced in recent months by the killing of innocent Black people by police and vigilantes.

This heated racial climate, often violent and lethal, highlights the importance of staying informed and demanding equality through civil disobedience.

Peace requires changes in social structures. Those changes must come about through peaceful, non-violent protest.

Participation in mass demonstrations may cause protesters to experience *de-individuation*: the loss of individual self-awareness and individual accountability (Festinger, Pepitone, & Newcomb, 1952; Zimbardo, 1969). De-individuation fosters a collective identity that affects behavior.

Passions run high during protests and tensions can quickly escalate to violence.

Responses to those protests must adhere to several principles in order to facilitate a peaceful outcome:

- *Protesters must be treated with respect.* Labeling them as "thugs," for example, exacerbates the problem and fails to address their motivation. This principle applies to media, law enforcement, and the public at large.

- *Use of force must be limited and proportionate.* Police must be trained to use the minimum force necessary for the situation, and such force should be proportionate to the conduct of the protesters.

- *Laws must be obeyed.* Illegal activity should be punished and legal activity should be permitted. Too often, law enforcement personnel are the ones who are in violation of the law.

We must not tolerate police brutality and other violence perpetrated against the innocent and those who exercise their right to lawfully protest. We must support and protect protesters as they bravely risk their own freedom and bodies to fight against social injustice.

We must join our fellow protesters in the struggle for World Peace.

References

Festinger, L., Pepitone, A., & Newcomb, B. (1952). Some consequences of deindividuation in a group. *Journal of Abnormal and Social Psychology*, 47, 382–389.

Reicher, S., & Stott, C. (2011). *Mad mobs and Englishmen? Myths and realities of the 2011 riots*. London: Constable and Robinson.

Zimbardo, P. (1969). The human choice: Individuation, reason and order versus deindividuation impulse and chaos. In W. J. Arnold & D. Levine (Eds.), *Nebraska Symposium of Motivation* (Vol. 17). Lincoln, NE: University of Nebraska Press

Editors' Discussion Questions

1. Do you agree with Martin Luther King, Jr.'s edict that "we must all protest"? Why or why not?

2. Martin Luther King, Jr. was arrested and jailed 29 times for breaking local laws. When is unlawful protest warranted, if ever?

Part 4
Attitudes, Behaviors and Persuasion

Turn on your TV. More bullets than kisses. Death as entertainment. What do we expect? America is a killing field on screen, on its streets, in its history, in its DNA. There should be less shock and more SHAME!

~ Marvin Sin

On Attitudes

In the early 20th Century, at the dawn of American social psychology, the concept of *attitudes* attracted a great deal of research attention. Attitudes may be expressed toward any person, place or thing, but social psychologists were particularly interested in *social* attitudes.

One of the earliest measures of social attitudes was the Social Distance Scale by Emory Bogardus (1925). This scale assessed attitudes toward various social groups (i.e., nationalities, racial groups), by asking respondents whether they would accept a person from a target group: (a) into their country, (b) into their city, (c) into their neighborhood, (d) as next door neighbors, (e) as a dinner guest, or (f) as a family member through marriage. These alternatives are ranked according to the "distance" that the respondent would like to maintain with the target person. This scale has been used in hundreds of studies (see Campbell, 1952).

That attitudes are *learned* has been widely accepted, yet Jhangiani and Tarry (2014) presented data that suggested some attitudes are resistant to change because they are *inherited* (Bourgeois, 2002, as cited by Jhangiani & Tarry, 2014). Yet, the assertion that attitudes toward roller coasters, abortion, or the death penalty are inherited (see Table 4.1 in Jhangiani & Tarry, 2014, p. 160) is both untestable and, on sober reflection, absurd.

Attitudes Have Three Components

The "tri-component" theory divides attitudes into three components: cognitive (thoughts, beliefs), affective (feelings, emotions), and behavioral intentions (proclivities to behave in a certain way). Attitudes toward war, for example, include cognitions (knowledge about past or current wars, ideas that war is necessary or evil), affects (feelings of pride or terror), and behavioral intentions (ambitions to become a soldier or peace activist).

Attitudes vary in their salience (how important they are), strength, and complexity. Attitudes that have the three components in alignment are stronger and more likely to predict behavior.

Cognitive Dissonance

People have attitudes about nearly everything and sometimes these attitudes come into conflict, creating what is known as **cognitive dissonance**. For instance, one's belief in the idea of "thou shalt not kill" would be in conflict with his or her support of the death penalty. Cognitive dissonance also arises when attitudes and behaviors are inconsistent. Attitudes and behaviors frequently collide, for example, when one espouses attitudes about good health but engages in self-destructive behaviors.

A national case of cognitive dissonance was the subject of Gunnar Myrdal's (1944) *The American Dilemma: The Negro Problem and Modern Democracy.* Myrdal, a Nobel laureate economist and sociologist from Sweden, described the conflict between American ideals of "freedom and equality" and the American realities of slavery, Jim Crow, and segregation. It is a dilemma that persists in the arenas of race and war and peace.

The A-B Relationship

The utility of the attitude concept has been due, in large part, to its presumed relationship to behavior.

The classic study that challenged this presumption was by Richard LaPiere (1934), who traveled the U.S. with a Chinese couple in the 1930s. During the tour, the trio stayed at a number of motels and ate at a number of restaurants. After the trip, LaPiere wrote the proprietors of the establishments they had visited, and asked whether they accepted Chinese guests. Many of those proprietors answered "no" (this was during a time of rampant anti-Chinese prejudice in many parts of the U.S.). This study launched many years of research on "the attitude-behavior relationship." The conclusion? Attitudes predict *some behaviors for some people, some of the time* (cf. Jhangiani & Tarry, 2014).

Attitude Change and Persuasion

Social psychologists' preoccupation with attitudes – what they are and how they are measured – naturally extended to how attitudes might be changed. Over $500 billion is spent every year, worldwide, on advertising aimed at influencing individuals' attitudes and behaviors.

Key terms in the literature on attitude change include messenger, message, and audience.

Messenger

Effective communicators are more likely to bring about attitude change than ineffective ones. To be effective, a communicator should be attractive and have charisma, credentials, and expertise (Jhangiani & Tarry, 2014). Communicators who speak quickly are often viewed as more confident, knowledgeable and trustworthy. Effective communicators may provide multiple points of view or demonstrate that they are not self-serving.

Message

Messages must grab the listener's attention to be effective. Effective messages offer something beneficial to the recipient. Messages may be geared toward one of the ABCs (attitudes, behaviors or cognitions), and may be one-sided or offer multiple viewpoints. Messages may be humorous, incite fear, or focus on self- or other-concern. Messages may be superficial – requiring little thought or reflection – or complex. Messages may be strong (supported with data) or weak (supported with opinion). Messages may be direct or indirect; obvious or subliminal.

Audience

The audience receives the messages and may be impacted by the attitude change efforts. An audience's receptiveness may depend on the relevance of the communication; or whether they have been forewarned or inoculated about the attempts to change their attitudes or behaviors (Jhangiani & Tarry, 2014, pp. 176-177).

Chapter Overviews

Chapter 17 (*Politicians and Attitudes: Using Persuasion to Create Change* by Alicia Breyer) describes how politicians use fear appeals to rise to power. Breyer urges the cultivation of more positive intergroup attitudes in order to bring about World Peace.

Chapter 18 (*On Dismembering LGBTQ Prejudice* by Madeleine Glouner) explores deeply ingrained attitudes towards the LGBTQ community and the issues that affect them. Glouner notes the value of celebrity endorsement and suggests that respect for others is a pathway to World Peace.

Chapter 19 (*Racial Tensions Cause an Unsafe World* by Gillian Hsieh Ratliff) reviews an article by Brent Staples that describes the plight of Black men in modern society. Hsieh Ratliff calls for an improvement in the projection of media images of Black men.

Chapter 20 (*The Power of Persuasion: Dzhokar Tsarnaev* by Sasha Forbath) provides a case study of one of the Boston Marathon Bombers. Forbath considers how the younger brother, Dzhokar, fell under his older brother's social influence.

Chapter 21 (*Global Warming and World Peace* by Samuel Martin) warns that climate change is a threat to World Peace. Martin views global warming as an opportunity for people to adopt a superordinate identity: "We're all in it together."

Chapter 22 (*A Sad Tale of Persecuted Minorities* by Halford H. Fairchild, Ph.D.) chronicles the tragedies that occur when discriminated against minorities share tension filled spaces. Fairchild recognizes that the basic features of our society set the stage for inter-ethnic conflict and violence.

Chapter 23 (*Obliterate Black-on-Black Violence for World Peace* by Earl M. Schultz) suggests that homicidal violence in Black communities is a product of systemic oppression and segregation. Schultz calls for the remediation of the social policies that corral Black people into destructive environments.

Chapter 24 (*Global Attitudes and World Peace* by Casey Chong) posits that global conflicts arise from a lack of intercultural understanding. Chong advocates for a shift from American individualism to a more global view if World Peace is to be achieved.

Chapter 25 (*The World Needs a Little Attitude Adjustment* by Therese Boter) applies the three components of attitudes – affect, behavior and cognition – to Australian citizens' attitudes towards refugees. Boter calls for an "attitude adjustment," where we see ourselves in others, in order to achieve World Peace.

Chapter 26 (*America Needs Many Tongues* by Halford H. Fairchild, Ph.D.) examines bilingual and foreign language education in the U.S. Fairchild considers bilingualism a cognitive asset that is increasingly necessary in international relations.

Chapter 27 (*The New American Dilemma* by Halford H. Fairchild, Ph.D.) recalls Myrdal's *An American Dilemma* which illustrated the conflict between American ideals of equal opportunity and the reality of *de jure* racial segregation. The new American dilemma exposes the continuing discontinuities between American ideals and the reality of waging war on comparatively defenseless populations, and massive wealth inequality.

References

Bogardus, E.S. (1926). Social distance in the city.*Proceedings and Publications of the American Sociological Society, 20*, 40-46.

Bogardus, E.S. (1947). Measurement of personal-group relations. *Sociometry, 10*(4), 306-311.

Bourgeois, M.J. (2002). Heritability of attitudes constrains dynamic social impact. *Personality and Social Psychology Bulletin, 28*(8), 1063-1072.

Campbell, D.T. (1952). The Bogardus Social Distance Scale. *Sociology & Social Research, 36*, 322-326.

Jhangiani, R., & Tarry, H. (2014). *Principles of social psychology – 1ˢᵗ international edition.* Licensed under a Creative Commons Attribution-NonCommerical-ShareAlike 4.0 International License.

LaPiere, R.T. (1934). Attitudes vs. actions. *Social Forces, 13*, 230-237.

Myrdal, G. (1944). *An American Dilemma: The Negro problem and modern democracy.* Oxford, England: Harper.

Editors' Discussion Questions

1. The editors suggest that the notion that attitudes towards roller coasters or the death penalty are inherited is "ridiculous." Do you agree? Why?

2. America professes freedom and liberty, yet millions of people live trapped in a cycle of abject poverty because they happen to be Black, Brown or Poor. How do you or others handle the dissonance caused by the inconsistencies between American ideals and realities?

Chapter 17

Politicians and Attitudes: Using Persuasion to Create Change

ALICIA BREYER

Abstract: Many factors affect intergroup attitudes. Hitler used *fear appeals* to rise to power. Current leaders threaten similar tactics when calling for a Muslim Registry. Instead of segregating ourselves from those who are different, we must be inclusive and celebrate our differences and our commonalities.

At an early age, we develop the attitudes that shape our beliefs and inform our actions. These are formed through conditioning and experience.

With developing technology and evolving perceptions of people and cultures, attitude change is a natural part of life.

Every day, we are bombarded by images and messages trying to persuade us to purchase products. Advertising and mass media are effective for changing attitudes through persuasion. Employing emotional appeals, advertising companies and politicians target cognitive processes to influence the way people think about an issue, situation or product. Attitude change can be achieved by making emotional appeals or by satisfying 'created needs.'

Fear is a large component of emotional appeals because it targets a person's motivation. Without motivation, attitudes remain static.

Throughout history, emotional appeals, specifically those utilizing fear, have been used for negative purposes. A prime example is Adolf Hitler, who notoriously used Nazi-propaganda and fiery oratory to rise to power and inspire a cult that led to the slaughter of an estimated 11 million Jews, Slavs, and the mentally and physically disabled in German-occupied Europe.

Hitler was an expert communicator, widely viewed as trustworthy by the German people. He used his knowledge of politics and the problems in post WWI Germany to project the image of himself as an expert. Known for his skillful speeches, Hitler used straightforward, confident and quick words to diminish counter-arguments and increase the effectiveness of his messages.

Employing these persuasive techniques (see Jhangiani & Tarry, 2014, chapter 4), Hitler used emotional appeals to argue – purportedly not for his self-interest, but in the interest of the people – that Germany had a right to be strong again. Spontaneous message processing (based on surface features or emotional content) encouraged listeners to find validity in his Nationalist messages.

Hitler gained the support of Germans by vilifying so-called "outsiders" (including criminals, gays, Jews, the disabled, etc.). In fact, "Germans generally turned out to be proud and pleased that Hitler and his henchmen were putting away certain kinds of people who did not fit in" (Gellately, 1996). Exploiting the German people's fear of the other, Hitler adroitly used his communication skills to foment those fears, and then provide a solution: containing and destroying the outsiders.

Even though Hitler is reviled as a murderous despot, and we think such atrocities could not happen again; similar techniques and ideas are still employed today.

Like Hitler, who required Jews to wear an identifying symbol; Donald Trump, the Republican candidate for U.S. president,[1] used fears of ISIS and terrorism to suggest that it might be necessary to "register Muslims in a database or [give] them a form of special identification that noted their religion" (Stone, 2015, p. 3).

While it may be true that many people believe Trump to be an outlier with a slim chance of actually succeeding to the presidency, he is currently leading the polls in states such as South Carolina, Virginia and Nevada. By using paths to persuasion such as authority, consistency and fear, Trump has gained millions of followers.

How is World Peace possible today, when there are still people in power influencing attitudes towards violence and dissent?

First, we must believe that World Peace is possible. Ending global conflict requires a paradigm shift in attitudes towards those who are different: from exclusion, isolation and apathy to inclusion, integration and compassion. We must embrace that which makes others different and

---

[1] Since the drafting of this chapter, Donald J. Trump was elected the 45th President of the United States.

unique, celebrate those qualities we share, and accept all people as partners in the pursuit of World Peace.

References

Gellately, Robert. (1996). Denunciations in twentieth-century Germany: Aspects of self-policing in the Third Reich and the German Democratic Republic. *Journal of Modern History, 68.* 931-67

Jhangiani, R., & Tarry, H. (2014). *Principles of social psychology – 1st international edition.* Licensed under a Creative Commons Attribution-NonCommerical-ShareAlike 4.0 International License.

Stone, Michael. (2015). *Trump goes full Nazi: Wants to close mosques, make Muslims wear ID.* Retrieved September 19, 2015 from www.patheos.com.

Editors' Discussion Questions

1. How is fear used in political campaigns? Can you think of specific examples?

2. Donald J. Trump was elected the 45th President of the United States. How do you evaluate his performance as Commander-in-Chief? Has his leadership led to harmony or disharmony in social relationships? Why?

Chapter 18
On Dismantling LGBTQ Prejudice

MADELEINE GLOUNER

Abstract: While social attitudes are generally malleable, attitudes towards the LGBTQ community are more deeply ingrained. One way to change attitudes is through good communication, and the LGBTQ community has enjoyed a number of celebrity personalities who have advocated for underrepresented groups. World Peace requires that all communities respect one another.

Humans learn to interact with others through experiences and attitudes that develop over time. Attitudes are evaluations that shape how we think and form opinions on a variety of topics, ranging from religion to sexuality.

Attitudes are generally malleable and subject to change. Our attitudes regarding issues or others often intensify when we have "direct positive or negative experiences with the attitude object" (Jhangiani & Tarry, 2014, p. 162). Yet some attitudes are deeply ingrained in personal bias or opinion.

Heterosexism and prejudicial attitudes towards the LGBTQ community, for example, are difficult to dismantle. Reducing homophobic beliefs and behaviors requires unique methods of persuasion.

One of the most important components of persuasion is good communication. Effective communicators are often seen as role models to whom people will listen. In fact, "research has demonstrated that the same message will be more effective if delivered by a more persuasive communicator... attractive communicators are frequently more effective persuaders" (Jhangiani & Tarry, 2014, p. 170) and can be advocates for change.

Celebrities like Caitlyn Jenner, Miley Cyrus, Lady Gaga, Frank Ocean and Ruby Rose have all been involved in the LGBTQ inclusivity movement that has produced millions of supporters. Their success is due, in large part, to their ability to communicate and advocate for underrepresented groups.

Direct experience with an attitude object can change a person's attitudes and behaviors towards that object. As the LGBTQ community gains exposure and acceptance, the dissonance that might arise in heteronormative communities may eventually dissipate.

Positive role models and interactions with the LGBTQ community will engender a more widespread acceptance.

To achieve World Peace, everyone, regardless of gender or sexual orientation, must be respected. Eliminating prejudice and recognizing that we all have something to contribute, will move us towards more social acceptance and eventual World Peace.

Reference

Jhangiani, R., & Tarry, H. (2014). *Principles of social psychology – 1ˢᵗ international edition.* Licensed under a Creative Commons Attribution-NonCommerical-ShareAlike 4.0 International License.

Editors' Discussion Questions

1. How have attitudes towards the LGBTQ community changed over the years? How much change is still needed? In what areas?

2. What strategies do you recommend for changing social attitudes?

Chapter 19

Racial Tensions Cause an Unsafe World

GILLIAN HSIEH RATLIFF

Abstract: Brent Staples' article, *Just Walk on By* (1986), discusses the experience that Black men often face in public: White women recoiling in fear. Television news, reality and drama shows reinforce many racial tensions that have consequences in the real world. Images of Black men need to be improved in order to reduce societal racism.

A White woman walks down the street as a Black man approaches from the opposite direction. The woman clutches her purse and avoids eye contact. This man could be wearing an expensive suit and tie or a sweatshirt and jeans, this woman would react the same because all she sees is the color of skin. Her non-verbal behavior sends a clear message that she is nervous and feels unsafe.

In *Just Walk on By,* Brent Staples – a Black man – recalls many instances in which White women would make these small adjustments when they were around him (Staples, 1986). Staples felt angry for being treated as if he were a criminal. A woman's fear becomes a racist stereotype when she reacts to *all* Black men as if they are criminals trying to steal her purse (Lowe, 2016).

An attitude is a manner of reacting to or thinking about a person, place or thing; and can range from a subtle (unconscious) evaluative reaction, to a more direct expression or overt behavior (Jhangiani & Tarry, 2014). Attitudes help people engage their social environment and express genuine connections with others (Smith, Mackie & Claypool, 2014). Attitudes are stronger when associated with a positive or negative experience.

For example, a woman might see a Black man on TV rob a White woman, thus creating a negative attitude towards Black men. It is common for television – news, reality, and drama – to portray Black men as criminals, which produce and reinforce many of the real-world racial tensions.

Attitudes have affective, behavioral, and cognitive components (Jhangiani & Tarry, 2014). Elaborating on the above example, that woman "learns" that Black men rob White women, so she responds in fear (affect), recalls past associations (cognitions) and clutches her purse (behavior).

Racial tensions are higher than ever, perhaps because of a pervasive lack of trust in our society and government. This lack of trust might be fueled by media portrayals or negative interactions. Tensions between Whites and Blacks are commonly shown in movies, especially in situations involving the police. It should be no surprise that these tensions are manifested nearly every day throughout the nation.

The media can play an important role in our quest for World Peace. By portraying positive images of Black men and featuring harmonious inter-racial interactions, the media may influence societal attitudes and behaviors to become more tolerant. It is only when we can live cooperatively and respectfully with others, that we can end global conflict.

References

Lowe, F. (2016). "The Clutch of Fear." *Chicago Reader*. 14 Feb. 2016.

Smith, E. R., Mackie, D. M., & Claypool, H. M. (2014). *Social psychology*. NY: Psychology Press.

Staples, B. (1986). Just Walk on By. *Ms. Magazine*. February 13, 2016.

Editors' Discussion Questions

1. Racial attitudes may be communicated verbally and non-verbally; they may be conscious or unconscious. What are some of the non-verbal, or unconscious expressions of racial prejudice?

2. How are different racial groups portrayed in television and motion pictures? What are the effects of these portrayals?

Chapter 20

The Power of Persuasion: Dzhokar Tsarnaev

Abstract: Dzhokar Tsarnaev, one of the Boston Marathon Bombers (April 15, 2013), was vilified in the press who made him out to be a monster and evil terrorist. Dzhokar's background and upbringing are reviewed. It is widely held that he came under the social influence of his older brother, Tamerlan. However, violence in the world does not emanate from evil individuals, rather from a variety of societal influences.

Following the Boston Marathon Bombing in 2013, news outlets made Dzhokar Tsarnaev out to be a monster and evil terrorist (Crouch, 2013).

Though Dzhokar Tsarnaev undoubtedly committed acts of terrorism, this does not necessarily mean that he was born evil or psychologically abnormal. Indeed, he had an unremarkable childhood and upbringing.

Born in Kyrgyzstan, a former region of the Soviet republic, he moved to the Republic of Dagestan before immigrating to the U.S. with his family (Sontag, Herszenborn & Kovaleski, 2013).

Tsarnaev's parents made a host of bad decisions while living in the U.S. and, after divorcing, both returned to Russia (Sontag et al., 2013) – leaving a young and impressionable Tsarnaev under the supervision and guidance of his older brother, Tamerlan.

Tsarnaev was well-liked and an apparently well-adjusted teenager with a vibrant social life and likeable personality (LoCicero, 2014). Unlike

---

[1] **Disclaimer**: Sasha Forbath attended the Cambridge Rindge and Latin School, the same high school as Dzhokhar Tsarnaev. Though she never knew him personally, they shared the same teachers and some friends. The arguments in this piece have not been verified by a legitimate source; but many members of the Cambridge community believe Dzhokar's participation in the Boston Bombing to be a result of persuasion.

Tsarnaev, who was popular and captained the wrestling team in high school; Tamerlan did not have an easy transition to the U.S. Tamerlan was a competitive boxer and national champion until he was barred from further participation in the "tournament of champions" due to a rule change in 2010, making only natural born citizens eligible to compete (Sontag, et al., 2013).

With the abrupt end of his boxing career, Tamerlan became much more devoted to Islam (Sontag, et al., 2013). Soon, this growing anti-American sentiment accelerated his radicalization. Indeed, sources suspect that Tamerlan had been radicalized even before his trip to Dagestan in 2012.

Investigators identified Tamerlan as the "main instigator" of the bombing; however the question remains, how and why would such a seemingly well-adjusted 19 year old like Tsarnaev agree to commit a horrific act of terrorism?

The evidence suggests that Tsarnaev was persuaded by his radicalized brother to participate in the Boston Bombing. Yet, it remains unclear exactly how Tamerlan convinced his brother to take part in the commission of such a heinous act.

Tamerlan was a skilled communicator; and Tsarnaev likely viewed him as trustworthy because he was family and knowledgeable about Islamic radicalism. Tamerlan presented an opinion that terrorist actions would effectively communicate anti-American sentiments, making his message even more powerful because it was an opinion held by few (Jhangiani & Tarry, 2014).

It may be that Dzhokhar initially dismissed his brother's invitation to conspire in the bombing, but experienced the *sleeper effect*. Though likely ambivalent and resistant to the idea, Dzhokhar eventually began to believe his brother's anti-American rhetoric and forgot that these comments came from an extremely biased source (Jhangiani & Tarry, 2014).

Perpetrators of violence, like Tsarnaev, act because of their environment and other influences. Violence is a systemic issue and the factors that cause a person to act violently must be identified and understood.

World peace will not be achieved until we recognize that violence is not caused simply by an individual's mental illness or social maladjustment; rather its origins are in the person's interactions with significant others. That interaction is embedded in the complex array of societal forces that propel individuals, groups and nations to violence.

References

Crouch, I. (2013, July 17). The Inconvenient Image of Dzhokhar Tsarnaev. *The New Yorker*. Retrieved March 1, 2016.

Holman, E. A., Garfin, D. R., & Silver, R. C. (2014). Media's role in broadcasting acute stress following the Boston Marathon bombings. *PNAS Proceedings of The National Academy of Sciences oOf The United States Of America, 111*(1), 93-98. doi:10.1073/pnas.1316265110

Jhangiani, R., & Tarry, H. (2014). *Principles of social psychology – 1ˢᵗ international edition.* Licensed under a Creative Commons Attribution-NonCommerical-ShareAlike 4.0 International License.

LoCicero, A. (2014). *Why 'good kids' turn into deadly terrorists: Deconstructing the accused Boston marathon bombers and others like them.* Santa Barbara, CA, US: Praeger/ABC-CLIO.

Sontag, D., Herszenhorn, D. M., & Kovaleski, S. F. (2013, April 27). A Battered Dream, Then a Violent Path. *The New York Times*. Retrieved March 1, 2016.

Editors' Discussion Questions

1. If Dzhokar was influenced by his brother to conspire in the bombing, does this excuse his behavior?

2. Can anyone use the excuse, "the situation made me do it" for misbehavior? Why or why not?

Chapter 21

Global Warming and World Peace

SAMUEL MARTIN

Abstract: Global warming threatens World Peace as the mal-distribution of wealth and natural resources place people in conflict. A focus on ameliorating the effects of global warming might help people to transcend their group interests and embrace a more global identity: *"We're all in it together."*

Global warming has made a future with higher temperatures and rising sea levels – accompanied by more frequent storms, droughts and floods – inevitable. With the accelerated changes in our environment, 'natural' disasters will become more frequent and cause great economic losses, and wildlife and human lives will be at risk (Nature.org, 2016).

One of the greatest threats to *World Peace* is the conflict over diminishing resources.

In 2014, this fear materialized in Syria when severe drought, exacerbated by a warming climate, forced farmers to abandon their crops and seek work in cities. This massive urban migration was a contributing factor to the Syrian Civil War, which ultimately fueled the rise of ISIL. This group of Islamic extremists seeks to establish a worldwide caliphate[1] and often employs terrorism as a means to that end (National Geographic, 2015).

How this regional-turned-global conflict will be resolved cannot be foreseen, but its causes can be identified. One contributing factor that should not be overlooked is climate change, which put all people and nation states at risk.

---

[1] **Editors' note:** "Caliphate" refers to an area that is under the control of a Muslim religious leader. The idea that ISIL or ISIS are seeking to establish a "global caliphate" is an idea propagated by apologists for the use of military force throughout the Middle East. Our view is that the violence in the Middle East is over the control of material resources (oil), not religious dogma. The seeds of contemporary violence were sown with the founding of the Anglo-Persian Oil Company, a British company, in 1908.

Climate change will worsen throughout our lifetimes, even if we stopped producing all greenhouse gases tomorrow. However, hope for reducing climate change's potentially devastating effects may lie in the recent UN Climate Change Conference in Paris, which established standards for reducing carbon emissions and switching to alternative energy sources. This is a start toward a more peaceful future.[2]

Indeed, simply focusing on climate change as a global problem can promote a "we're-all-in-it-together" attitude. It has been demonstrated that increasing attention on international issues, particularly global warming, decreases support for war (Pyszczynski, Motyl, Vail, Hirschberger, Arndt & Kesebir, 2012). Conflicts over dwindling resources, especially those in underdeveloped nations, may be alleviated with diplomatic and economic assistance from third parties (Winter, 2007). The world's biggest polluters should be held accountable and made responsible for providing that diplomatic and economic assistance.

Climate change and its sequelae pose a serious threat to our planet. We must address climate change head on and afford it the serious attention it deserves. We must create a sustainable world, where all share equally in the Earth's precious resources, if we are to achieve an enduring World Peace.

References

National Geographic (2015). http://news.nationalgeographic.com/news/2015/03/150302-syria-war-climate-change-drought/

Nature.Org. (2016). http://www.nature.org/ourinitiatives/urgentissues/global-warming-climate-change/threats-impacts/

Pyszczynski, T., Motyl, M., Vail, K. I., Hirschberger, G., Arndt, J., & Kesebir, P. (2012). Drawing attention to global climate change decreases support for war. *Peace and Conflict: Journal of Peace Psychology, 18*(4), 354-368. doi:10.1037/a0030328

Winter, D. D. (2007). Understanding identification with the natural environment. *Peace and Conflict: Journal of Peace Psychology,13*(2), 247-250. doi:10.1080/10781910701271028

Editors' Discussion Questions

1. What is the author's point of view regarding global warming and human conflict? Do you agree or disagree? Why?

2. Global warming is a big political issue. Why do people deny the reality of climate change? Who benefits from that denial? Who loses?

---

[2] **Editors' note:** Subsequent to the writing of this article (Spring 2016), U.S. President Donald J. Trump withdrew from the Paris Climate Accord, dismantled environmental regulations, and promoted the renewed exploitation of fossil fuels.

Chapter 22
A Sad Tale of Persecuted Minorities[1]

HALFORD H. FAIRCHILD, PH.D.

Abstract: Fifteen-year-old Latasha Harlins was killed by Soon Ja Du, a Korean American merchant. This tragedy reveals the complexities of cross-ethnic relationships in America's inner cities. To prevent tragic recurrences, we must: increase sensitivity to one another; grapple with differences in cultures; develop nonviolent means to resolve conflicts and recognize that basic features of our society set the stage for inter-ethnic conflict and violence.

Latasha Harlins, a 15-year-old African-American school girl, is dead from a gunshot wound to the head after trying to buy orange juice in a South Central Los Angeles convenience store. A 51-year-old Korean-American businesswoman, Soon Ja Du, is in jail for pulling the trigger.[2] But we cannot begin to count all of the victims in this American tragedy.

Clearly, Harlins is a victim. Du is both victimizer and victim. Their families and communities are victimized by grief, and we are left with the need to repair the damage to Korean-Americans' and African-Americans' relations.

The 20th Century is marked by the urbanization of African-Americans. Structural inequality, exacerbated by residential segregation, resulted in isolated communities that remain hard pressed to secure basic economic goods and services. This economic impotence of the African-American community opened the door for non-African-American entrepreneurs to fill the commerce vacuum,

---

[1] This Chapter is revised from an op-ed published in the Opinion Section of *The Los Angeles Times* on March 24, 1991. The murder of Latasha Harlins was on March 16, 1991.

[2] Soon Ja Du spent several days in jail, and was found guilty of manslaughter with a maximum sentence of 16 years in prison. She was awarded probation, sentenced to 400 hours of community service, and fined $500 (Jennings, 2016).

typically at a price that included the added cost of doing business in economically depressed areas.

In many predominantly African American communities, a majority of the convenience stores are owned and operated by Korean-American families. These circumstances are echoed in New York City and other metropolitan areas.

The foregoing economic reality highlights the limited range of opportunities immigrant Koreans have in America. They continually face discrimination in education and employment. Entrepreneurship offers them a reliable path to economic success.

African-Americans, on the other hand, have virtually no meaningful chances to take control of their community's economy. Lack of education and training, as well as employment discrimination, diminishes their economic empowerment. Sadly, their economic peril is historically ingrained and appears intractable.

The ethnic diversification of America necessarily carries with it many dangers. In particular, the confluence of African-American and Korean-American cultures invites conflicts in language, behavioral styles, customs, ideologies and values.

Korean merchants, like any others, face conflicts with customers, competitors and workers. But when customers and merchants are members of groups who each have long and bitter histories of racial and ethnic discrimination, the simple act of buying orange juice, as in the Latasha Harlins' case, can become an occasion for lethal violence.

Several Korean merchants have been killed in the Los Angeles area. It is, therefore, easy to understand why they arm themselves for self-defense. Latasha Harlins was not the first customer to be killed in a store owned by Koreans – she will not be the last. Guns in America have increasingly become the final arbiters of interpersonal and intergroup disputes.

The media contribute to the potential for violent conflict by latching on to images that degrade African-Americans and Asian-Americans. When a group of people are routinely dehumanized in popular culture, as African-Americans are; it is not surprising to see them as frequent victims of nightsticks and guns. A disturbing and enduring lack of fundamental respect for African-Americans connects the beating of Rodney G. King by the LAPD and the murder of Latasha Harlins. African-Americans are the most vulnerable – and victimized – group in American society.

Yet understanding these issues – of structured inequity, of racism, of media prejudice, of cultures in conflict – does not make solutions any easier to identify. Clearly, racism must be eliminated; equal opportunity must become a reality; and sensitivity to different peoples and cultures stressed.

We must translate these broad initiatives into individual practices that reduce prejudice, intolerance and the potential for violent conflict. We must be re-socialized to view the use of lethal force as a method of *no resort*.

Tragedy is certainly not a new theme in America's interracial relationships. The slaying of Latasha Harlins forces us to develop increased sensitivity to differences in cultures and provides an incentive for nonviolent conflict resolution. Fifteen-year-old Natasha Harlins' death is a reminder that basic features of our society set the stage for inter-ethnic conflict and violence.

Editors' Discussion Questions

1. What is the nature of race relations in your city or community? How might they be improved?

2. How do the "basic features of our society set the stage for inter-ethnic conflict and violence"?

3. Should gun laws be made more restrictive? Why or why not?

Chapter 23

Obliterate Black-on-Black Violence for World Peace

Earl M. Schultz

Abstract: The violent crime rate in Chicago is symptomatic of the larger problem of Black-on-Black violence. Because that violence is a product of toxic environments and systematic oppression, we must fix the societal issues that corral Black people into destructive environments.

Chicago is one of the most violent cities in America. Only 7 days in 2015 passed without a shooting or a homicide. The number of Black homicide victims, 399 in total, was nearly 5 times more than any other racial category. Of those victims, more than 96 percent of their alleged assailants were Black, highlighting the enormity of Black-on-Black violence (Illustrating Chicago Crime, 2016).

The media oversimplifies Black-on-Black violence by misrepresenting its causes. Contrary to media portrayals, much of the inner-city violence is not the result of gang related conflicts.

Societal structures produce a vicious cycle of Black-on-Black violence. Black people, particularly those trapped in dilapidated inner cities, are systematically oppressed. They too often lack the resources and opportunities to succeed in American society. Their communities are often unsafe and fail to offer the same educational opportunities to Black youth that are afforded to White youth.

The toxic environments that Black people inhabit expose them to violence, often in their childhood. As a result, many Blacks suffer from a form of post-traumatic stress disorder (PTSD) that may predispose them to violence.[1]

---

[1] These environmental conditions afflict many economically depressed communities, particularly those inhabited by Hispanics, Native Americans, Asian Immigrants and poor Whites.

73

... [A] cavalier attitude towards death grows out of a very limited view of life. Many are uncertain about how long they are going to live and believe they could violently die at any time. They accept this fate; they live on the edge. Their manner conveys the message that nothing intimidates them... (Anderson, 1994, as cited by Newman & O'Brien, 2000, p. 106).

PTSD influences its sufferer's thoughts, which may cause some to feel irritable or be easily provoked. Those suffering PTSD may perceive surrounding threats, even in their absence. These thoughts can influence their actions, causing them to respond aggressively to perceived threats as other more positive, non-violent responses are not readily available (Newman & O'Brien, 2000).

The cycle of Black-on-Black violence runs deeper than simple gang conflicts. The attitudes of many Black people are shaped by their experiences and exposure to violence, which creates paranoia and the proclivity to respond to threats with violence. The violence that plagues most inner cities also permeates American life and culture from this country's founding (Fairchild, 2016).

We must fix the societal issues that corral Black people into destructive environments. We must eliminate inequalities in the workplace and repair our broken school systems that limit opportunities for Blacks and other oppressed people. We need to rebuild infrastructures from the ground up and eliminate corruption from the top. We must put an end to homelessness and provide affordable health care for everyone.

References

Anderson, E. (2002). The code of the streets. Pp 293-304 in S. Gabbidon, H.T. Greene, & V.D. Young (Eds.), *African American classics in criminal justice*. Thousand Oaks, CA: Sage Publications.

Chance the Rapper Talks SNL, Fatherhood, Chi-Raq and much more with the Chicago Morning Takeover [Interview by K., K. G., & L.]. (n.d.). In *WGCI*. Chicago, IL: 107.5 FM.

Fairchild, H.H. (2016). (Re)Solving violence in America. Chapter 11 (pp. 87-100) in H.H. Fairchild (Ed.), *(Re)Solving violence in America*. Delhi: Indo American Books.

Illustrating Chicago Crime, Murder and Mayhem at heyjackass.com. (n.d.). Retrieved February, 2016, from http://heyjackass.com/category/2015-chicago-crime-murder-stats/

Newman, D. M., & O'Brien, J. (2000). *Sociology: Exploring the architecture of everyday life: Readings* (7th ed.). Thousand Oaks, CA: Pine Forge Press.

Editors' Discussion Questions

1. How are African Americans (and other minorities and poor people) "corralled" into toxic environments? What should be done to correct this problem?

2. How is "Black-on-Black violence" a misnomer? What terminology would be more accurate?

Chapter 24
Global Attitudes and World Peace

CASEY CHONG

Abstract: Global conflicts arise from the lack of intercultural understanding and respect. American individualism hinders intercultural interaction and understanding. America should shift its emphasis on the individual and adopt a more global perspective if World Peace is to be achieved.

Many global conflicts arise from a lack of intercultural understanding and respect. In order to achieve World Peace, we must overcome that barrier and embrace cultural differences.

Attitude refers to "our relatively enduring evaluation of something" (Jhangiani & Tarry, 2014, p. 160). Social psychology recognizes the importance of attitudes in daily life.

Everyone holds thousands of attitudes, ranging from relatively weak to very strong. Attitudes are shaped through social interactions, may be formed quickly, and often influence one's behaviors.

The United States is a country that celebrates individualism. Although the appreciation and celebration of self and one's own culture can be beneficial, one drawback is that it can also marginalize or ignore others.

American children often grow up interacting only with others from similar backgrounds. Socialized to view other cultures as "different," Americans tend to lack empathy and have close-minded attitudes towards other cultures. Such attitudes hinder Americans from effectively engaging and connecting with other cultures, which must occur if World Peace is ever to be realized.

To create and sustain a more globally empathetic climate in the United States, Americans must make a concerted effort to experience and enjoy the variety of cultures within its borders and beyond. We must be capable of viewing the world through the eyes of others. The United States must shift its emphasis from the individual (and that which is exclusively American), and adopt a more global perspective. Only then will America be able to engage in a productive conversation that leads towards World Peace.

Reference

Jhangiani, R., & Tarry, H. (2014). *Principles of social psychology – 1ˢᵗ international edition.* Licensed under a Creative Commons Attribution-NonCommerical-ShareAlike 4.0 International License.

Editors' Discussion Questions

1. How does American *individualism* contribute to problems in intercultural understanding? What other issues contribute to these problems?

2. What strategies do you suggest for enhancing intercultural understanding? How might these strategies be used to bring about World Peace?

Chapter 25

The World Needs an Attitude Adjustment

THERESE BOTER

Abstract: Attitudes are comprised of three components: affect, behavior and cognition. These components are revealed in Australian citizens' attitudes towards refugees. Their affect is outrage and fear, their behavior is reflected in negative terminology, and their cognitions treated the refugees as "poor" or "trespassers." An 'attitude adjustment' is needed so that we can see ourselves reflected in others, only then can we achieve World Peace.

"A positive attitude causes a chain reaction of positive thoughts, events and outcomes. It is a catalyst and it sparks extraordinary results."

~ Wade Boggs

Attitude – a degree of feeling towards something or someone – is powerful. It influences how we interact with others (Jhangiani & Tarry, 2014). For example, a person who is angry towards an individual is more likely to be aggressive. Conversely, a person is more likely to engage in polite behavior towards someone for whom he or she admires or has affection. To better understand social interaction, we must first consider attitudes.

The recent refugee crisis in Australia illustrated how negative social attitudes resulted in poor outcomes.

In 2015, the Australian government rejected 15 boats filled with refugees from countries like Afghanistan, Iran, and Sri Lanka before they ever reached land ("Australia asylum: Why is it controversial?" 2015). In 2016, the government was set to deport 37 refugee babies and 90 refugee children ("Asylum seeker families face deportation to Nauru after High Court ruling," 2016). This response to refugees can be readily explained using the components of attitude – *affect, behavior and cognition.*

Affect: Hartley and Pederson (2015) found that many Australian citizens felt outrage and fear toward refugees. Those feelings derived from the perception that non-European refugees would disrupt Australia's cultural, moral and religious values. Based on these feelings, many Australians developed a negative attitude towards refugees and endorsed tougher restrictions against them.

Behavior: Many Australians referred to refugees as "boat people" and the words "illegal" or "criminal" were also commonly expressed. While affect can determine attitude, so too does behavior. In this case, the derogative terms often used by Australians evinced their negative attitude.

Cognition: Louis, Duck, Terry, Schuller and Lalonde (2006) reported that refugees were perceived as of lower socio-economic status than Australians. The belief among Australians that refugees are "poor" or "trespassers" also played a role in their negative attitude towards asylum seekers.

Our attitudes influence how we treat others. Due to the prevailing negative attitudes, Australia experienced strong resistance and refugees suffered.

We need an 'attitude adjustment' – not just for our individual benefit, but for the sake of our planet. We must shift our affect, behavior and rhetoric from fear to empathy. Our cognition must dignify refugees, rather than disparage them, because it is only when we see ourselves reflected in others that we can achieve an enduring World Peace.

References

Asylum seeker families face deportation to Nauru after High Court ruling. (2016, February 3). Retrieved February 27, 2016, from http://www.sbs.com.au/news/article/2016/02/03/high-court-throws-out-legal-challenge-australias-offshore-detention-policies

Australia asylum: Why is it controversial? – BBC News. (2015, November 9). Retrieved February 27, 2016, from http://www.bbc.com/news/world-asia-28189608

Hartley, L. K., & Pederson, A. (2015). Asylum Seekers and Resettled Refugees in Australia: Predicting Social Policy Attitude from Prejudice Versus Emotion. *Journal of Social and Political Psychology*, 3(1), 179-197. Doi:10.5964/jspp.v3i1.476

Jhangiani, R., & Tarry, H. (2014). *Principles of social psychology – 1st international edition*. Licensed under a Creative Commons Attribution-NonCommercial-ShareAlike 4.0 International License.

Louis, W.R., Duck, J.M., Terry, D.J., Schuller, R.A., & Lalonde, R.N. (2007). Why do citizens want to keep refugees out? Threats, fairness and hostile norms in the treatment of asylum seekers. *European Journal of Social Psychology*, 37(1), 53-73.doi:10.1002/ejsp.329.

Editors' Discussion Questions

1. How is the Australian response to the refugee crisis repeated in Europe? In America? What are the similarities and differences?

2. How is it possible to develop cognitions of refugees that recognizes their dignity as human beings?

Chapter 26

America Needs Many Tongues[1]

Halford H. Fairchild, Ph.D.

Abstract: In the U.S., bilingual education is given short shrift in public and private schools. Linguistic minorities confront bewildering challenges in acquiring the *Three Rs* and foreign language education is notably ineffective. Bilingualism must be recognized as a cognitive asset, particularly in the international arenas of business, science, politics and culture.

Language is the medium of human exchange. Language – written and spoken – delimits our species.

The United States is a "salad bowl" of nationalities, ethnicities and languages. Within our borders are individuals who represent hundreds of cultures, languages and dialects.

But language has become heavily politicized and is frequently used as a vehicle for entho-centrism, xenophobia and racism. Language too often serves as a barrier to intercultural awareness and understanding.

Despite our diversity, bilingual education is given short shrift in our public and private schools, and "linguistic minority" children are confronted with the bewildering task of acquiring the *Three Rs*[2] in a language that they can scarcely understand. Our "sink-or-swim" teaching methods deny these children an equal educational opportunity, setting them back for the rest of their lives.

In the context of tight budgetary realities, bilingual education is often last in line for funding and allocation of resources. In Los Angeles, several thousand teaching aides – most of them bilingual – are striking for modest working conditions: four-hour minimum work days, sick pay and medical benefits.

---

[1] This Chapter is revised from an op-ed published in the Opinion Section of *The Los Angeles Times* on December 5, 1990.

[2] Reading, wRiting and aRithmetic.

81

Our colleges are poorly equipped to train teachers in bilingual education, with most programs emphasizing the teaching of English to non-English speakers. This "subtractive bilingualism" is consistent with a value system that degrades languages and dialects other than "standard" English.

Demographic projections point to the increasing heterogeneity of the U.S. population into the 21st Century. Yet our educational systems appear neither willing, nor able to provide relevant learning experiences for the increasingly diverse student bodies that attend our schools.

Bilingual education, in the rest of the world, is the norm – not an odious program fraught with political bickering and divisiveness. Indeed, in most of the world today, the majority of populations are necessarily bilingual or multilingual.

Education in other countries take linguistic diversity into explicit account, where the expectation is that the well-educated person is conversant in two or more languages.

Schools in large metropolitan areas necessarily have linguistic diversity among pupils. Students with proficiencies in languages other than English can (and should) serve as linguistic role models for native English speakers. Instead, they are segregated in classrooms that retard their academic development in the interest of making them fluent speakers of English. The grim reality is that they lose their native language proficiency, while falling behind their English-speaking counterparts in basic academic skills.

Our research indicates that bilingualism is a cognitive asset. Instead of being perceived as a hindrance, bilingualism affords the individual enhanced learning flexibility and a more empathic awareness and understanding of different cultures and world views.

Foreign-language education in the United States typically treats the study of another language as an object of inquiry, rather than as a tool for communication and intercultural understanding. Although the average American college student has been exposed to several years of foreign-language instruction, the majority of college graduates cannot engage in meaningful conversation in any language other than English for more than a few minutes.

International business and commerce require a sensitivity to other cultures and language systems. This demands innovative language-education programs that celebrate the linguistic diversity of students. It requires a desire and a willingness for most of us to acquire the ability to read, write, speak and understand a language other than English. It requires the recognition that the influx of immigrants into the United States presents an opportunity, not a challenge.

A survey of bilingual education in the U.S., and language education in general, exposes some fundamental flaws in the American education system.

By attempting to resolve the issues surrounding language education, we also seek democracy in public education; the enhancement of the intellectual and social development of our populations; increased sensitivity to other peoples of the world; and competitiveness in the international arenas of business, science, politics and culture.

Editors' Discussion Questions

1. Why do many people in the U.S. hold onto an "English Only" mentality? What, if anything, can be done to change that?

2. What are the benefits of bilingualism? Multilingualism?

3. How do some bilingual education programs engage in "language subtraction"?

4. How are the issues raised in this chapter related to the pursuit of World Peace?

Chapter 27

The New American Dilemma

HALFORD H. FAIRCHILD, PH.D.

Abstract: America's ideals of freedom and democracy are in conflict with its foreign policy. This conflict produces a *cognitive dissonance* that should lead to genuine efforts to cease American war making.

Published in 1944, Gunnar Myrdal's *An American Dilemma* illustrated the inconsistencies in American ideals and its racial realities. America professed equal opportunity, but practiced racial segregation. Myrdal's analysis illustrated a *national cognitive dissonance* that was reduced, in part, by the passage of the 1954 *Brown Decision* that ordered the desegregation of public schools in the U.S.

America has long prided itself on freedom and democracy. But, its foreign policy has been antithetical to those very ideals. The 2003 invasion of Iraq was hailed as *"Operation Iraqi Freedom."* Yet, during this "liberation" of the Iraqi people, the U.S. dropped millions of pounds of bombs that destroyed much of the civilian infrastructure, killed thousands of innocent civilians and tens of thousands of men and women serving in the Iraqi military. U.S. soldiers searched house to house and arrested and imprisoned thousands of innocent men; many were tortured and killed. More than 100,000 innocent men, women and children were killed in the search for non-existent Weapons of Mass Destruction. Freedom?

How do we profess *freedom* and *democracy*, while bombing the cities and towns of defenseless people? How are the discrepancies between these beliefs and practices resolved in the American psyche?

The dominant reaction in the U.S. has been to affirm the ideals – however false – while justifying the war-making by demonizing the targets of American weaponry. U.S. citizens avoid the new American dilemma by convincing themselves that wars are for good causes (*freedom* and *democracy*) and the opposition is deserving of "fire, fury and total destruction."[1]

The only way to eliminate the dissonance from U.S. war making is to get the U.S. to stop waging war.

Perhaps cognitive dissonance theory can be useful in the pursuit of peace, not by reducing the tension in the collective American consciousness, but by *increasing* it. This may bring into sharp focus the true nature of the dilemma we face.

American wars are predicated on spreading and defending ideals of freedom, liberty and democracy. Surely these ideals include the right to live.

Yet, wars cause casualties and destroy towns and ways of life. Since World War II, the U.S. is responsible for millions of deaths in dozens of countries (Lucas, 2015). If the American public were made more aware of the horrors our military has wrought on defenseless people, it would raise sufficient psychic discomfort so that people might band together to demand the cessation of war.

Only through anti-war activism, and the eventual elimination of war, will the new American dilemma be resolved.

References

Fairchild, H.H. (2017). (Re)Solving violence in America. Chapter 11 in H.H. Fairchild (Ed.), *(Re)Solving violence in America (Second Edition)*. Delhi: Indo American Books.

Lucas, J.A. (2015). The U.S. has killed more than 20 million people in 37 nations since WWII. https://popularresistance.org/us-has-killed-more-than-20-million-in-37-nations-since-wwii/.

Myrdal, G. (1944). *An American Dilemma: The Negro problem and modern democracy*. Oxford, England: Harper.

Editors' Discussion Questions

1. How do Americans insulate themselves from experiencing dissonance given the discrepancy between their ideals of freedom and democracy and the invasion and bombing of sovereign nations?

2. What strategies might be used to increase the public's awareness of the true motives and consequences of U.S. military interventions and energize them to demand change in U.S. foreign policy?

---

[1] These were the unfortunate words used by Donald J. Trump in reference to North Korea in 2017. They are reminiscent of the "shock and awe" rhetoric employed by the U.S. government when its military invaded Iraq in 2003.

Third Interlude

Kaddish for Lebanon

ROSS ALTMAN

Have you read *The Prophet*
By Kahlil Gibran?
Did you know that all that wisdom
Came from Lebanon,
Underneath the rubble
That used to be Beirut?
How many future Kahlil Gibrans
Lie mute?

       Chorus:
       There must be a better way
       Than this ancient code
       "There are no roads to peace
       Peace is the road."[1]

How many Lebanese refugees
Will it take to break your heart?
How many dead civilians
And families torn apart?
They're only pawns in the game between
Israel and Hezbollah
How many more must die before
A cease-fire? (*Chorus*)

---

[1] This line was written by 20th Century American pacifist A. J. Muste.

Bridge:
An eye for an eye
And a tooth for a tooth
Makes the whole world blind
Ain't that the truth –

They don't need Moses
To part the Red Sea;
They don't need Jesus
In Galilee;
They don't need a miracle
Just common sense—
Someone to help them break
The cycle of violence. (Final Chorus)

Part 5
Person Perception

Be the change you wish to see.

~ Mahatma Gandhi

The essence of social psychology is the study of interpersonal interaction. How important are first impressions? What factors are involved in making initial impressions? How do we think about the motivations of others? How do people differ in their ability to perceive others? These are the questions addressed in Part 5.

First Impressions are Lasting Impressions

The old adage, "first impressions are lasting impressions," appears to be true. Dozens of studies have demonstrated that initial impressions provide the template against which all new information is evaluated. First impressions often become ingrained and are hard to change.

Physical attractiveness has an inordinate influence on interpersonal interaction, especially at the all-important moment of making first impressions. The physically attractive also enjoy *the halo effect,* wherein those who are considered attractive are also perceived as good, competent and worthy. The physically *un*attractive, in contrast, are frequently regarded negatively and less competent.

Unfortunately, attractiveness is determined by the beauty standards of the dominant "race."[1] Racial minorities, therefore, are at a disadvantage in any context where Eurocentric standards of beauty are prevalent.

Non-verbal Behaviors

First impressions are predicated on many stimuli other than physical attractiveness.

---

[1] The term "race" is used with caution (see Yee, Fairchild, Wyatt & Weizmann, 1993; Fairchild, Yee, Wyatt & Weizmann, 1995). "White" beauty standards are propagated throughout the world – but they are based on the "Whites" of Northern European extraction.

A person's style of clothing, walking, talking and gesturing are all factored into making first impressions. People often advertise their values and attitudes through clothing and hair styles, accessories, tattoos, piercings, flags or colors. Manner of speech, tone, gestures, posture and eye contact also influence first impressions.

Studies have shown that persons who are introduced to an audience as either "warm" or "cold" are evaluated in significantly different ways, even when it is the same person giving the same speech. The "warm/cold" effect has been confirmed in dozens of studies (Babad, Kaplowitz & Darley, 1999).

Attribution Theory and Person Perception

Attribution theory, first articulated by Harold Kelley (1967), is concerned with how people infer the causes of their own and others' behavior. Attribution theory – the cornerstone of *social cognition* – focuses on how people think about *why* people do the things they do.

Attributions involve three dimensions: *internality* (whether the cause of behavior was dispositional, due to something inside of the actor); *controllability* (the degree of control the person has over his or her behavior); and *stability* (the degree to which the motivating factor was long-standing or episodic).

Although attribution theory is typically applied to an individual's thoughts about others, it also may be applied to social groups and nation states. For example, survivors of the Jewish Holocaust attributed the atrocities committed by the Nazis to their disposition; whereas German citizens attributed those same atrocities to more situational determinants (Doosje & Branscombe, 2003).

Attributions vary depending on whose behavior is being evaluated and the nature of their actions.

When assessing the behavior of others, *the fundamental attribution error* frequently comes into play and we perceive the behavior of others as due to internal or dispositional causes. However, when evaluating our own behavior, *the self serving bias* features prominently, as we tend to attribute our successes to our internal qualities, and our failures to situational factors.

These attributional biases are revealed in justifications for war. Heinous acts are attributed to the dispositions of our enemies; whereas the atrocities that we commit are attributed to situational demands. In war, each side justifies their actions by the situations that drew them into conflict – often invoking the demonization of the enemy. This is an example of the "mirror-image misperception" as a cause of war (White, 1966).

Chapter Overviews

Chapter 28 (*The Three Evils of War: A Review of White [2004]* by Justin Blankson-Phipps) reviews Ralph White's classic article on "misperception" and war. Blankson-Phipps concludes that the demonization of the enemy contributes to armed conflicts.

Chapter 29 (*The Gun Debate: From Blaming Mental Illness to Sensible Gun Laws* by Alicia Breyer) examines America's culture of violence and the ready availability of guns. Breyer suggests that attributing gun violence to mental illness is an instance of the fundamental attribution error.

Chapter 30 (*Images of the Enemy: When Hatred Wins* by Aidan Hall) explores the role of dehumanization in intergroup violence. Hall cautions against undifferentiated prejudice against Muslims.

Chapter 31 (*A Wake-up Call for Peace* by Halford H. Fairchild, Ph.D.) is a response to the terrorist attacks of September 11, 2001. Written in the days after the attacks, Fairchild calls for peace, not war.

Chapter 32 (*Tackling Health Inequities* by Erick Cruz Grave) describes how the fundamental attribution error can lead to blaming the victims for their poor health. Cruz Grave asserts that healthcare should be a fundamental right throughout the world.

Chapter 33 (*Attribution Bias and the American Dream* by Carla Casares) invokes the fundamental attribution error and just world hypothesis to understand the problem of poverty. Casares explains that understanding the perils that confront people is necessary to achieve World Peace.

Chapter 34 (*Student Labeling and Miseducation* by Casey Chong) considers the problem of labeling and student outcomes. Chong warns that labeling often results in a self-fulfilling prophecy.

Chapter 35 (*Understanding Poverty* by Halford H. Fairchild, Ph.D.) suggests that the fundamental attribution error leads to a blaming of the victim for his or her plight. Understanding the circumstances confronting people living in poverty leads to more comprehensive and effective policy interventions.

Chapter 36 (*How Africa Developed the World* by Halford H. Fairchild, Ph.D.) challenges the stereotypical view of Africa as "undeveloped." Fairchild demonstrates that more advances in human development have taken place in Africa than anywhere else.

References

Babad, E., Kaplowitz, H., & Darley, J. (1999). A 'classic' revisited: Students' immediate and delayed evaluations of a warm/cold instructor. *Social Psychology of Education, 3*(1-2), 81-102.

Doosje, B., & Branscombe, N.R. (2003). Attributions for the negative historical actions of a group. *European Journal of Social Psychology, 33*(2), 235-248.

Fairchild, H.H. (2017). A truly new world order. In H.H. Fairchild (Ed.), *Black Lives Matter: Lifespan Perspectives*. Delhi: Indo American Books.

Kelley, H.H. (1967). Attribution theory in social psychology. *Nebraska Symposium on Motivation, 15*, 192-238.

White, R.K. (1966). Misperception and the Vietnam War. *Journal of Social Issues, 22*(3), 1-164.

Yee, A.H., Fairchild, H.H., Weizmann, F., & Wyatt, G.E. (1993). Addressing psychology's problems with race. *American Psychologist, 48*(11), 1132-1140.

Editors' Discussion Questions

1. Given our own biases, and those of others, is the true understanding of someone's behavior hopelessly elusive? Why or why not?

Chapter 28

The Three Evils of War:
A Review of White (2004)

Justin Blankson-Phipps

Abstract: Ralph K. White (2004) described war as the result of "misperception." Both sides of armed conflicts demonize the enemy, while extolling their own virtues. The enemy is reviled and underestimated. The belief that war is inevitable leads to a self-fulfilling prophecy. Demonizing others, while rationalizing one's own warlike behavior, must end if we are to resolve global conflicts.

> *"People are not normally constituted for war without a supporting emotion, be it hate or fear"*
>
> ~ Ralph K. White

In 2004, Ralph K. White published his definitive essay, "Misperception and War," in *Peace and Conflict: Journal of Peace Psychology*. This chapter reviews that classic effort.

The average person is not born with the capacity to kill. The ability to take a life generally must be developed through hatred and fear. So how is it that within the past 100 years, over 100 million people died in war?

Demonizing and underestimating the enemy, and *rationalizing war-like behavior,* are the "three evils" of war and a by-product of fear and hate.

Before a country goes to war, it must first garner the support of its people. To that end, governments *demonize* the enemy using propaganda to brainwash its citizens.

Once at war, *rationalizing one's own war-like behavior* becomes necessary. This provides soldiers with a reason to fight – whether it be fear of what the enemy can/will do or pure hatred of what the enemy has done.

The prelude to the United States' war against Iraq is a recent example of the foregoing. The terrorist attacks on September 11, 2001 caused Americans to fear terrorism on their soil. President George W. Bush then used the rationale of defending our country to stoke fear in Americans and launch wars against Afghanistan and Iraq.

Rationalizing one's own war-like behavior can be used to justify murder. Soldiers in combat often believe they have no alternative but to fight.

The belief in the inevitability of armed conflict is a *misperception* because wars are, in most cases, unnecessary and/or avoidable (White, 2004).

In the surprise military attack on the U.S. naval base at Pearl Harbor, the Japanese underestimated America's strength. When the U.S. responded by dropping atomic bombs on the largely civilian populations of Nagasaki and Hiroshima, Japan surrendered days later.[1] This conflict could have been avoided without the attack on Pearl Harbor.

The third evil, *underestimating the enemy*, has led to countless unnecessary deaths. Events like the Vietnam war, the bombing of Pearl Harbor and the U.S. war in Afghanistan are recent examples that give testament to the perils of *underestimating the enemy*.

Underestimating the enemy includes a miscalculation of your opponent's military force, and a failure to appreciate the enemy soldiers' level of conviction and commitment. Generally, if soldiers believe they are fighting for a just cause, they will be hard to defeat.

Before a nation attacks another, it should first put itself and its citizens in the proverbial shoes of the enemy, and then decide whether war makes sense and if armed conflict is the best way to achieve the intended result.

When leaders stop demonizing other nations to rationalize their own avarice and war-like behavior, then a meaningful reduction in global conflicts is possible.

References

White, R. K. (2004). Misperception and war. *Peace and Conflict: Journal of Peace Psychology, 10*, 399-409.

Editors' Discussion Questions

1. How are the "misperceptions" described by White (2004) applicable to the conflicts happening around the globe?

2. How does understanding "misperceptions" provide a path toward World Peace?

---

[1] Within the first two to four months of the bombings on August 6th and 9th 1945, the acute effects of the atomic bombings killed an estimated 146,000 people in Hiroshima and 80,000 in Nagasaki.

Chapter 29

The Gun Debate: From Blaming Mental Illness to Sensible Gun Laws

ALICIA BREYER

Abstract: Attributing gun violence to mental illness is an instance of the fundamental attribution error – a failure to identify circumstances that give rise to acts of gun violence. The upward trend in gun violence is largely the result of America's culture of violence, the ready availability of guns, the glorification of violence in the mass media, and profit motives of the gun industry.

To achieve *World Peace*, the U.S. must have peace within its borders. Divides based on race, sexual preference, religion and class hinder social harmony in America.

The ongoing debate over the Second Amendment exposes the conflict between the right to bear arms and the right to be free of gun violence.

Many observers blame gun violence on mental illness, rather than on lax gun control laws or easy access to military-style assault weapons (Fairchild, 2016a; Farris, 2016). Americans have become inured to gun violence.

Causal attribution refers to how people explain the motives behind their own – and others' – behavior (Jhangiani & Tarry, 2014, p. 219). The *fundamental attribution error* occurs when an individual's behavior is seen as dispositional (part of who they are as an individual), rather than situational (due to circumstances). Attributing gun violence to mental illness is an instance of this error.

For example, in the case of the Aurora, Colorado mass shooting, the media was quick to blame mental illness as the cause (Ferner, 2013). But this overly simplistic explanation ignored the circumstances surrounding the shooter, including a culture of violence and the ready availability of military-style assault weapons.

> ...where there are more guns, there is more homicide.
>
> (Alcohol, Drugs, and Firearms, 2013, p. 17).

The U.S. ranks number one in the world in firearm ownership. In 2011, firearms were involved in 32,163 injuries, 11,101 homicides, 19,766 suicides, and 851 accidental deaths (Alcohol, Drugs, and Firearms, 2013).

In regards to suicide and self-harm:

> Differences in mental health do not appear to explain why gun owners and their families are at higher risk for completed suicide than non-gun owning families... Household handgun ownership itself...appears to be positively correlated with suicide (Alcohol, Drugs, and Firearms, 2013, p. 45).

Efforts to prevent gun violence often focus on mental health and access to treatment. While these are legitimate concerns, the real solutions lie in meaningful gun control legislation and enforcement.

The fundamental attribution error – ascribing violent behavior to personal factors (in this case mental illness) – is corrected by shifting attention to a broader array of situational determinants of gun violence:

> ...a culture of violence, an American love affair with guns and the Second Amendment, permissive gun laws, the glorification of violence in the mass media, a rapacious profit motive in the gun industry, and millions of dollars of political puppeteering (Fairchild, 2016b).

Resolving gun violence is vital for achieving World Peace.

References

Alcohol, Drugs, and Firearms. (ADAI Info Brief). Prepared by Meg Brunner, MLIS, and Nancy Sutherland, MLS for the UW Alcohol & Drug Abuse Institute, February 2013.   URL: http://adai.uw.edu/pubs/infobriefs/ADAI-IB-2013-01.pdf

Fairchild, H.H. (2016a). Gun violence in America. Chapter 2 (pp. 17-24) in H.H. Fairchild (Ed.), *(Re)Solving violence in America*. Delhi: Indo American Books.

Fairchild, H.H. (2016b). Personal communication. February 25, 2016.

Farris, M. (2016). Rampage killings. Pp. 69-70 in H.H. Fairchild (Ed.), *(Re)Solving violence in America*. Delhi: Indo American Books.

Ferner, Matt (2013). *Secret James Holmes mental health report completed, given to court*. Retrieved September 9, 2013 from www.huffingtonpost.com.

Jhangiani, R., & Tarry, H. (2014). *Principles of social psychology – 1st international edition*. Licensed under a Creative Commons Attribution-NonCommerical-ShareAlike 4.0 International License.

Editors' Discussion Questions

1. In the U.S., military-style assault weapons are readily available. Should there be restrictions on civilian access to military-style assault weapons? Why or why not?

2. In what ways is violence celebrated in American culture? What, if anything, should be done about this?

3. Why has it been so difficult to pass meaningful gun control legislation in the U.S.?

Chapter 30

Images of the Enemy: When Hatred Wins

AIDAN HALL

Abstract: Dehumanization features prominently in intergroup violence. During the Cold War, the Soviet Union was demonized as an evil empire bent on the destruction of democracy and the American way of life. The new enemies of the West are Muslim fighters, and when we dehumanize them, hatred wins and violence will continue to spread across the globe.

Dehumanization is the behavior or process that undermines the individuality and humanity of others. It features prominently in intergroup violence as it is often the harbinger of moral exclusion[1]. Generally, one cannot inflict serious harm on another without first dehumanizing the victim in one's mind so as to rationalize and justify the violence.

Advocates of war regularly dehumanize the enemy. To justify the fight against "evil", governments create propaganda with the singular purpose of making the enemy seem sub-human to garner support for a war that murders tens of thousands. These blurred images of reality are the by-products of "conflicts between nations" (Miles, 2012).

An example of a demonized enemy ingrained in popular culture is that of the Soviet Union. During the era of the cold war (from 1947 until the collapse of the Soviet Union in 1991), the West came to see Soviets as enemies of democracy and the American way of life.

For the West, the current image of fear is the "radical Islamic terrorist," which has led to a backlash against all Muslims.

---

[1] Moral exclusion is the process whereby stigmatized groups are perceived as outside the boundaries in which moral values, rules, and considerations of fairness apply.

In the wake of the 9/11 attacks and the rise of terrorist organizations like Al-Qaeda and ISIL, anti-Muslim rhetoric and attacks have spiked. In fact, the FBI reported a seventeen-fold increase in anti-Muslim crimes (Human Rights Watch, as cited by Abu-Raiya, et al., 2011).

With origins in fear and a desire for vengeance, the dehumanization of Islamic terrorists has, for some, resulted in the dehumanization of all Muslims. If we allow the image of the *Radical Islamist Terrorist* to become synonymous with all Muslims practicing Islam, then we have allowed hatred to win.

References

Abu-Raiya, Hisham, Pargament, Kenneth I., & Mahoney, Annette. (2011). Examining Coping Methods with Stressful Interpersonal Events Experienced by Muslims Living in the United States following the 9/11 Attacks. *Psychology of Religion and Spirituality* 3(1), 1-14. Retrieved on *PsycINFO*. Web. 25 Feb. 2016.

Miles, Hannah. (2012). WWII Propaganda: The Influence of Racism. *Artifacts Journal RSS*. University of Missouri, Mar. 2012. Web. 25 Feb. 2016.

Editors' Discussion Questions

1. How do you feel about Muslims? How do you feel about the Islamic religion? What are the origins of these attitudes?

2. Many "Radical Islamic Terrorists" have used religion to justify their violence. How do you think terrorists view the targets of their violence? Why do they feel justified in terrorist violence?

3. How was religion implicated, or not, in the U.S. decision to invade Iraq in 2003?

Chapter 31

A Wake-up Call for Peace[1]

HALFORD H. FAIRCHILD, PH.D.

Abstract: The terrorist attacks on September 11, 2001 are a case of the proverbial "chickens coming home to roost." The U.S. has waged war against people in the Middle East for many decades, destroying cities and resulting in tens of thousands of civilian deaths. The United States has been at perpetual war since its founding. The 9/11 attacks should serve as a wake-up call for peace.

September 11, 2001:

I offer my sincerest condolences to the families of the thousands of innocent civilians killed in the terrorist attacks in New York, Washington, D.C. and Pennsylvania.

This unimaginable tragedy must serve as a wake-up call to end war and engender peace in a world shared by billions.

Days after President John F. Kennedy's assassination (November 22, 1963), Malcolm X, the national spokesman of the Nation of Islam, likened the killing as a case of the "chickens coming home to roost." The public and the mass media promptly excoriated him for the remark, as did the leader of the Nation of Islam, the late Elijah Muhammad.

Although his analogy may have been offensive to many, Malcolm simply meant that the assassination of the iconic U.S. President was a case of violence begetting violence.

The retaliation against the United States on September 11, 2001 was an even more apt example of the "chickens coming home to roost."

For decades, the U.S. has waged a one-sided war against people of color in the Middle East. It has supported nation states that have used

---

[1] This Chapter is revised from an article of the same title, published in *Psych Discourse: The Newsjournal of The Association of Black Psychologists,* Volume 32, No. 10, pp. 18-19 (2001).

"made-in-America" weaponry to kill many thousands of civilians. The U.S.'s own militia continues to strike from afar – using stealth bombers, cruise missiles, so-called smart bombs and drones – and cause terror in the hearts and minds of people in Iran, Kuwait, Afghanistan, Sudan, and similar locales.

In this ongoing conflict, the United States has engaged in an "inversion of reality." The U.S. views its military as just, noble and courageous; whereas "terrorists" are seen as evil, depraved and cowardly. Yet while the U.S. strikes in relative safety by employing stealth technology and bombing from afar, those who fight against the mammoth U.S. military machine sacrifice their lives to do so. This begs the question: Who is showing the most bravery?

Of course, we must decry the killing of innocent civilians for any reason. Nothing can justify the hijacking of four U.S. commercial jetliners and crashing them into the World Trade Center, the Pentagon, and the fields of Pennsylvania. Yet while we mourn the loss of American lives, let us be reminded of the lost lives of Palestinians, Iranians, Afghanis, and others who have witnessed the destruction and terror of American "smart bombs" for years, and who have suffered tens of thousands, if not hundreds of thousands, of casualties.

It is ironic that U.S. politicians describe the attacks on September 11, 2001 as "acts of war." Yet, this country has waged war around the globe for more than 200 years. Indeed, the settlement of North America by European malcontents occurred in the context of war waged against the Indigenous Americans and African populations. Early European immigrants generated unimaginable wealth by stealing African people to work land stolen from Indigenous Americans. These colonial wars of conquest are now a *fait accompli*. The Indigenous populations of North America have either been exterminated or remanded to desolate "reservations," Africa remains under the yoke of European (neo)colonialism, and the descendants of African slaves are effectively neutralized through policies of mental, physical and socio-economic incarceration.

The United States has dominated the world through the doctrine of "might makes right." We have a military force that is unassailable. Only the U.S. can fly from Missouri to Afghanistan, refuel in mid air, drop 20,000 pounds of high explosives, and return to Missouri unscathed, indeed, unseen. In this context, it is laughable to see U.S. fighter planes now patrolling the skies over major metropolitan areas. No one in the world can mount the kind of long distance attack on the U.S. that the U.S. can mount on others.

Instead, those who retaliate against the U.S. must sacrifice their lives in hideous suicide missions.

Most troublesome is the talk of war and the undoubtedly severe retaliation that will soon be meted out in the Middle East. Already, the U.S. Embassy in Afghanistan has been shuttered and its diplomats called home, as have various relief agencies in that country. These actions presage a violent and deadly use of force to punish those suspected of being responsible for the unprecedented destruction on U.S. soil during the 9/11 attacks. But what warmongers fail to realize is that the acts of "terrorism" against the U.S. were themselves retaliation for the terror being rained on Middle East populations for decades. So as we retaliate against their retaliation, what is the likely result? Surely, we are on the precipice of a very dangerous and deadly time in world affairs.

Instead of retaliating against the suspected perpetrators, the U.S. should see the violence of September 11, 2001 as a wake-up call for peace. Just as Japan soberly awakened to the futility of war against the U.S. when the U.S. dropped atomic bombs on the civilian populations of Hiroshima and Nagasaki in 1945; so too the U.S. should recognize that the suicidal tactics of committed freedom fighters cannot be prevented. Only peace can prevent a recurrence of the terrible tragedy of September 11th.

It is natural, perhaps normal, to seek retribution for the taking of thousands of American lives in New York, and hundreds more in Washington, D.C. and Shanksville, Pennsylvania. However, it is pure insanity to strike back at shadows, killing thousands of innocent civilians. Each civilian killed by made-in-America weapons creates scores of individuals ("terrorists") committed to retribution – *Death to America!*

Violence begets violence. We must have the courage to say, "I have seen the enemy, and he is us!"

The only rational solution to this crisis is for the U.S. to stop exporting violence and negotiate with those who have legitimate grievances against this country. This is not to say that the U.S. must surrender, as Japan did after the atomic bombings of two of its cities. Rather, it simply means that we must do everything in our power to ensure that such violence does not recur.

The only lasting solution to international conflict is earnest and committed diplomacy.

The U.S. spends more than $600 billion every year on military preparedness (in 2017). To appreciate this staggering figure, $650 billion a year equates to $1.8 billion a day, $74 million an hour, more than $1,230,000 every minute, $20,600 a second. The Bush administration asked congress for an emergency appropriation of $20 billion to respond to the 9/11 attacks; Congress awarded $40 billion. In 2017, President Donald J. Trump proposed a $50 billion dollar increase in military spending; meanwhile, the U.S. is engaged in a trillion dollar upgrade of its nuclear arsenal.

The better solution is to appropriate monies for peace. Even allocating one billion dollars annually – a paltry sum in comparison to military spending – may help lead to world peace. Funds earmarked for peace could be spent on education and bringing leaders and citizens to forums designed to articulate and iron out differences in attitudes and beliefs. Transferring military spending into spending for the pursuit of peace could go a long way toward eradicating the underlying sources of un-ease in our world: hunger, poverty, ignorance, and preventable illnesses. Solving the problem of terrorism – by nation states and individuals – is as simple as allocating the funds to pursue the peaceful resolution of conflicts.

Instead of demonizing our enemies, we must recognize their humanity. Instead of assuming that the individuals who committed heinous acts of terrorism were filled with hate, we should understand that they were also capable of and filled with love: Love for their families, love for their homes, love for the innocents killed in their countries, love for their religion, love for their leaders, love for humanity. They were also filled with hope that their deaths, and the deaths of innocent Americans, would lead to a change for the better. Their deaths, and the deaths of victims on both sides of the Atlantic, must not be in vain.

Let us commit ourselves to the abolition of war.[2]

Editors' Discussion Questions

1. What were the terrorists' motivations for the attack on September 11, 2001? How do different presumed motives lead to different solutions to the conflict?

2. Do you agree that the 9/11 terrorists were "capable of and filled with love"? Why or why not?

---

[1] Since the writing of this article in 2001, the U.S. invaded Afghanistan and Iraq. More than 100,000 innocent civilians were killed. Thousands of U.S. soldiers were killed. A trillion dollars was spent. The U.S. military budget has doubled. The Islamic State was born. Terrorism around the world became commonplace.

Chapter 32

Tackling Health Inequities

Erick Cruz Grave

Abstract: The victims of health inequities are often blamed for their condition. This is an instance of the fundamental attribution error or blaming the victim. More attention should be paid to the situational determinants of inequities in our healthcare system. Healthcare should be a fundamental human right and is necessary for creating a true global community.

Of all the forms of inequality, injustice in health care is the most shocking and inhumane.
~ Martin Luther King, Jr.

Environmental factors within a person's life give rise to health inequities. One's socioeconomic status, living conditions within his or her community, governmental policies, and other factors are all crucial in shaping an individual's overall health.

We often use trait-based, personality-driven, and dispositional factors in explaining the behavior of others. The *fundamental attribution error* is the process for *blaming the victim* (cf. Ryan, 1971). For example, an ill patient may be blamed for his or her deteriorating health, or labeled "too lazy" to obtain regular checkups. It is easier to castigate the patient, rather than repair our broken healthcare system. The *fundamental attribution error* exemplifies how we tend to overestimate the role of the individual and overlook, or at the very least underestimate, the impact of one's circumstances or social environment (Jhangiani & Tarry, 2014, p. 226).

Society tends to discount the power of circumstances to influence all aspects of a person's life. We fail to take into account environmental factors that affect individuals and generally focus on a person's negative traits as the cause of his or her struggles.

Why are some people not receiving proper screenings or basic medical care? What influences a person's decision to not go to a doctor? Language barriers, access to health care, poverty, transportation, are all very significant problems that must be addressed. We must take a holistic approach to healthcare, one that tackles the systemic causes of inequities in our healthcare system. Instead of focusing on ameliorating the symptoms of disease or illness, we should turn our efforts to identifying and eliminating the socio-economic and environmental causes.

We must direct our attention to these social inequities, increase our cultural awareness, provide greater access to public health programs, and expand employer-sponsored health coverage.

Healthcare is a fundamental human right and must be treated as such. Universal health care is one path to creating a true global community.

References

Jhangiani, R., & Tarry, H. (2014). *Principles of social psychology – 1ˢᵗ international edition*. Licensed under a Creative Commons Attribution-NonCommerical-ShareAlike 4.0 International License.

Editors' Discussion Questions

1. What are the "situational determinants" of inequities in health care? How might they be ameliorated and eventually eliminated?

2. What is your opinion about universal health care, wherein everyone receives free healthcare paid for by the government?

Chapter 33

Attribution Bias and the American Dream

CARLA CASARES

Abstract: The *American Dream* – of hard work leading to success – is illusory for many. Yet this belief in the American Dream, combined with the *fundamental attribution error* and *just world hypothesis*, leads to justifications for inequality that blame the poor for their condition. World Peace requires looking beyond dreams, and recognizing the true perils confronting people in their lives.

> *The American Dream: "...that dream of a land in which life should be better and richer and fuller for everyone, which opportunity for each according to ability or achievement .... A dream of social order in which each man and each woman shall be able to attain the fullest stature of which they are innately capable, and be recognized by others for what they are, regardless of fortuitous circumstance of birth or position."*
>
> ~ James Tinslow Adams

One may ponder: What makes America so great?

Democracy? Civil Rights? Liberty? Opportunity? Equality?

The national ethos of the United States, the *American Dream*, is based on the ideals articulated by James Tinslow Adams. The American ideal of *freedom* necessarily includes the *opportunity* for *prosperity* and *success*. It stands for the proposition that, regardless of social class or circumstances of birth, everyone should have equal opportunity for upward mobility if they work hard. In this utopian American meritocracy, hard work is the pathway to a successful and prosperous life.

105

This *American Dream*, however, is illusory to most. The reality is that everyone is not born 'equal,' nor with the same access to opportunities.

In reality, the *American Dream* parallels biases in social psychology that attribute the behavior of others to some personal quality or characteristic, rather than to situational or environmental circumstances.

The *fundamental attribution error* is the tendency to overestimate the role of individual factors, and overlook the impact of situations (Jhangiani & Tarry, 2014). When too much import is given to the individual and not enough attributed to the situation, environment or circumstances, society begins to blame the victims for their victimization. This victim-blaming is related to the *just world hypothesis*, the belief that the world is fundamentally fair (Jhangiani & Tarry, 2014).

Those who believe in the *American Dream* accept the notion that people's outcomes and experiences are necessarily fair. To wit, if a person is successful, then his or her success is attributed to that individual's hard work. This mentality becomes particularly dangerous when people begin to believe that 'good things happen to good people, bad things happen to bad people.' This common aberration of the *American Dream* is often used to rationalize and justify inequality and oppression (Oldmeadow & Fiske, 2007).

The *just world hypothesis* causes people to believe that every person gets what he or she deserves, whether good or bad. People begin making internal attributions about others and eventually start to blame them for their problems (Rubin & Peplau, 1973).

The *fundamental attribution error* and *just world hypothesis* work in concert and place the blame of an individual's plight squarely on the victim's shoulders, while ignoring the socio-economic conditions that created his or her challenges. These challenges, like racism and discrimination, are historically ingrained, intractable and might appear impossible to overcome. This is particularly true given people often view others more harshly than themselves, and tend to blame victims for events that are beyond their control (Lerner, 1980).

This *attribution bias* in the *American Dream* can cloud people's judgment as it obscures the realities of life in America: where people of color are often corralled in poor inner cities with failing schools, under- and unemployment, and afforded little, if any, opportunity to improve their circumstance and escape the cycle of poverty.

World Peace requires looking beyond the *American Dream,* and recognizing the true perils that people confront in their lives. Then we must ask ourselves, how do we create a future reality where every person (in America and around the globe) lives with dignity, without want for the basic necessities of life, and enjoys the same opportunities to reach his or her full potential? We must grapple with that question before we can achieve World Peace.

References

Jhangiani, R., & Tarry, H. (2014). *Principles of social psychology – 1ˢᵗ international edition.* Licensed under a Creative Commons Attribution-NonCommerical-ShareAlike 4.0 International License.

Lerner, M. J. (1980). *The belief in a just world: A fundamental delusion.* New York, NY: Plenum.

Oldmeadow, J., & Fiske, S. T. (2007). System-justifying ideologies moderate status = competence stereotypes: Roles for belief in a just world and social dominance orientation. *European Journal of Social Psychology*, 37(6), 1135-1148. doi:10.1002/ejsp.428

Rubin Z., & Peplau L.A. (1973). Belief in a just world and reactions to another's lot: A study of participants in the national draft lottery. *Journal of Social Issues*, *29*, 73–93.

Editors' Discussion Questions

1. How does the *American Dream* fall short of reality?

2. What is "meritocracy"? Why do some people call it a "myth"? What is your opinion?

3. What obstacles, if any, do you face in achieving your life's ambitions? What are the origins of those obstacles?

Chapter 34
Student Labeling and Miseducation

CASEY CHONG

Abstract: Many children face a myriad of challenges in obtaining a quality education, including being labeled "learning disabled" or "a problem child." Such labels often result in a self-fulfilling prophecy. Teachers should ignore labels and treat each student as an individual in order to enhance their educational outcomes. We must educate future generations, equip them with the tools to shape geo-political relations and, most importantly, inspire them to strive for World Peace.

Education features prominently in the quest for World Peace. In order to meaningfully discuss global issues, future generations need to be educated and *informed*.

Yet, obtaining such an education is often difficult or impossible. While one would hope that teachers would try their hardest to ensure that each child receives the education they need and deserve, this is often not the reality. Sadly, many teachers use their *person-perception* to negatively label certain children, which can adversely affect their educational future.

Person perception, or the process of learning about other people, is a human skill wherein we use social cues to form impressions of others quickly and easily (Jhangiani & Tarry, 2014). Initial perceptions of an individual, regardless of their accuracy, can affect future interactions. Negative perceptions of others occur regularly in human interactions. However, when such negativity occurs in the context of a teacher-student relationship, it can have devastating consequences.

For example, if a teacher in an elementary school decides that a child has an attention deficiency, that label often follows the child throughout his or her educational experience. When a child is labelled as having a "learning problem," his or her schedule may be modified in order to address the purported "disability." Subsequent teachers, aware of the label, may

108

expect this child to be distracted and disruptive and, therefore, reprimand the child more frequently and more harshly than others.

Students labeled "a problem" early in their schooling are often perceived as such by subsequent teachers. The initial label becomes a "self-fulfilling prophecy" (Rosenthal & Jacobson, 1968). These "problem" students do not receive the attention necessary to excel in the classroom, and their positive achievements are often overlooked or downplayed. When students feel they cannot escape their "problem child" label, they may be discouraged from continuing their education.

The initial perception of a single teacher can affix a label on a student that deeply affects the remainder of that child's school experience. A good education is difficult to obtain when the very person charged with educating the student has formed a negative perception that works against him or her.

To guard against the foregoing, teachers must commit fully to giving each child the education that he or she deserves. Teachers should not be influenced by the labels placed on children who do not fit the "perfect student" mold, and recognize that each student is unique and may have different ways of learning. Educators should focus on the positive attributes and individuality of students, instead of negative labels.

The students of today are the ones who will one day work toward World Peace. Educators, therefore, should do everything within their power to ensure that they are prepared to do so.

References

Jhangiani, R., & Tarry, H. (2014). *Principles of social psychology – 1st international edition.* Licensed under a Creative Commons Attribution-NonCommerical-ShareAlike 4.0 International License.

Rosenthal, R., & Jacobson, L. (1968). *Pygmalion in the classroom: Teacher expectation and pupils' intellectual development.* New York: Holt, Rinehart & Winston.

Editors' Discussion Questions

1. Many students are labeled with various disorders early in their schooling. ADHD (Attention Deficit Hyperactivity Disorder) is one of the more popular labels in recent years. What are the effects of this labeling?

2. How would educational practices change if all children were presumed to be gifted?

Chapter 35
Understanding Poverty

HALFORD H. FAIRCHILD, PH.D.

Abstract: Attributional biases lead many to blame the poor for their impoverishment. Such victim blaming is then codified in unpalatable and ineffective policies. Shifting the focus to the circumstances that confront the poor suggests more feasible solutions for the eradication of poverty.

William Ryan developed the *Blaming the Victim* thesis (Ryan, 1971), wherein people use attributional biases to justify their own station in life and to disparage those less fortunate than themselves.

Attribution theory is concerned with how people think about the *causes* of behavior (Kelley, 1967). These causes – or attributions – vary on a number of dimensions: *internality* (in the disposition of the person or due to external circumstances), *stability* (whether on-going or episodic) and *controllability* (under the person's control or not) (Kelly, 1967).

Those with attributional biases believe the poor are poor because they: (a) are of poor genetic stock; (b) have low ambition; (c) are too lazy to work; and/or (d) are embedded in a "culture of poverty" and are poor by their own design. These attributions are internal, stable and controllable. Taken together, they perfectly illustrate the *blaming the victim* problem.

If the victim can be blamed for his or her plight, then society is absolved from meaningful interventions.

Attributing the causes of poverty to impoverished individuals – that is, blaming the victim – leads to unpalatable policies. Some of the more odious "solutions" have been to limit population growth of minority and poor people through voluntary or forced sterilization. Others have adopted draconian punishments for populations "more prone to crime" – including an increased readiness to impose the death penalty (Herrnstein & Murray, 1994).

Only by shifting our focus to the *situational* circumstances confronting people living in poverty can we hope to create more compassionate, comprehensive and effective policies.

Poverty is a man-made[1] condition, created through hundreds of years of appropriating native lands and enslaving millions, murdering millions of others, and remanding their descendants into ghettoes, barrios, reservations and townships. The person born into an impoverished environment may suffer malnutrition, shelter instability, violent neighborhoods, and non-existent or failing schools. The escape from poverty is all but impossible.[2]

Impoverished communities are characterized by schools that fail their students (Fairchild & Fairchild, 2017). Students are then almost forced to enter informal economies that place them in frequent contact with law enforcement. Such contacts lead to arrests, criminal records, incarceration and sometimes death.

Identifying the causes of poverty in the *situations* of impoverished persons suggest clear policy initiatives: advancing educational opportunities by investing in schools, personnel and curricula; demanding equal educational outcomes; and creating jobs (and eradicating poverty) through infrastructure revitalization.

Public safety must be redefined from policing and incarceration to investments in human capital (in schools and jobs). At the national level, priorities must shift from military dominance to domestic and human development (Fairchild & Fairchild, 2017).

A proper understanding of the causes of poverty is required before lasting solutions may be crafted and implemented.

The eradication of poverty is a necessary condition for achieving World Peace.

References

Fairchild, H.H. & Fairchild, H.F. (2017). Reflections on Black Lives Matter. Afterword (Pp. 307-316) in H.H. Fairchild (Ed.), *Black Lives Matter: Lifespan Perspectives*. Delhi: Indo American Books.

---

[1] "Man-made" is a male-centric term, generally to be avoided, but used intentionally in the current context.

[2] The escape from poverty is not impossible; just improbable. Success stories of individuals escaping harsh childhood environments are the 'exceptions that prove the rule.'

Herrnstein, R., & Murray, C. (1994). *The bell curve: Intelligence and class structure in American life.* NY: Free Press.

Kelley, H.H. (1967). Attribution theory in social psychology. *Nebraska Symposium on Motivation, 15*, 192-238.

Editors' Discussion Questions

1. How do "schools fail their students"?

2. What, in your opinion, are the causes of poverty? Based on each of the causes you list, what are the solutions?

Chapter 36

How Africa Developed the World[1]

HALFORD H. FAIRCHILD, PH.D.

Abstract: Despite the popular belief that Africa is "undeveloped," "less developed" or "under-developed;" Africa is the birthplace of humanity, and is the locus of the longest period of human development. The great leaps forward in human development were achieved in Africa, before recorded history. African progress was interrupted by *The Maafa's* 400 years of conquest, enslavement, segregation and discrimination. Through the theft of land, people and labor, Africans developed the modern world.

The idea of an undeveloped Africa dies hard. Contemporary discourse includes phrases such as "undeveloped," "less developed," "under developed" or "developing" to characterize the "Third World," particularly Africa.

A Black Studies perspective, however, recognizes the strange perversion of the *Truth* when it comes to Africa. Far from being underdeveloped or developing, it is more accurate to recognize that human development began in Africa and continued there for a much longer period of time than anywhere else on the face of the earth.

European scholars have portrayed Africa as a continent of "stagnated development." Captain Richard Burton, the nineteenth century British explorer, suggested that Africans had failed to develop from the primitive to the civilized and had reached a point of "helplessness" that could not be improved (Davidson, 1969, p. 24). Sir Samuel Baker, in 1866, claimed that the African "...mind is as stagnant as the morass which forms its puny world" (cited in Davidson, 1969).

---

[1] This paper is revised from one published in 2000 in *Psych Discourse*, Volume 31 (10), 12-13. It was originally written as an instructor's example of a response to a week's readings in Introduction to Black Studies, taught at The Claremont Colleges, Fall, 2000.

The First People

Basil Davidson (1969) and other scholars in the African-centered tradition, including Cheikh Anta Diop, Jacob Carruthers and John Henrik Clarke (see Karenga, 1993), have thoroughly debunked the notion of "stagnated development" in Africa.

The fact that human development originated in Africa is conceded even in Western (White) archeology, specifically in the highly regarded research of Louis and Mary Leakey and their colleagues (Leakey, 1933, 1935). This research established, without equivocation or debate, that the human species originated in Africa. The origins of *homo sapiens* (the sentient or thinking beings) were in Africa as were our nearest phylogenetic ancestors. Today, there is no serious debate about the fact that all human beings have African ancestry. (This observation may one day lead to a more collective identity that defeats racism and nationalism.)

For many thousands of years, the human race progressed in Africa. The challenges confronting early humans were daunting: a harsh environment with extreme climates, a huge land mass, and myriad predators that posed life-and-death dangers (see Davidson, 1969). African people, undoubtedly dark skinned and superficially similar to Africans today, not only survived these rigors of existence – but they thrived. Their population mushroomed from a mere handful to many millions. Early Africans invented language, were the first to use tools and fire, developed agriculture, animal husbandry and created community organization. These great leaps forward in human achievement laid the foundation for human culture: the arts, literature, religion and science.

Many credit the ancient Greeks with establishing civilization out of thin air; but the historical record clearly situates these achievements in Africa, many thousands of years before the first Greek learned the alphabet. Ancient Africans provided the bedrock upon which all other human cultures are built (cf. Davidson, 1969). *Africa developed the world.*

The Ancients

From the head start given to them by tens of thousands of years of human development, ancient Nubian and Ethiopian cultures flourished in the Nile River Valley. Following the northerly flow of the 3000-mile-long Nile River (the Great African Highway), African civilization reached its apex in Egypt (Karenga, 1993). This south-to-north movement was enhanced through reciprocal influences in West Africa, Europe, the Middle East, the Indian subcontinent and elsewhere. Evidence of the African influence on world cultures is apparent in creation myths, linguistics, music and the arts (see Davidson, 1969). The oldest scripts are of African origin, as are the oldest books (Karenga, 1993).

The Greeks (500-350 BC, nearly 2500 years *after* the building of the first Egyptian pyramid) plagiarized much of Egyptian philosophy (see George G.M. James' *Stolen Legacy*, and Martin Bernal's *Black Athena*).

Africans explored and settled the world. Can you imagine the surprise on the European explorers' faces when they found dark skinned peoples in Australia, New Zealand, Fiji, Tonga, India, Sri Lanka, Cambodia and virtually every "new land" they "discovered"? As Fryer (1984) noted, Africans were in Britain before the English.

The African *Maafa*

The *Maafa,* a term advanced by Drs. Marimba Ani (1994), Wade Nobles and others, refers to the 400-year period of African enslavement, degradation and dehumanization. It is an experience that is unprecedented in human history.

The rapacious appetite of the European Conquerers (Los Conquistadores) raped and pillaged people and places. Their insatiable greed demanded free (or near free) labor to maximize their accumulation of capital. When they encountered indigenous people in the Caribbean and Americas, they killed the men, raped the women, stole the land, and destroyed their culture (Shepherd, 1999). The resistance of Caribbean women was so great that many of them sacrificed their children – through infanticide – so that they would not have to suffer the dehumanizing treatment of the colonizers (Shepherd, 1999). Who, then, are the true barbarians?

Plantation economies in the Americas demanded a ready supply of land and labor. As Williams noted, "Negroes…were stolen from Africa to work the lands stolen from the Indians in America" (1994, p. 9). It was a strange case of "survival of the fittest": African laborers were superior to Native American and White laborers, and therefore contributed to the strengthening of the 'peculiar institution' of slavery throughout the Americas (Williams, 1994). The White captors acted as parasites on the Black masses and depended on them for their own survival.

For another three hundred years (including the present), Africans developed the world through their stolen land and their stolen bodies. Africa (with its abundant natural and human resources) fed the coffers of the European capitalists. African labor, forced through captivity, created enormous wealth for those who enslaved others. It was this great accumulation of capital that gave impetus to the Industrial Revolution and all of the other hallmarks of Western "civilization."

Today, America is regarded as a rich and powerful country. Many Western European countries, including Australia and South Africa, are correctly viewed as controlling massive resources and a disproportionate share of the world's wealth. A proper understanding of this (mal)distribution of resources can only be obtained by re-examining the history of European and American expansionism and colonialism.

Africans (along with the indigenous populations in the Americas, the South Pacific, and Asia) developed the world.

References

Ani, M. (1994). *Yurugu: An Afrikan-centered Critique of European Cultural Thought and Behavior*. Trenton: Africa World Press, 1994.

Bernal, M. (1987). *Black Athena: The Afroasiatic roots of classical civilization*. Rutgers University Press.

Davidson, Basil. (1969). *The African Genius: An introduction to African social and cultural history* (Part 1, Pp. 23-41). Boston: Little, Brown & Company.

Fryer, Peter. (1984). 'Those kind of people.' Chapter 1 (pp. 1-13) in *Staying power: The history of Black people in Britain*. London: Pluto Press.

James, G.G.M. (1954, 1985). *Stolen Legacy* (Reprint Edition). San Francisco, CA: Julian Richardson Associates, Publishers.

Karenga, Maulana (1993). Black History (chapter 2.1 – 2.3). Pp., 69-108 in *Introduction to Black Studies*. Los Angeles, CA: University of Sankore Press.

Leakey, L.B. (1933). *Adam's ancestors*. Oxford, England: Longmans.

Leakey, L.B. (1935). *The stone age races of Kenya*. Oxford, England: Univ. Press.

Shepherd, Verene, A. (1999). Indigenous Caribbean women. Chapter 1 (pp. 1-19) in *Women in Caribbean women history*. Oxford: James Curry.

Williams, Eric. (1994). The origin of Negro slavery. Chapter 1 of *Capitalism and Slavery*. Chapel Hill: University of North Carolina Press.

Editors' Discussion Questions

1. If the human species originated in Africa, does that make everyone "African descended"? Why would such an idea be resisted? What benefits might be derived from this awareness?

2. On a global level, wealth is mal-distributed. A small number of people are extremely rich, while hundreds of millions live in extreme poverty. Should wealth be re-distributed? Why or why not?

Fourth Interlude
Marie

ANDY MANOFF

Marie

If I don't make it home tonight
Give my love to Marie
And tell her that I've gone away
And not to wait for me

    Cause when they called me
    I could not turn away
    This is your country
    It's her that you must save
    Don't turn away

Now they say these are the sands of time
And I must learn to be a man
But filled with fear and hunger for my home,
And my Marie
A stranger in this land

    And when they showed me
    Who I'd have to kill
    I looked in their eyes
    I could not find the will
    I turned away

Now I'm holding on to memories
Of things I used to know so well
Like my Marie
If I don't find a way
To get back home and see her soon
I'll fade away

Just a different point of view
And they would still be left alive
But waiting in these lonesome sands of time
Ten thousand future soldier's graves and they're
piling high

If I don't make it
Back to my Marie
Will you please hold her
In your arms for me
And say good-bye

© 1990 Words and music by Andy Manoff

Part 6
Conformity and Obedience

*I oppose the war in Vietnam because I love America.
I speak out against it not in anger but with anxiety
and sorrow in my heart, and above all, with a
passionate desire to see our beloved country stand
as a moral example of the world.*
~ Martin Luther King, Jr.

Social psychology is the science of how an individual's attitudes, feelings and behaviors are affected by others.

In Part 6, we explore how individuals *conform* their attitudes, beliefs and behaviors to those of others. Social influence also occurs at the behest of authority figures. Whether we *obey* or not depends on many situational factors, including the *power* wielded by leadership.

These issues – conformity, obedience and submission to authority – were illustrated dramatically in two prison studies: one simulated and one real.

Conformity

Conformity happens every day to everybody. We conform in every social sphere we occupy – from our families, neighborhoods, schools, communities, nation states, and the global community. Bronfenbrenner's theory of nested spheres of social influence is useful in this context.

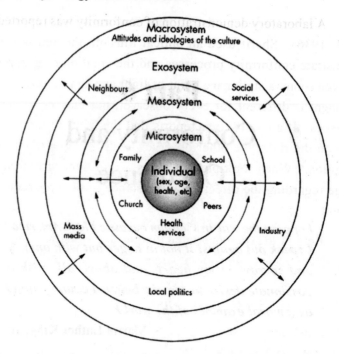

The individual is nested within ever-broadening spheres of social influence. At the *micro* or familial level, we conform to the requirements of living in shared spaces (assuming we want to live in harmony). At the *meso*-level, we conform to the norms that govern neighborhoods and schools – in dress and personal conduct. At the *exo*-level, we conform to the rules of the road and workplace. At the broader *macro*-level, we conform to certain ideologies – capitalism, consumerism, racism, religious dogma and the like. These social systems move through time (the *chronos*-system), and conform to mores and values that have shaped human existence since the origin of the species.

Conforming To Be Right

People conform to be right. We like to feel that we have "correct" information, and conform our opinions to those of experts. In this process of *informational social influence* (Jhangiani & Tarry, 2014), we compare our attitudes and beliefs with those of others, and adjust them to be in agreement with what we perceive to be correct. This process is similar to *social comparison* (Festinger, 1954), wherein we compare our beliefs, attitudes and behaviors with those of similar others.

A laboratory demonstration of conformity was reported by Muzafir Sherif (1936). Sherif used an optical illusion, the auto-kinetic effect, to demonstrate conformity processes and the creation of group norms. In a darkened room, a stationary point of light appears to move. The apparent movement is different for every observer, but may be affected by social influences. If a co-observer reports that the point of light is moving two inches to the right, the other observer tends to agree (conform) with this perception. When multiple observers are present, group norms quickly emerge regarding the direction and distance of the apparent movement of the light.

Berg (1962) demonstrated that the auto-kinetic effect was sensitive to racial attitudes in inter-racial situations. Whites with negative attitudes towards Blacks were less likely to conform their perceptions in the auto-kinetic paradigm compared to Whites with more positive racial attitudes.

Conforming To Be Liked

Solomon Asch (1956, 1961) published some of the most influential experiments in social psychology on conformity. The "Asch Paradigm," as it became known, involved the situation wherein a research participant sat among a group of other research participants who, in reality, were "confederates" of the researcher. The researcher asked them to judge the length of lines: was a target line equal in length to which of three comparison lines? The lines varied significantly in length, and only one of the three was clearly correct. The task appeared easy.

Yet, one-by-one, the research "confederates" gave an incorrect response to the question. When it was the real participants' turn, most of them conformed to the majority opinion – even when that opinion was obviously incorrect. These amusing experiments were captured on film, and may be found on YouTube (search for Asch conformity studies).

The conformity processes reported by Asch were a form of *normative social influence* – conforming to be liked and to avoid rejection (Jhangiani & Tarry, 2014). Such processes may be influenced by the social status of others – including sex and race (Berg, 1962; Janney, Mallory, Rossitto & Simon, 1969). People are more likely to conform to high status others.

Obedience to Authority

Stanley Milgram (1963) conducted one of the most controversial series of studies in social psychology. He wanted to better understand the horrors of the Holocaust. How could thousands of German soldiers be complicit in the murder of millions of people? To answer that question, Milgram (1963) invited ordinary citizens to come to a laboratory for a study ostensibly about learning; but in reality, they entered what was to become a torture chamber for many of the research participants.

The research participant was paired with a confederate of the researcher. In what appeared to be a random process, the confederate was assigned the role of "learner," while the research participant was assigned the role of "teacher." The teacher "taught" the learner a list of word pairs and, during the testing phase, "punished" the learner with an electric shock whenever he or she made a mistake. In reality, no electric shocks were delivered to the learner, who played a pre-recorded schedule of correct and incorrect answers during the testing phase of the experiment.

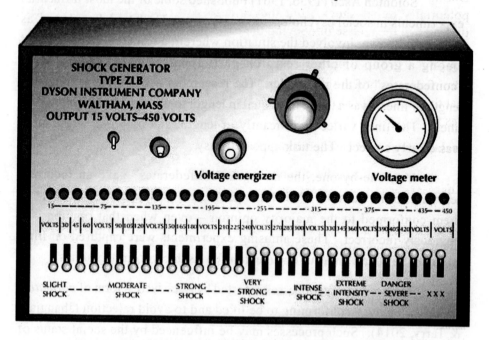

The teacher was told to administer increasing levels of shock intensity, in 15 volt increments, starting at 15 volts to a maximum of 450

volts (see the "shock generator," above). The shock generator was labeled with ominous warnings, and the "learner's" tape recorded responses included cries of pain. In fact, the learner stopped responding at 350 volts. The learner's failure to respond from that point forward suggested that he or she was unconscious or dead. Nevertheless, the majority of "teachers" obeyed instructions to administer shocks up to 450 volts, and administered that level of shock *three times* before the experiment was terminated.[1]

Milgram conducted this experiment in many different configurations – changing settings, "authority figures," scripts, etc. – but the overarching conclusion was the same: most people would comply with the authority figures' instructions all the way to the potentially lethal end of the shock generator.

This experiment was important for several reasons. It demonstrated that ordinary people can be coerced to engage in potentially lethal behavior towards others – albeit under the guise of "obedience to authority."

The Milgram Experiment was also instrumental in revising guidelines and ethical standards for the treatment of research participants. During the course of the experiment, the majority of "teachers" administered potentially lethal shocks, but they did so with considerable emotional turmoil. In the course of obeying the experimenter's instructions, most of the participants exhibited extreme nervousness and stress. Although they were later debriefed – and relieved to learn that they had not actually administered any real shocks to the "learner" – they left with the knowledge that they could have killed someone just because someone told them that it was necessary for an experiment.

Social Power and Leadership

Everyone has the potential to influence others. French and Raven (1959) described five forms of *social power*: *reward* (providing benefits); *coercive* (providing punishments); *legitimate* (earned status, such as teachers); *referent* (persons with whom we might identify, such as celebrities); and *expert* (knowledge based). These forms of social power combine within different leader personalities to produce greater or lesser social influence.

---

[1] One of the best video summaries of the Milgram experiment may be found here: https://youtu.be/eTX42lVDwA4. Milgram made a 42 minute documentary that is available here: https://youtu.be/1HcMWlnTtFQ.

Leaders might be *charismatic* (using the force of their personality), *transactional* (focusing on getting the job done) or *transformational* (willing to make more dramatic changes). The *contingency model of leadership effectiveness* (Jhangiani & Tarry, 2014) asserts that a leader's effectiveness is determined by the interactions between the qualities of the leader and the characteristics of those being led.

The Power of the Situation: Imprisonization

Philip Zimbardo's simulated prison in the basement of the psychology department at Stanford University was one of the most important social psychological studies ever conducted (Haney, Banks & Zimbardo, 1973; also see Haney & Zimbardo, 1998).

Zimbardo and his students, Curtis Banks and Craig Haney, recruited college aged men to live in a simulated prison for several weeks. Each man tested within normal psychological profiles, and was randomly assigned to the role of "guard" or "prisoner." The guards wore a uniform and mirrored sun glasses (depersonalizing features); the prisoners wore smocks and were treated in dehumanizing ways (referred to as numbers instead of names, strip searched, blind folded, etc.).

Researchers were compelled to terminate the experiment after only six days due to the extraordinary reactions of the young men. Some of the guards became sadistic, shielded by the anonymity of their roles. Some of the prisoners suffered emotional breakdowns, with one begging to be released after only two days.[2]

The "power of the situation," as demonstrated in Zimbardo's simulated prison, was tragically replicated in the real world prison, Abu Ghraib (Zimbardo, 2007, 2008).[3]

In March, 2003, the United States invaded Iraq, ostensibly in search of (non-existent) weapons of mass destruction. After weeks of bombardment, ground forces conducted house to house searches and arrested tens of thousands of Iraqi citizens – mainly adult men, many of whom were imprisoned at Abu Ghraib (a former Iraqi prison).

---

[2] Zimbardo produced an hour-long documentary of the experiment, which can be found on YouTube.

[3] The Ghosts of Abu Ghraib, an HBO documentary, may be found here: https://youtu.be/FGpaOp6_I7M.

In April 2004, a cache of photographs was made public that revealed horrible scenes of torture within the prison. Prisoners were stripped naked, forced to engage in homosexual acts, covered in excrement, bitten by dogs, and tortured in ways designed to humiliate and cause death. The sadism at Abu Ghraib was eerily reminiscent of the abuses that emerged in Zimbardo's simulated prison (Zimbardo, 2008).

Social influence occurs on many levels. The state-sponsored violence in Afghanistan and Iraq has led to the retaliatory terrorism that we have witnessed in recent years – in New York, Washington, D.C. and Pennsylvania on September 11, 2001; and horrific attacks on civilians in Paris, San Bernardino, Orlando, London, Brussels, Istanbul and Barcelona. These connections must be acknowledged and remedied if we are ever to achieve World Peace.

Chapter Overviews

Chapter 37 (*Conforming During the Japanese-American Internment* by Therese Boter) considers the reasons why people conform. Boter considers a case of non-conformity during the Japanese Internment period in U.S. history.

Chapter 38 (*Pioneers of Peace Psychology: Herbert Kelman* by Tianze Cheng) reviews Herbert Kelman's autobiography (Kelman, 2010). Cheng describes Kelman's career as a "model of social responsibility."

Chapter 39 (*Prescriptions for Women's Faces: Flipsides of the Same Misogynistic Coin?* by Halford H. Fairchild, Ph.D. and Oona Doyle) is a collection of three photographs (by Fairchild) and a drawing (by Doyle). After viewing the artwork, Fairchild and Doyle challenge readers to answer the question posed in the title.

References

Asch, S. E. (1956). Studies of independence and conformity: I. A minority of one against a unanimous majority. *Psychological Monographs: General and Applied, 70*(9), 1-70. doi:10.1037/h0093718

Asch, S. E. (1961). Issues in the study of social influences on judgment. In I. A. Berg, B. M. Bass, I. A. Berg & B. M. Bass (Eds.), *Conformity and deviation* (pp. 143-158). New York, NY, US: Harper and Brothers. doi:10.1037/11122-005

Berg, K. R. (1962). Ethnic attitudes and agreement of White persons with a Negro person in the autokinetic situation. *Dissertation Abstracts, 33*(1), pp. 334.

Festinger, L. (1954). A theory of social comparison processes. *Human Relations,* *7,* 117-140.

French, J. R. P. J., & Raven, B. (1959). The bases of social power. In D. Cartwright, & D. Cartwright (Eds.), *Studies in Social Power* (pp. 150-167). Oxford, England: University of Michigan.

Haney, C., Banks, C., & Zimbardo, P. (1973). Interpersonal dynamics in a simulated prison. *International Journal of Criminology & Penology, 1*(1), 69-97.

Haney, C., & Zimbardo, P. (1998). The past and future of U.S. prison policy: Twenty-five years after the Stanford prison experiment. *American Psychologist, 53*(7), 709-727. doi:10.1037/0003-066X.53.7.709

Janney, F., Mallory, S., Rossitto, R., & Simon, J. (1969). Conformity as a function of race and age. *Psychological Reports, 25*(2), 591-597. doi:10.2466/pr0.1969.25.2.591

Jhangiani, R., & Tarry, H. (2014). *Principles of social psychology – 1ˢᵗ international edition.* Licensed under a Creative Commons Attribution-NonCommerical-ShareAlike 4.0 International License.

Milgram, S. (1963). Behavioral study of obedience. *The Journal of Abnormal and Social Psychology, 67*(4), 371-378. doi:10.1037/h0040525

Sherif, M. (1936). *The psychology of social norms.* Oxford, England: Harper.

Zimbardo, P. (2007). *The Lucifer effect: Understanding how good people turn evil.* New York, NY, US: Random House.

Zimbardo, P. G. (2008). The journey from the Bronx to Stanford to Abu Ghraib. In R. Levine, A. Rodrigues, L. Zelezny (Eds.), *Journeys in social psychology: Looking back to inspire the future* (pp. 85-104). New York, NY, US: Psychology Press.

Editors' Discussion Questions

1. Describe how conformity issues are evident in your everyday behavior.

2. What are some "less obvious" forms of conformity?

Chapter 37

Conforming During the Japanese-American Internment

Therese Boter

Abstract: People conform with others to be liked and to avoid rejection. These processes were evident during the days of the Japanese-American Internment. Fred Korematsu conformed to dominant values by altering his physical appearance and changing his name, yet he refused to comply when it came to Internment. Breaking free of the pressure to conform is, at times, necessary to fight for what matters.

> *The opposite of bravery is not cowardice but conformity.*
>
> ~ Robert Anthony

People like to feel accepted. In an effort to feel like they belong, they often will alter their behavior, beliefs, or opinions to fit in with the majority – this is called *conformity*. A variety of conformities exist; but under *normative social influence*, people conform *to be liked* and *to avoid rejection* (Jhangiani & Tarry, 2014).

To Be Liked

Many Japanese-Americans began conforming when they faced rising anti-Japanese sentiment during WWII. After the 1941 attack on Pearl Harbor, the fear of another Japanese infiltration permeated the U.S. This prompted President Roosevelt to sign Executive Order 9066, which authorized the military to relocate American citizens with Japanese ancestry to concentration camps (Robinson, 2001).

The order to inter Japanese-American citizens prompted many of them to conform to American beliefs in order to gain acceptance by Whites. In response, the Japanese American Citizens League was formed to help second generation Japanese (the *Nisei*) assimilate to American ideals and prove that they were devoted citizens (Spickard, 1996).

To Avoid Rejection

Fred Korematsu, a Japanese-American citizen, conformed in various ways. He reshaped his eyes with plastic surgery to look less Japanese and changed his name to Clyde Sarah (Danico & Ocampo, 2014, p. 614).

By conforming, people lose their sense of individuality. Many Japanese-Americans sacrificed their identity as Japanese to become part of a larger group of Americans. For Korematsu, he altered his physical self, changed his name and embraced American values over his cultural heritage – all in an effort to be accepted by White America.

Though conforming to avoid rejection from White Americans, Korematsu refused to comply with internment in concentration camps. He defied military authority and went against crowds of Japanese-Americans who obeyed the internment order. Yet by refusing to leave his home and appealing his conviction to the Supreme Court, Korematsu fought for justice for all Japanese-Americans.

When faced with social injustice of any kind – from internment camps, to mass incarceration or failing schools, we all must be brave and resist. We must not fear rejection or exclusion from the majority; instead, we must be steadfast in our fight for social justice – wherever that battle lies.

References

Anthony, R. (1986). *The Ultimate Secrets of Total Self-Confidence*. Penguin.

Danico, M. Y., & Ocampo, A. C. (Eds.). (2014). *Asian American society: An encyclopedia* (Revised, annotated ed.). Los Angeles, Calif.: SAGE Reference.

Jhangiani, R., & Tarry, H. (2014). *Principles of social psychology – 1st international edition*. Licensed under a Creative Commons Attribution-NonCommercial-ShareAlike 4.0 International License.

Robinson, G. (2001). *By order of the president: FDR and the internment of Japanese Americans*. Cambridge, Mass.: Harvard University Press.

Spickard, P. R. (2009). *Japanese Americans: The formation and transformations of an ethnic group*. New Jersey: Rutgers University Press.

Editors' Discussion Questions

1. How is conformity necessary in human affairs?

2. Why is conformity often a problem?

Chapter 38

Pioneers of Peace Psychology: Herbert Kelman

TIANZE CHENG

Abstract: Herbert Kelman's autobiography (Kelman, 2010) details his efforts to resolve the Palestinian-Israeli conflict. After fleeing the devastation of WWII, Kelman developed his passions for psychology and the pursuit of peace.

This chapter provides a summary of a classic autobiography in peace psychology, that of Herbert Kelman (2010). Kelman chronicles his efforts to resolve the Palestine-Israeli conflict. He describes his early start in anti-war movements, then recounts his education in social psychology and his interest in the Palestine conflict.

Born in 1927 to a Jewish family in Vienna, Kelman and his sister joined a Zionist organization as teenagers.

Later, his family fled the devastation of WWII and emigrated to the U.S. They settled in New York and it was there, at age 18, that Kelman published his first articles on what would become his life's work – the pursuit of peace. Determined to pursue his passion for peace and justice, Kelman matriculated to Yale University in 1947 and earned his Ph.D. in social psychology.

A devoted peace researcher during the 1950s, Kelman joined other academics to establish The Department of Behavioral Sciences at Stanford University.

Kelman suffered a stroke in late 1972. Cognizant of his mortality, he committed fully to work in interactive problem solving, specifically conflict resolution in the Middle East.

Kelman contributed to peace scholarship at various institutions of higher learning in the U.S. and abroad.

The former director of the Program on International Conflict Analysis and Resolution at Harvard University's Weatherhead Center for International Affairs, Kelman was also the recipient of the Association for Psychological Science's 2000 James McKeen Cattell Fellow Award for being "a model of the social responsibility of psychologists" and "always placing the moral dimension at the center of his work" (James McKeen Fellow Award 2000).

Herbert C. Kelman's biography is a clarion call to all who seek World Peace.

References

Herbert C. Kelman (2010) Looking Back at My Work on Conflict Resolution in the Middle East. Peace and Conflict, 16:361-387, Taylor Francis.

James McKeen Cattell Fellow Award (2000). Herbert Kelman, Harvard University.

Editors' Discussion Questions

1. Is social psychology the ideal discipline to address issues of peace and justice? Why or why not?

2. What will it take to bring about peace in the Israeli/Palestinian conflict? Are Israeli settlements in Palestinian territory a problem? Why or why not?

Chapter 39

Prescriptions for Women's Faces: Flipsides of the Same Misogynistic Coin?[1]

HALFORD H. FAIRCHILD, PH.D. AND OONA DOYLE

Abstract: The title of the chapter poses a question to the reader based on the images of women from different cultures.

---

[1] Photographs by the author; taken from Facebook images available to the public.

Editors' Discussion Questions

1. How do you answer the question posed in the title of the article?

2. When women dress in order to emphasize certain features or parts of their bodies, does this take away from their internal qualities? Is it fair to say that these cultural practices are misogynistic? Why or why not?

Part 7
Close Relationships

If we ... define love as caring behavior that confers survival benefits, then love is a decisive aspect of our evolution.

~ Ashley Montagu

The study of close relationships is an integral part of social psychology, and features prominently in the social sciences. At least two journals are devoted to this topic: *Journal of Social and Personal Relationships*, and *Journal of Family Psychology*. Division 43 of the American Psychological Association, Society for Couple and Family Psychology, focuses on these issues. Other divisions have strong emphases in close relationships (Division 44, Society for the Psychological Study of Lesbian, Gay, Bisexual and Transgender Issues; Division 45, Society for the Psychological Study of Culture, Ethnicity and Race; and Division 51, Society for the Psychological Study of Men and Masculinity).

Part 7 explores initial attraction, close relationships, romance and love.

Initial Attraction

Physical Attractiveness

In Western cultures, an inordinate emphasis is placed on physical attractiveness. Unfortunately, attractiveness is narrowly defined in culturally and ethnically/racially specific ways. "Ken and Barbie" might be thought of as the prototypical beautiful people: young, White, affluent, blonde and thin. These culturally-determined beauty standards have persisted for many years.

First impressions are largely based on physical appearance, and "attractive people" enjoy the "halo effect" of also being thought of as good, intelligent and successful (Dion, Bersheid & Walster, 1972). This halo effect influences many of our relationships and may contribute to discrimination in all spheres of social life.

Gender Differences in Perceived Attractiveness

The widely accepted theory of gender differences in perceived attractiveness is that men are primarily attracted to physical features (youthfulness, facial attractiveness, hip-to-waist ratios), whereas women are more attracted to social status. Jhangiani and Tarry (2014) rely on evolutionary psychologists, such as Rhodes (2006), to offer a *natural selection* explanation for these gender differences. According to Rhodes (2006), men are attracted to young, curvaceous women because they are more likely to provide reproductive success; whereas women are attracted to men of high status because they can best provide for their offspring. Other evolutionary theorists have posited that men are more likely to philander so as to enhance the probability that their genes will be transmitted to future generations (Wilson & Daly, 1993).

Debunking Evolutionary Theory

These evolutionary explanations are, however, seriously flawed. As noted elsewhere in this text, evolutionary psychology suffers from the problem of teleology – assuming that end results are the product of a natural process. What better natural process than Darwinian evolution to explain gender differences? Debunking Darwinian theory is necessary because it serves as the intellectual cornerstone of the *isms* that give rise to imperialism, racism, sexism, genocide and war.

A more plausible explanation for gender differences in perceived attraction may be that it is simply the product of more than two thousand years of male usurpation of social and material power.

Somewhere in our ancestral past, men and women were egalitarian and lived harmoniously. However, for most of *recorded* Western history, men have ruled families, societies and nations.

Evolutionary explanations for male dominance suggest that men rose to prominence because of natural or biological forces (Wilson & Daly, 1993).

The problem is that Darwinian theory applies exclusively to the evolution of *species*; and not to the evolution of *cultural practices*.

An alternative and more likely explanation is that men have usurped social power with the false ideology of male supremacy, and have maintained that power differential through rituals and traditions that have survived for the past two thousand years or more. Male-centered ideologies that derogate women justify these unbalanced social relations.

It may be that men desire younger women because they are more easily dominated. It may be that women prefer men with higher social status because men generally have superior social statuses – bestowed upon them by generations of misogynistic customs.

The emphasis on physical attractiveness has other perils. Women, in particular, are objectified. In most cultures, women are objectified through cosmetics, hair styles and clothing that draw attention to their bodies, body parts and facial features. The extent to which emphasis is placed on the exterior – the face and body – is the extent to which the internal qualities of the person are under-emphasized. Yet, the objectification of women is nearly universal across the globe. *Objectification is dehumanization.*

A second peril derives from the culturally defined standards of beauty – and the hegemony of White Euro-American definitions of attractiveness. Most of the world is not White. Yet, most of the world is victimized by White/European cultural imperialism – from Hong Kong to Johannesburg to Sao Paolo to Tokyo – people of color spend considerable proportions of their time and resources to "look White." This is seen in the eye surgery popular among Asian people to "Westernize" their eyes (Shirakabe, Kinugasa, Kawata, Kishimoto & Shirakabe, 1985). It is evident in African women's emulation of straight hair styles (Patton, 2006). It is demonstrated in the light colored contact lenses that are popular among all people – but especially among people of color (Redway, 2015).

What are the psychological costs of emulating the physical appearance of a powerful group that disparages one's own? What are the psychological benefits and costs of being a member of the idolized group or race?

Propinquity

Close relationships are more likely among people who live in close proximity. Bossard's classic study reported that among 5,000 consecutive marriage licenses issued in Philadelphia, one-third of the couples lived within half a mile of each other prior to marriage (Bossard, 1932). The percentage of licenses decreased as the distance increased between the couples getting married.

We are much more likely to meet, fall in love, and marry someone in our community than a person living in another state or continent. Friendships form among peers in closer contact with each other. People in close geographic proximity interact more and familiarity breeds liking (Reis, Maniaci, Caprariello, Eastwick & Finkel, 2011).

Similarity

People are drawn to *similar* others. This attraction is predicted by social comparison theory – we validate our own attitudes, beliefs and behaviors against those who are similar to ourselves. We are not going to judge our success in life against that of Bill and Melinda Gates (the billionaire Microsoft philanthropists); however, we are more likely to compare ourselves to people who are in, more or less, similar circumstances.

In like manner, we are more likely to have interactions with those with similar demographics to our own. Over the course of human history, people living in close proximity grew more similar by virtue of selective inbreeding. Cultural, racial and linguistic groups formed tens of thousands of years ago, in remote geographical locales.

Residential living patterns have been shaped by the history of racial/ethnic isolation. People are attracted to others who, more often than not, are of similar racial, ethnic, linguistic, and/or economic background. This is true for casual and intimate relationships.

Close Relationships

Many factors contribute to long-lasting close relationships (including physical attractiveness, propinquity and similarity). Close relationships are characterized by intimacy, self-disclosure, and a sense of "we-ness" (Aron, Aron, Tudor & Nelson, 1991).

Relationships serve different purposes. Some relationships are *communal*, marked by interdependence and sharing; others are based on *social exchange*, wherein the participants weigh the costs and benefits in maintaining the relationships. Relationships are most enduring when the partners are committed and love each other.

Love

One of the most cited definitions of love is Sternberg's *Triangular Model of Love* (Sternberg, 1986).

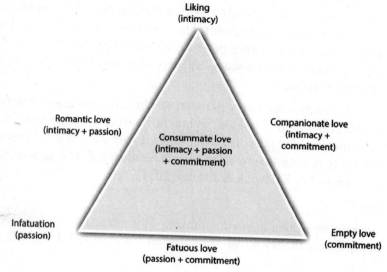

The corners of Sternberg's triangle are Passion, Intimacy and Commitment. Sternberg conceptualized various forms of love according to the level of emphasis on each of these three poles. The "highest" and perhaps most satisfying form of love, according to Sternberg, is Consummate Love (when Intimacy, Passion and Commitment combine).

Attachment Styles

The success or failure of personal relationships depends largely on each individual's *attachment style*. Decades of research, mostly in child development, have identified a variety of attachment styles: secure, anxious/ambivalent, avoidant and disorganized. The most successful relationships occur when both partners exhibit secure attachment styles (Shaver & Brennan, 1992).

Millennial Relationships

Recent technological developments affect personal relationships; particularly the proliferation of smart phones and social media which enable nearly constant interaction with significant or anonymous others. Close relationships may be enhanced, for example, by going "Facebook official." On the other hand, relationships may be destroyed in social media by violations of trust through bullying or posting embarrassing information.

Chapter Overviews

Chapter 40 (*Loving Your Self and Valuing Personalities* by Carla Casares) decries the emphasis placed on physical attractiveness. Casares urges more focus on partners' inner qualities and shared attitudes and values.

Chapter 41 (*Hyper-Masculinity Is Not Hot* by Madeleine Glouner) exposes hegemonic masculinity as a contributor to the subjugation of women and racial minorities. Glouner calls for an emphasis on equality and respect as a route toward World Peace.

Chapter 42 (*It's Hard Out There for a Female* by Madeleine Glouner) considers the problem of gender inequality in the corporate world. Glouner offers strategies to empower women in the workplace.

References

Aron, A., Aron, E.N., Tudor, M., & Nelson, G. (1991). Close relationships as including other in the self. *Journal of Personality and Social Psychology, 60*(2), 241-253.

Bossard, J. H. (1932). Residential propinquity as a factor in marriage selection. *American Journal of Sociology*, 219-224.

Dion, K., Berscheid, E., & Walster, E. (1972). What is beautiful is good. *Journal of Personality and Social Psychology, 24*(3), 285-290.

Jhangiani, R., & Tarry, H. (2014). *Principles of social psychology – 1ˢᵗ international edition*. Licensed under a Creative Commons Attribution-NonCommerical-ShareAlike 4.0 International License.

Patton, T. O. (2006). Hey girl, am I more than my hair?: African American women and their struggles with beauty, body image, and hair. *NWSA journal, 18*(2), 24-51.

Redway, L. (2015). Black folks and colored contacts: Tips to avoid looking a mess. Ebony (June 3). http://www.ebony.com/style/black-folks-and-colored-contacts-tips-to-avoid-looking-a-mess-504#axzz4ObruCTFi

Reis, H. T., Maniaci, M. R., Caprariello, P. A., Eastwick, P. W., & Finkel, E. J. (2011). Familiarity does indeed promote attraction in live interaction. *Journal of personality and social psychology, 101*(3), 557.

Rhodes, G. (2006). The evolutionary psychology of facial beauty. *Annual Review of Psychology, 57*, 199-226.

Shaver, P. R., & Brennan, K. A. (1992). Attachment styles and the" Big Five" personality traits: Their connections with each other and with romantic relationship outcomes. *Personality and Social Psychology Bulletin, 18*(5), 536-545.

Shirakabe, Y., Kinugasa, T., Kawata, M., Kishimoto, T., & Shirakabe, T. (1985). The double-eyelid operation in Japan: its evolution as related to cultural changes. *Annals of plastic surgery, 15*(3), 224-241.

Sternberg, R. (1986). A triangular theory of love. *Psychological Review, 93*, 119-135.

Wilson, M., & Daly, M. (1993). An evolutionary psychological perspective on male sexual proprietariness and violence against wives. *Violence and victims, 8*(3), 271.

Editors' Discussion Questions

1. How do technology and social media affect relationships?

2. How has technology affected your relationships?

3. What safeguards can be implemented to reduce the detrimental effects of technology on close relationships?

Chapter 40

Loving Your Self and Valuing Personalities

CARLA CASARES

Abstract: Too much emphasis is placed on physical attractiveness. Popular beauty standards are unattainable for most, and emphasize outer physical features at the expense of inner qualities. We should value the inner qualities of our partners and shared attitudes and beliefs.

Physical attractiveness influences relationships. People generally prefer those who are young and who have symmetrical facial features and bodies (Jhangiani & Tarry, 2014). Advertisers feature unusually attractive people to promote their products.

Physical attractiveness plays a major role in people's lives and influences social interaction. Which begs the question, "What influences what we find attractive?"

For decades, mass media have distorted our perception of what is considered beautiful. Images of women, for example, have been manipulated so dramatically that "beauty" may feel unattainable to most. This is problematic when young adults spend considerable amount of money on cosmetics and plastic surgery to make themselves more "attractive."

With so much value placed on being "perfect" in the media, expectations of one's own appearance may be unrealistic. A clear connection can then be made of images of "perfect people" in the media and low self-esteem. When we compare ourselves to others, we undermine and under-value our true identity. Thus, to attain inner peace, we must learn to love ourselves as we are.

Although attractiveness is important, we should stress other characteristics. We should encourage people to place more importance on

139

personalities, rather than physical attributes. When contemplating a serious relationship, a person should consider a potential partner's values and beliefs. Close relationships are more successful when a couple shares similar attitudes and values (Jhangiani & Tarry, 2014).

When people are happy in a close relationship, they experience high self-efficacy, self-esteem and positive mood (Jhangiani & Tarry, 2014). We are more secure in life and with ourselves when we know someone who truly cares about and supports us. This, too, will contribute to a higher level of inner peace.

Finding someone who shares your values and with whom you are compatible is more important to sustaining a relationship than physical attraction.

Achieving World Peace will not be easy; nevertheless, we have a good idea where to start: within yourself. When you challenge the popularized media concepts of beauty, and realize that these images have been manipulated; you can begin to accept who you are and begin to celebrate your own unique beauty.

Self-acceptance and finding a companion that shares common values and beliefs will help both partners find inner peace.

References

Jhangiani, R., & Tarry, H. (2014). *Principles of social psychology – 1ˢᵗ international edition.* Licensed under a Creative Commons Attribution-NonCommerical-ShareAlike 4.0 International License.

Editors' Discussion Questions

1. How does the emphasis on physical appearance differ for men and women? What accounts for these differences?

2. How do beauty standards affect you?

3. Many women around the world wear some type of facial makeup. Is this a symptom of self objectification? Why or why not?

Chapter 41

Hyper-Masculinity Is Not Hot

Madeleine Glouner

Abstract: Men who appear to be masculine – strong, aggressive, macho – are generally viewed as more desirable. But the hegemonic masculinity that permeates American society contributes to the global subjugation of women and racial minorities. World Peace requires the dismantling of these prevailing values and replacing them with an emphasis on equality and respect.

Although intimate relationships are based on more than physical appearance, attraction is very important in the initial stages of a romantic relationship. For example, females who look "youthful" are perceived as being more attractive. Males who appear to be masculine – strong, aggressive, macho – are viewed as more desirable (Jhangiani & Tarry, 2014, p. 299).

But the perception of masculinity as more attractive – and thus, more valuable – can be harmful.

Hegemonic masculinity permeates American society. The traditional definitions of the *masculine ideal* – which gives license to male dominance in social spheres – is "the most valued, most accepted, and most legitimate form of masculinity" (Bloksgaard, et. al., 2015). This provides the ideological justification for the global subordination of women – and of racial, ethnic, and sexual minorities – to White heterosexual men. *Hegemonic masculinity* idealizes patriarchy, and loathes (and/or fears) homosexuality and femininity (Kimmel, 1996).

This emphasis on hyper-masculinity as being most desirable has proven problematic in the U.S., where men are valued for being tough and aggressive (Hofstede, 2003). Western masculinity is a source of the rampant violence in the U.S. and provides the rationale for the subordination women and minorities.

World Peace requires the dismantling of these predominant values and replacing them with an emphasis on equality and respect for all.

References

Bloksgaard, L., Christensen, A., Jensen, S. Q., Hansen, C. D., Kyed, M., & Nielsen, K. J. (2015). Masculinity Ideals in a Contemporary Danish Context. *NORA: Nordic Journal of Women's Studies*, *23*(3), 152-169. doi:10.1080/08038740.2015.1046918

Hofstede, G. (2011). Dimensionalizing Cultures: The Hofstede Model in Context. *Online Readings in Psychology and Culture, 2*(1). http://dx.doi.org/10.9707/2307-0919.1014

Jhangiani, R., & Tarry, H. (2014). *Principles of social psychology – 1st international edition.* Licensed under a Creative Commons Attribution-NonCommerical-ShareAlike 4.0 International License.

Kimmel, M. (1996). *Manhood in America: A Cultural History.* NY: The Free Press.

Editors' Discussion Questions

1. In what ways is *hegemonic masculinity* manifested in American society? In other cultures?

2. What will it take to dismantle the prevalent over-valuation of masculinity and replace it with an emphasis on equality for all?

Chapter 42

It's Hard Out There for a Female

MADELEINE GLOUNER

Abstract: Gender inequality pervades the workplace due to corporate culture. In her TED talk, Sheryl Sandberg, Facebook C.O.O., urged women to be more assertive. Strategies to empower women in the workplace are offered.

Gender inequality and stereotypes continue to permeate workplace dynamics. Gender representation in upper level corporate positions is imbalanced due to the long history of gender bias in business and the world at large.

Working women often suffer from "acceptance of one's own low status as part of the proper and normal functioning of society" (Jhangiani & Tarry, 2014, p. 511), which contributes to the lack of female leaders in many professions. Women who are motivated to climb the corporate ladder face many obstacles. This "glass ceiling" is a barrier that keeps women from obtaining more powerful positions (Cotter, Hermsen, Ovadia & Vanneman, 2001).

Sheryl Sandberg, Facebook C.O.O., has undertaken a major initiative to address gender inequalities in the workplace. Her TED talk, "Why We Have Too Few Women Leaders", addresses key behaviors that women need to exhibit in order to achieve leadership positions and success (Sandberg, 2010). The most important piece of advice she offers is to "sit at the table." Women systematically underestimate their abilities to be a part of the conversation.

In order to succeed in the male dominated workplace (and society), women *must* assert themselves – which is no easy feat. Because leadership in the workplace is overwhelmingly male, women in positions of power face the adverse effects of in-group favoritism (*the tendency to respond more positively to people from our in-groups than we do to people from out-groups)* (Jhangiani & Tarry, 2014, p. 481). Consequently, female leaders are often isolated and lack support of male coworkers.

The perception of women in leadership positions reflects a gender bias in the appraisal of a leader's likeability, competence and effectiveness. Butler and Geis (1990) reported that, when proposing the same initiatives, women leaders elicited more negative non-verbal emotional responses than their male counterparts.

The "boys club" mentality pervades the corporate environment. To empower females to aspire to leadership roles, we must make dramatic changes in corporate culture. Providing female mentors, implementing more inclusive methods of hiring, and equalizing pay to those of their male counterparts, will go a long way towards eliminating gender bias and creating a more diverse work environment.

References

Butler, D., & Geis, F. L. (1990). Nonverbal affect responses to male and female leaders: Implications for leadership evaluations. *Journal of Personality and Social Psychology, 58,* 48-59.

Cotter, D., Hermsen, Ovadia, S. & Vanneman, R. (2001). The glass ceiling effect. *Social Forces, 80,* 655-682.

Jhangiani, R., & Tarry, H. (2014). *Principles of social psychology – 1ˢᵗ international edition.* Licensed under a Creative Commons Attribution-NonCommerical-ShareAlike 4.0 International License.

Sandberg, S. (2010). Sheryl Sandberg: Why we have too few women leaders. [Video file] Retrieved from http://www.ted.com/talks/ sheryl_sandberg_why_we_ have_too_ few_women_leaders.html.

Editors' Discussion Questions

1. What strategies should women use to gain respect in the workplace?

2. What can be done to bring about gender equality in all aspects of societal functioning? Is it possible? Do you believe you will see true gender equality in your lifetime? Why or why not?

Fifth Interlude

Letter From The Front

ANDY MANOFF

Letter From The Front

I fought your god damn war
Dug my own grave
I followed all your rules
No one was saved

You've got no answers
You've got no guts
Your head is screwed on wrong
You must be nuts

I thought you knew us
I thought you cared
We all have one dream
And this ain't fair

We have the ways
We have the means

But what about freedom
What about justice for all
And what about liberty
You made this call

Where's your kindness
Let's save the human race

And what about peace
What about peace
What about peace
What about peace

Bout 9/11
Don't seem just right
Just one more reason
For another fight

You pushed us all
You dragged us into war
It's time to stop right now
We don't want no more

You think you fooled us
We know you lied
You brought this all on
Now you can't hide

We're gonna see
The day you fall
And I think
It's right about now

And what about freedom
What about justice for all
And what about liberty
You made this call

Where's your kindness
Let's save the human race

And what about peace
What about peace
What about peace
What about peace

Part 8

Pro-Social Behavior and Altruism

The choice is not between violence and non-violence,
but between non-violence and non-existence.
~ Martin Luther King, Jr.

Although violence and aggression appear ubiquitous among humans (Bohm, Rusch & Gurerk, 2015), altruistic and pro-social behaviors are even more common (Kolm, 2006). We explore the social psychology of aggression in Part 9. But what do we know about pro-social behaviors?

Pro-Social Behaviors

Pro-social or altruistic behaviors range from everyday courtesies (allowing someone to merge into traffic, opening doors, helping a stranger fix a flat or giving money to the homeless), to the heroic (risking one's own safety or life to help others).

The collective action of the passengers on United Flight 93 on September 11, 2011 was a tragic demonstration of "extraordinary heroism" (Gunn, 2006). Flight 93 was one of four planes hi-jacked on that fateful day (two others were flown into the World Trade Center in New York, and one crashed into the Pentagon, and the fourth – United Flight 93 – crashed in an open field near Shanksville, Pennsylvania). Transcripts from phone conversations between passengers of Flight 93 and their families and friends revealed the decision-making by passengers to over-take the hi-jackers, even if it meant crashing the plane (Quinn &Worline, 2008).[1]

Understanding Altruism

Evolution or Propinquity?

Jhangiani and Tarry (2014) offered evolutionary explanations for altruism. Most of these explanations suffer from the same conceptual flaws identified earlier: the explanations are not testable (or falsifiable), are teleological, and serve as the cornerstone to scientific racism, sexism,

---

[1] This "extraordinary heroism" was made into a docu-drama directed by Paul Greengrass (Gunn, 2006).

conflict and war. For example, McAndrew (2002) argued that humans are more likely to help a family member (than a stranger) because it helps to perpetuate their genetic code. This requires the implausible existence of a seventh sensory sense: the ability to detect genes in others, and an unconscious motivational system embedded in our own DNA. A simpler and more plausible explanation is that we help family members because we know them, we live near them, and we love them.

Social Norms

Many social norms encourage altruism and are present in nearly every culture: reciprocity, social responsibility, and the Golden Rule (treat others as you would want to be treated).

Mood

We are more likely to help others when we are in a good mood, or to alleviate guilt – the so-called "Macbeth effect" (Jhangiani & Tarry, 2014).

Kitty Genovese and the Diffusion of Responsibility

One of the most famous case studies in American psychology is that of Catherine "Kitty" Genovese, a 29 year old woman who was murdered on the streets of New York City on March 13, 1964 (Manning, Levine & Collins, 2007). Ms. Genovese was stalked by a man wielding a knife and stabbed repeatedly on a busy street. Her screams were heard and the attack was witnessed by more than three dozen onlookers. The murder occurred over more than a 10-minute period and yet, not a single onlooker intervened or called the police. Why?

John Darley and Bibb Latané (1968) pioneered the area of research currently known as the *bystander phenomenon*. Through a series of ingenious experiments, they concluded that the number of onlookers influences whether any particular individual will help in a crisis. The more onlookers there are, the more *diffusion of responsibility* occurs so that individuals feel absolved from helping. For example, a typical experiment involves a research participant filling out a questionnaire when smoke seeps into the room from under a door. When only a single participant is present, he or she is quick to alert someone about the problem. When three or four participants are present, they are collectively much slower to respond to the apparent emergency.

Other Determinants of Pro-Social Behavior

Individual Differences

Pro-social and anti-social behaviors fall on a continuum. People vary in "pro-sociality" or their willingness to be helpful to others. Some people exhibit a more "altruistic personality" and are more concerned for others than themselves. Others, more self-centered, may be less likely to help others.

Religion

A compelling study explored whether religious practitioners were more altruistic than atheists or the non-religious (Batson, Oleson, Weeks, Healy, Reeves, Jennings & Brown, 1989). Batson, et al. (1989) reported that the individuals who were most altruistic were not those who were non-religious or religious; but those who were "quest oriented" (viewing religion as a vehicle for answering life's bigger questions).

Sex Differences

Although sex differences in helping behavior are highly dependent on the situation, women are more pro-social and altruistic. Due to the profound effect of sexual socialization on gender roles, men and women differ in the nature of their helping behaviors (men are more likely to change a tire; women a diaper). Men are more likely to work in occupations – firefighter, police officer – in which coming to the aid of others is part of their job description. Surprisingly, then, in a study of extreme heroism – situations wherein the altruist assists another person at great personal risk or cost – women were *equal to or more* heroic than men (Becker & Eagly, 2004).

Attributions and Helping

We are more likely to help those we deem worthy of the assistance. A disabled veteran is deemed more worthy of a handout than someone who advertises, "I'm honest, I need a beer." People are more likely to donate blood to an AIDS patient if the patient contracted the disease through a blood transfusion rather than through unprotected sex (Dooley, 1995).

Cultural Issues

As mentioned, several norms are culturally universal: responsibility, reciprocity and the Golden Rule. And yet, cultures can differ significantly in the expression of those norms. Collectivist cultures – in Asia, Africa and much of the Third World – emphasize more concern for others than individualistic ones. These collectivist cultures are more altruistic because of the value placed on interdependent relationships.

Increasing Pro-Social Behaviors

Increasing pro-social behaviors requires challenging individualism and self-concern, and promoting a more collectivist orientation. Helping others should be an integral part of childhood socialization; parents and teachers should find ways to encourage and reward pro-social behaviors.

Research on the diffusion of responsibility illustrates the powerful influence of situational factors on altruism. People need to be aware that when multiple onlookers are present, they must overcome bystander inaction and employ "active bystandership" (Staub, 2013).

To render assistance to those in need, we must value groups that have been historically devalued and ignored – minorities, the poor – and encourage a norm of "inclusive caring" (Staub, 2013, 2014).

Western societies may become more caring by modeling others. A Tibetan society, known as the Ladakh, is a remarkably altruistic community (Gielen, 2004). Their conception of "no-self," coupled with Buddhism's emphasis on compassion for all sentient beings, contributes to their non-violent worldview. Gielen (2004) concluded:

> The argument advanced is that the aggressive and expressive forms of individualism prevailing in the United States stand in stark contrast to the restrained, synergistic, cooperative forms of social interaction found in Ladakh and other peaceful societies. It also is argued that because modern psychology is a manifestation of individualism, it unwittingly contributes to the forces of fragmentation that undermine American society, leading to social disorganization and violent behavior (abstract).

Altruism must be viewed as an antidote to the indifference to human conflict and the suffering of others (Oliner, 1991). Harrison (2014) called for a "cosmic revolution" to transform a "paranoid" world into one that is "pronoid," wherein the norm of reciprocity prevails and we begin to engage in win-win thinking.

Pro-Social Television: Star Crusaders

Near the beginning of my career in Psychology and Afro-American Studies at the University of California, Los Angeles (UCLA), I consulted on a project to develop a pilot for children's television to address issues of intergroup attitudes and behaviors. One evening, my research on intergroup relations, television's effects and childhood socialization coalesced and inspired the creation of a pilot television program, *Star Crusaders*. Borrowing on the tenets of Allport's contact hypothesis, the Star Crusaders were a group of young adults – ethnically and gender diverse – who worked cooperatively in the pursuit of common goals.

Set in the future when space travel is commonplace, each of the actors was cast in a counter-stereotypical role: the Asian woman was the strategist, the White male displayed extraordinary physical abilities, the Black male had high intellect, and the Latino male was the technical specialist. This talented crew travels to a distant planet and work together to bring an end to intergroup conflict among the people living there (Fairchild, 1981, 1984; Japenga, 1985).

One way to enhance pro-social behaviors is to develop television programming that socializes children to appreciate the benefits of altruism, cooperation, and the non-violent resolution of conflict.

Chapter Overviews

Chapter 43 (*Helping Should Not Be Exclusive* by Therese Boter) observes that altruism is typically restricted to ingroup members. Boter asserts this is reflected in conservatives' indifference to the needs of the poor. She urges that altruistic actions be extended to all.

Chapter 44 (*Prosocial Behavior for World Peace* by Samuel Martin) suggests that prosocial behaviors are part of human nature, although we are more likely to help similar others. Martin concludes that altruism benefits all – the person helped, the helper, and broader society.

References

Allport, G. (1954). *The nature of prejudice.* Oxford, England: Addison-Wesley.

Batson, C.D., Oleson, K.C., Weeks, J.L., Healy, S.P., Reeves, P.J., Jennings, P., & Brown, T. (1989). Religious prosocial motivation: Is it altruistic or egoistic? *Journal of Personality and Social psychology, 57*(5), 873-884.

Becker, S.W., & Eagly, A.H. (2004). The heroism of women and men. *American Psychologist, 59*(3), 163-178.

Darley, J.M., & Batson, C.D. (1973). "From Jerusalem to Jericho": A study of situational and dispositional variables in helping behavior. *Journal of Personality and Social Psychology, 27*(1), 100-108.

Darley, J.M., & Latané, B. (1968). Bystander intervention in emergencies: Diffusion of responsibility. *Journal of Personality and Social Psychology, 8*(4, Pt. 1), 377-383. Doi: 10.1037/h0025589.

Fairchild, H. H. (1984). Creating, producing, and evaluating pro-social TV. *The Journal of Educational Television, 10*(3), 161-183.

Fairchild, H. H. (1988). Creating positive television images. Pp. 270-279 in S. Oskamp (Ed.), *Television as a social issue. (Volume 8 of the Applied Social Psychology Annual).* Newbury Park, CA: Sage Publications.

Gunn, F.X. (2006). United in the face of evil. *PsycCRITIQUES, 51*(36).

Gabriel, U., & Banse, R. (2006). Helping behavior as a subtle measure of discrimination against lesbians and gay men: German data and a comparison across countries. *Journal of Applied Social Psychology, 36*(3), 690-707. doi:10.1111/j.0021-9029.2006.00025.x

Gabriel, U., Beyeler, G., Däniker, N., Fey, W., Gutweniger, K., Lienhart, M., & Gerber, B. L. (2001). Perceived sexual orientation and helping behaviour: The wrong number technique, a swiss replication. *Journal of Cross-Cultural Psychology, 32*(6), 743-749. doi:10.1177/0022022101032006008

Gaertner, S., & Bickman, L. (1971). Effects of race on the elicitation of helping behavior: The wrong number technique. *Journal of Personality and Social Psychology, 20*(2), 218-222. doi:10.1037/h0031681

Japenga, A. (1985). Promoting social harmony with positive TV images. *Los Angeles Times, View*, Part 5, pp. 1 & 8 (January 9, 1985).

Manning, R., Levine, M., & Collins, A. (2007). The Kitty Genovese murder and the social psychology of helping: The parable of the 38 witnesses. *American Psychologist, 62*(6), 555-562. doi:10.1037/0003-066X.62.6.555

McAndrew, F.T. (2002). New evolutionary perspectives on altruism: Multilevel-selection and costly-signaling theories. *Current Directions in Psychological Science, 11*(2), 79-82.

Montanye, T., Mulberry, R.F., & Hardy, K.R. (1971). Assessing prejudice toward Negroes at three universities using the lost-letter technique. *Psychological Reports, 29*(2), 531-537. doi:10.2466/pr0.1971.29.2.531

Quinn, R.W., & Worline, M.C. (2008). Enabling courageous collective action: Conversations from United Airlines Flight 93. *Organization Science, 19*(4), 497-516.

Staub, E. (2013). Building a peaceful society: Origins, prevention, and reconciliation after genocide and other group violence. *American Psychologist, 68*(7), 576-589. doi: 10.1037/a0032045

Staub, E. (2014). Reconciliation between groups: Preventing (new) violence and improving lives. In P.T. Coleman, M. Deutsch, E.C. Marcus, (Eds.), *The handbook of conflict resolution: Theory and practice, 3rd Edition* (pp. 971-997). San Francisco, CA, US: Jossey-Bass.

Wispe, L.G., & Freshley, H.B. (1971). Race, sex, and sympathetic helping behavior: The broken bag caper. *Journal of Personality and Social Psychology, 17*(1), 59-65. doi:10.1037/h0030462

Editors' Discussion Questions

1. What accounts for individual differences in pro-sociality? In anti-sociality?

2. Is the accumulation of wealth inherently anti-social? Why or why not?

Chapter 43

Altruism Should Not Be Exclusive

THERESE BOTER

Abstract: Altruism tends to be restricted to people close to us (friends, relatives). Altruism is more likely for *ingroup* members and less likely for *outgroup* members. A real-world application is the indifference, and in some cases antipathy, that many of those who identify as politically conservative have for those in need. Altruism should be extended to broader society, not just one's *ingroup*.

When people help others, they build a community around one another. However, when people become selective in those they choose to help, that community becomes exclusive.

Altruism occurs when people perform selfless acts without the desire for a direct reward (Jhangiani & Tarry, 2014). Yet humans naturally offer more help to members in their *ingroup* – people that are viewed as similar and important because of close, shared connections (Jhangiani & Tarry, 2014). For example, a person will preferably spend the entire weekend fixing a friend's car as opposed to repairing one for a stranger.

Humans inherently exhibit *kin selection* – favoring the success of a relative even at the cost of one's own survival (Jhangiani & Tarry, 2014). Altruistic behaviors can depend on *who* is being helped – i.e., whether the person in need is a friend or a relative in the *ingroup*. Members of the *outgroup* – people who are not viewed as similar or important – do not receive as much help as their *ingroup* counterparts. For example, a father works overtime to help put his children through school, but not to fund a scholarship for an anonymous student.

Many conservatives are opposed to welfare and government spending for the poor (Lakoff, 2002). Because of differences in status and income, the poor are considered an *outgroup* to the higher-income class. As such, wealthier individuals are more likely to offer help to those with whom they share similarities. Since the poor are the *outgroup*, the support they receive from upper-income individuals is comparatively low.

Helping others should not be limited to our *ingroup*, but extended to broader society. By increasing our connection with those outside our ingroup, we can influence altruistic behavior and begin to offer help to *all those in need* – moving us one step closer to achieving World Peace.

References

Jhangiani, R., & Tarry, H. (2014). *Principles of social psychology – 1st international edition.* Licensed under a Creative Commons Attribution-NonCommercial-ShareAlike 4.0 International License.

Lakoff, G. (2002). Moral Politics: How Liberals and Conservatives Think, by George Lakoff, an excerpt. Retrieved March 06, 2016, from http://www.press. uchicago. edu/ Misc/ Chicago/467716.html

Editors' Discussion Questions

1. What steps can be taken to encourage the affluent to be more altruistic, particularly towards the poor?

2. Social media connects people to a larger network of friends and acquaintances. Over time, do you think this will lead to improved intercultural relations? Why or why not?

Chapter 44

Prosocial Behavior for World Peace

Samuel Martin

Abstract: Altruism is part of human nature, but we are more likely to help family members or people who are similar to ourselves. Help may be offered with the expectation of reciprocity or motivated by the social responsibility norm. Aiding others benefits those being helped, those offering assistance and the broader society.

> *"Every man must decide whether he will walk in the light of creative altruism or in the darkness of destructive selfishness."*
> ~ Martin Luther King, Jr.

Context

Performing favors for others is a common form of altruism. Favors are acts of assistance that may or may not be reciprocated. Favors can be solicited by explicit requests ("Can you do me a favor?"), or may be offered when observing someone in need.

Helping others is basic to human nature, but we all have biases relating to how often, to whom, and in what situations we offer assistance. We are more likely to help family members and others who are similar to ourselves. We are also more likely to help if we perceive a high chance of success or reward and that assistance comes at a low cost.

Some people are more inclined to assist those who have the capacity to return the favor in the future, an approach called *reciprocal altruism*. Others may act with the *social responsibility norm* in mind, offering assistance to those with no expectation of return. A third group might lack the willingness to help others.

The Importance of Prosocial Behavior

Assisting those in need influences others to act in kind. Studies have shown that recipients of generosity behave more generously towards others (Liu, Safin, Yang & Luhmann, 2015). Whether reciprocating help to the original altruist, or paying the assistance forward to another deserving person, prosocial behavior makes for a better world.

Prosocial behaviors also benefit the helper. In helping others, the altruist can achieve internal peace by working toward a moral purpose – making a difference in the lives of others – and becoming a part of something greater than themselves (Coles, 1993).

Altruism promotes beneficial relationships among people, regions, and nations. Working with others allows one to identify and empathize with the struggles of others (Tappen, 2014).

Conclusion

Regardless of the situation, everyone benefits from increased altruism. A world that assists those in need, and endeavors to level the playing field for all, is undoubtedly a more peaceful one.

References

Coles, R. (1993). *The Call of Service: A Witness to Idealism*. Boston, MA: Houghton Mifflin.

Jhangiani, R., & Tarry, H. (2014). *Principles of social psychology – 1st international edition*. Licensed under a Creative Commons Attribution-NonCommerical-ShareAlike 4.0 International License.

Liu, P., Safin, V., Yang, B., & Luhmann, C. C. (2015). Direct and indirect influence of altruistic behavior in a social network. *Plos ONE, 10*(10),

Tappen, K. C. (2014). Brief mindfulness training: Can a single session of mindfulness influence altruism, trust, and cooperation among college students? *Dissertation Abstracts International, 74*.

Editors' Discussion Questions

1. Some people are helpful to others, while others are selfish and indifferent. Why?

2. How can altruism be promoted throughout the U.S. and the world?

Part 9
Aggression

True peace is not merely the absence of tension; it is the presence of justice.
~ Martin Luther King, Jr.

Social psychology is more than the science of how people influence each other; it has long been concerned with pressing social issues and alleviating human suffering. Problems of interpersonal and intergroup prejudice, racism, discrimination – and violence and war – have been at the forefront of social psychology since its inception.

Mass killings have been prevalent throughout recorded history (Berkowitz, 2012). Modern manifestations of violence, at home and abroad, plague the modern world (Anderson, Bushman, Donnerstein, Hummer & Warburton, 2015; Berkowitz, 2012; Fairchild, 2016a; Krahe, 2013).

What is Aggression?

Aggression is any intentional behavior that harms another person, animal or object. Aggression may serve an instrumental purpose (to achieve a goal) or may be in reaction to strong emotions (Angus, Schutter, Terberg, van Honk & Harmon-Jones, 2016).

Violence is behavior intended to inflict physical harm, often with severe injury or death as a goal (Fairchild, 2016a).

Aggression and violence may be emotional and impulsive, or more meticulously planned.

Aggression and violence take many forms (verbal or physical abuse, bullying, terrorism, war) and can range from the minor (a harsh rebuke) to the genocidal killing of thousands of innocents (Fairchild, 2016a).

The Causes of Violence and Aggression

Violence and aggression have many causes that range from the biological to the social. In this section, we review the literature on the biological causes of aggression – in particular evolutionary theory – and debunk its major tenets.

We also explore the social causes of violence and aggression including modeling, the mass media, video games and a variety of cultural influences.

Biological Causes

Evolutionary Heritage. One of the widely accepted explanations for human violence and aggression is that it is part of our evolutionary heritage (Friend & Thayer, 2015). Sigmund Freud's theory about Life and Death Instincts (*Eros* and *Thanatos*) embedded these constructs in our biological inheritance. Others have suggested that humans are tribal creatures with a history of "coalitions of male warriors" competing for scarce resources (Van Vugt, 2009).

Brain Mechanisms. Discoveries in neuroscience link certain brain structures with violent behavior (DeWall & Chester, 2015). The amygdala serves at least a mediating role (Angus, et al., 2016). Neuroscience research has identified neural markers associated with violent video games, and has documented physiological desensitization caused by exposure to violence (Engelhardt, Bartholow, Kerr & Bushman, 2011).

Hormones. It is generally accepted that men are more aggressive and violent than women, and researchers have attributed this sex difference to either neurological or hormonal mechanisms (Angus, et al., 2016; Berkowitz, 2012; DeWall & Chester, 2015; Friend & Thayer, 2015).

Debunking Biological Explanations

The problem with biological explanations is their inherent *pessimism* and the futility it breeds. If violence is part of our evolutionary heritage, we might as well just learn to live with it. If violence is in our genes, then not much can be done about it. If violence and aggression are hard wired into our brains, nothing can be done to quell our savage nature short of psychosurgery or pharmacological intervention.

As noted elsewhere in this text, evolutionary explanations are problematic on many levels. Regarding violence and aggression, evolutionary theories fail due to several undeniable observations: (1) most humans are not violent; and (2) some humans are decidedly non-violent (Mahatma Gandhi and Martin Luther King, Jr. readily come to mind). If violence and aggression were truly part of our evolutionary heritage, then it must be present in every member of the species. Instead, violence is the exception.

Most violence in the world is politically and economically motivated; and these motivations have nothing to do with evolutionary forces. Wars are fought by the rich and powerful to protect their economic interests. The wars in the Middle East are a case in point.

Though war and violence are present throughout most of modern human history (Friend & Thayer, 2015), it is important to note that the vast majority of human history is *unrecorded*.

Our True Evolutionary Heritage

Modern humans (*homo sapiens*) arose from a Southern African savannah 200,000 to 300,000 years ago (Stringer, 2016). Imagine what the first human experiences were like: a small clan exploring a vast surround. The earliest humans numbered in the dozens, then the hundreds, and eventually a few thousand. As they grew in number, they began to disperse, eventually inhabiting the entirety of Africa and migrating to the rest of the world.

We imagine that, for most of that time, the exigencies of daily living required cooperative social relationships. The earliest humans were too few in number to aggress against each other. Resources were too plentiful to compete over; and survival demanded cooperation and coordination of efforts. We were born – as a species – familial, communal and cooperatively interdependent. (Not unlike our evolutionary predecessors – the great apes.)

Competition for the control of ideas and resources creates aggression, violence and war. We propose that such competition arose from the creation of nation states within the past few thousand years, in concert with the maldistribution of wealth and the growing disparities between the rich and the poor.

Modeling Aggression:
Mass Media, Video Games and State-Sanctioned Murder

Albert Bandura's "Bobo doll" experiments demonstrated that children learn aggressive attitudes and behaviors from adult models. In a number of filmed studies, Bandura (Bandura, Ross & Ross, 1961, 1963) allowed children to watch a film of an adult tossing around an inflated "Bobo doll" and assaulting it in various ways. Children, more often than not, imitated the specific behaviors performed by the adult.

Hundreds of studies on the effects of television violence have shown that viewers were more likely to tolerate or engage in violence, or to be less sensitive to it when it occurred (Anderson, et al., 2015; Donnerstein, 2011; Farris, 2016; Krahe, 2013). These findings extend to the increased violence associated with many video games (Engelhardt, et al., 2011).

Capital punishment is state-sanctioned murder and sends the message that the killing of defenseless people can be rationalized. (The State of Texas executed 538 prisoners from 1976 to 2016.) In like manner, when national governments wage war on others – killing people by the tens of thousands – it makes it virtually impossible to communicate credibly to its citizens the more noble idea that *thou shall not kill.*

Cultural Influences

Violence and aggression are part of Western culture, especially in the United States. American culture is steeped in violence – from the emphasis on military spending to the marketing of war in children's toys, television and motion pictures. This culture of violence is exported throughout the world via the mass media and the sales of armaments to foreign countries.

The culture of violence in the United States provides the context for understanding individual differences in violence and aggression. More than 300 million guns circulate in the U.S. More than 30,000 people in the U.S. die every year from gun violence (Fairchild, 2016b).

Violence is celebrated in the U.S., from the launching of new battleships to handheld combat games to award winning motion pictures.

Chapter Overviews

Chapter 45 (*Instrumental Aggression: A Means to an End* by Alicia Breyer) concludes that terrorism, like war, is planned and has instrumental purposes. Breyer calls for open channels of communication and the non-violent resolution of conflict.

Chapter 46 (*Gaming, Media, and Violence* by Kassidy Cuccia-Aguirre) notes that technological progress is reflected in violent video gaming, wherein players engage in realistic lethal violence. Cuccia-Aguirre urges video game designers and manufacturers to develop exciting but *non-violent* video games.

Chapter 47 (*Relational Aggression in Cyberspace Hinders Peace* by Sasha Forbath) considers the problem of cyberbullying on the internet. Forbath recommends that children be taught to use social media in socially responsible ways.

Chapter 48 (*Confronting White Supremacy* by Halford H. Fairchild, Ph.D.) comments on the arrest of a group of White Supremacists who sought to launch a race war by killing innocent Black people in Los Angeles. Fairchild argues that the depth and breadth of White Supremacy must be recognized and acknowledged in order for it to be effectively eliminated.

References

Abdullah, M. (2017). Black lives matter: Past, present and future. Foreword (pp. xxiii to xxix) in H.H. Fairchild (Ed.), *Black Lives Matter: Lifespan Perspectives*. Delhi: Indo American Books.

Anderson, C. A., Bushman, B. J., Donnerstein, E., Hummer, T. A., & Warburton, W. (2015). SPSSI research summary on media violence. *Analyses of Social Issues and Public Policy (ASAP), 15*(1), 4-19. doi:10.1111/asap.12093

Andreas, J. (2015). *Addicted to war: Why the U.S. can't kick militarism.* Oakland, CA: AK Press.

Angus, D. J., Schutter, D.J.L.G., Terburg, D., van Honk, J., & Harmon-Jones, E. (2016). A review of social neuroscience research on anger and aggression. In E. Harmon-Jones & M. Inzlicht (Eds.), *Social Neuroscience: Biological approaches to social psychology* (pp. 223-246). New York, NY, US: Routledge/Taylor & Francis Group.

Bandura, A., Ross, D., & Ross, S. A. (1961). Transmission of aggression through imitation of aggressive models. *Journal of Abnormal and Social Psychology, 63,* 575-582.

Bandura, A., Ross, D., & Ross, S. A. (1963). Imitation of film-mediated aggressive models. *Journal of Abnormal and Social Psychology, 66,* 3-11.

Berkowitz, L. (2012). A history of social psychological research on aggression. In A.W. Kruglanski & W. Stroebe, (Eds.), *Handbook of the history of social psychology* (pp. 265-282). New York, NY, US: Psychology Press.

Clifford, C. (2017). These 14 billionaires just promised to give away more than half of their money like Bill Gates and Warren Buffet. *CNBC.com.* (May 31, 2017). https://www.cnbc.com/2017/05/31/14-billionaires-signed-bill-gates-and-warren-buffetts-giving-pledge.html.

DeWall, C. N., & Chester, D. S. (2015). The neurobiology of aggression: Looking underneath the hood. In M. DeLisi, & M. G. Vaughn (Eds.), *The Routledge international handbook of biosocial criminology* (pp. 251-262). New York, NY, US: Routledge/Taylor & Francis Group.

Donnerstein, E. (2011). The media and aggression: From TV to the internet. In J. P. Forgas, A. W. Kruglanski & K. D. Williams (Eds.), *The psychology of social conflict and aggression* (pp. 267-284). New York, NY, US: Psychology Press.

Engelhardt, C. R., Bartholow, B. D., Kerr, G. T., & Bushman, B. J. (2011). This is your brain on violent video games: Neural desensitization to violence predicts increased aggression following violent video game exposure. *Journal of Experimental Social Psychology, 47*(5), 1033-1036. doi:10.1016/j.jesp.2011.03.027

Fairchild, H.H. (Ed.) (2016a). *(Re)Solving violence in America.* Delhi: Indo American Books.

Fairchild, H.H. (2016b). Gun violence in America. In H.H. Fairchild (Ed.), *(Re)Solving violence in America* (pp. 17-24). Delhi: Indo American Books.

Farris, M. (2016). Violence in the popular culture. Chapter 4 (pp. 33-38) in H. Fairchild (Ed.), *(Re)Solving violence in America.* Delhi: Indo American Books.

Friend, J. M., & Thayer, B. (2015). War and aggression. In V. Zeigler-Hill, L.L.M. Welling, T. K. Shackelford (Eds.), *Evolutionary perspectives on social psychology* (pp. 375-386). Cham, Switzerland: Springer International Publishing. doi:10.1007/978-3-319-12697-5_29

Gallagher, J.J., & Shapiro, E. (2017). Chicago's 'out of control' violence produces 762 homicides in 2016. *ABC News*. http://abcnews.go.com/US/chicagos-control-violence-produces-762-homicides-2016/ story?id= 44402951.

Krahé, B. (2013). *The social psychology of aggression., 2nd ed.* New York, NY, US: Psychology Press.

Lucas, J.A. (2015). The U.S. has killed more than 20 million people in 37 nations since WWII. https://popularresistance.org/us-has-killed-more-than-20-million-in-37-nations-since-wwii/.

SIPRI. Stockholm International Peace Research Institute. (2017). *SIPRI Military expenditure database, April, 2017*. Peter G. Peterson Foundation. http://www.pgpf.org/chart-archive/0053_defense-comparison.

Stringer, C. (2016). The origin and evolution of Homo sapiens. *Philosophical Transactions Of The Royal Society B: Biological Sciences, 371*(1698), 1-12. doi:10.1098/rstb.2015.0237

Van Vugt, M. (2009). Sex differences in intergroup competition, aggression, and warfare: The male warrior hypothesis. In O. Vilarroya, S. Altran, A. Navarro, K. Ochsner & A. Tobeña (Eds.), *Values, empathy and fairness across social behaviors* (pp. 124-134). New York, NY, US: New York Academy of Sciences.

Editors' Discussion Questions

1. Are human beings inherently violent and warlike? What are the implications of your answer?

2. What are your experiences with violent video games? What are the pros and cons of their popularity?

Chapter 45

Instrumental Aggression: A Means to An End

ALICIA BREYER

Abstract: Terrorism affects people in all corners of the globe and, like war, is planned and has instrumental purposes. World Wars I and II witnessed widespread attacks on civilian targets, culminating with the bombing of Hiroshima and Nagasaki by the United States. Today, terrorists target innocent civilians in a tragic imitation of larger nation states. The solution is to identify and understand the reasons why groups resort to terrorism, and open channels of communication for diplomacy.

Terrorism – the intentional use of indiscriminate violence intended to further political or religious ideologies – now affects people in all corners of the globe. The United States' Code of Federal Regulations describes it as "the unlawful use of force and violence against persons or property to intimidate or coerce a government, the civilian population, or any segment thereof, in furtherance of political or social objectives" (FBI, 2005, p. 9).

Terrorist attacks do not occur at random. Instrumental aggression and recent wars have justified attacks on civilians.

Instrumental aggression is defined as "aggression that is intentional and planned" (Jhangiani & Tarry, 2014, p. 376). War is "instrumental" because it seeks to satisfy the needs of a group; the aggression is usually a means to an end.

For thousands of years, wars have been fought on battlefields, soldier against soldier, and sword against sword.

However, with recent technological developments, war has become genocidal. Today, nations are armed with weapons of mass destruction capable of killing millions, destroying cities, cultures and devastating the land.

World War I marked the beginning of modern state-sponsored attacks on civilians. Germany conducted air raids on Britain, who retaliated with food blockades to starve the German population.

At the beginning of World War II, the leaders of the United States and Britain regarded civilian attacks as savage and ruthless. Once Germany began dropping bombs on London, Britain responded in kind. The United States soon joined in the bombing of civilian targets.

The U.S. commenced bombing raids on Japan and, one night in 1945, "300 U.S. B-29 bombers" targeted Tokyo. "By dawn, more than 100,000 people were dead, a million were homeless, and 40 square kilometers of Tokyo were burned to the ground" (Spitzer, 2012, p. 1). Sadly, this was only the beginning of devastating civilian attacks. On August 6, 1945, the U.S. dropped the first atomic bomb on Hiroshima, killing an initial 80,000. A second bomb dropped on Nagasaki, days later, demonstrated the depths of state-sponsored violence.

These attacks on civilians were intended to force surrender. Hundreds of thousands of innocent civilians were sacrificed.

Today, terrorists target innocent civilians in a tragic imitation of what larger nation states have done in the Middle East and around the globe.

While terrorism might appear random, it is actually an expression of instrumental aggression with the goal of ending U.S. bombing in, and military occupation of, their sovereign lands.

The solution is to understand and acknowledge what motivates terrorists and inspires violent attacks. We must open channels of communication to give diplomatic solutions a chance.

Diplomacy is the only road to World Peace.

References

Federal Bureau of Investigation. (2005). *Terrorism 2002-2005*. Retrieved 2005 from www.fbi.gov

Jhangiani, R., & Tarry, H. (2014). *Principles of social psychology – 1st international edition*. Licensed under a Creative Commons Attribution-NonCommerical-ShareAlike 4.0 International License.

Spitzer, Kirk. (2012). *A forgotten horror: The great Tokyo air raid*. Retrieved March 27, 2012 from http://nation.time.com

Targeting Civilians. Retrieved from http://cs.stanford.edu

Editors' Discussion Questions

1. When are attacks on civilian targets permissible?

2. Is the threat of nuclear war a form of terrorism?

3. How are terrorist acts a form of "instrumental aggression"? Is violence ever random?

Chapter 46

Gaming, Media and Violence

KASSIDY CUCCIA-AGUIRRE

Abstract: Technological progress is reflected in violent video games, wherein players are active participants in lethal violence. Research has linked these video games with violent behavior, including mass shootings. Video game manufacturers have a responsibility to create exciting yet non-violent games.

In violent video games, the player is an *active participant* involved in *causing* the violence. A player in "Call of Duty," for example, engages in violent combat with other players and success is measured in the number of enemies killed. The violence in video games is interactive, which begs the question: how readily can it translate from virtual to real?

As Rapping (2016) explained, "common sense tells us there is some kind of relationship between what we see and what we believe and do."

The American Psychological Association (APA, 2016a) concluded that "video game use and aggressive outcomes" were strongly correlated. Exposure to video game violence can increase interpersonal aggression, including verbal behaviors such as taunts or insults (Farris, 2016).

The National Institute of Mental Health similarly concluded that children who regularly watched violence on television "may be more likely to behave in aggressive or harmful ways toward others" (APA, 2016b). Both witnessing violence and participating in simulated violence may contribute to aggressive behavior.

After several recent mass shootings, including those at Sandy Hook and Columbine, the media attempted to tie the shooter's use of violent video games with the event. However, other data suggests that, despite the proliferation in violent video games, "violent crime has fallen by 51 percent since 1991" (Cooke, 2016).

The APA's "Resolution on Violent video Games" attributed violence to a variety of risk factors, including exposure to video games. This report also concluded that players of violent video games have less empathy, are less morally engaged, and are less likely to engage in prosocial behaviors (APA, 2016a).

A review of the literature on violence in the popular culture reported causal links between playing violent video games and aggressive attitudes and behaviors (Farris, 2016).

One reviewer of this literature concluded:

> Video game manufacturers ought to turn their creativity to the development of exciting but non-violent games, or games that challenge the problem-solving abilities of its players without the imaginary violence to people, places or things (Fairchild, 2016, p. 93).

The correlation between exposure to violence and violent behavior is well established. Until we stop promoting violence as entertainment, the upward trend in mass shootings will continue and the world will never be at peace.

References

APA. (2015). "APA Review Confirms Link Between Playing Violent Video Games and Aggression". *Apa.org.* 13 August 2015. Web. 25 March 2016.

APA. (2016a). "Resolution on Violent Video Games". *Apa.org.* Web. 25 March 2016.

APA. (2016b). "Violence in the Media". *apa.org.* Web. 24 March 2016.

Cooke, C. W., (2016). "Careful with the Panic: Violent Crime and Gun Crime Are Both Dropping", *nationalreview.com.* 30 November 2015. Web. 24 March 2016.

Fairchild, H.H. (2016). (Re)Solving violence in America. Chapter 11 (pp. 87-96) in H.H. Fairchild (Ed.), *(Re)Solving violence in America.* Delhi: Indo American Books.

Farris, M. (2016). Violence in the popular culture. Chapter 4 (pp. 33-37) in H.H. Fairchild (Ed.), *(Re)Solving violence in America.* Delhi: Indo American Books.

Rapping, Elayne. (2016). "Like Money in the Bank: Understanding Media's Investment in Violence", *Medialit.org.* Web. 24 March 2016.

Editors' Discussion Questions

1. What are some examples of violent video games? Describe the nature of that violence. What effects do you think violent video games have on people who play them?

2. How should the mass media be regulated, if at all, regarding the portrayal of violence in television, motion pictures, games and news?

Chapter 47

Relational Aggression in Cyberspace Hinders Peace

Sasha Forbath

Abstract: Technology allows us to communicate on a global scale. Although internet campaigns have produced some good, the internet has been used as a platform for cyberbullying with potentially lethal consequences. To reduce and eventually eliminate social aggression in cyberspace, children should be taught to use social media responsibly.

Technological advancements enable communication on a global scale. Today, communication is more efficient and easier than ever. Technology has provided an interface for social movements, such as the Ice Bucket Challenge, to gain international attention (Haythornthwaite, 2005). While the internet can be used for philanthropic endeavors or to promote a cause, it can also provide a platform for aggression.

Cyberspace creates an air of anonymity and impersonality. As a result, many individuals, particularly adolescents, use the Internet to bully their peers. In 2010, the suicide of Rutgers University student Tyler Clementi highlighted a nationwide suicide epidemic among bullied young adults (Jhangiani & Tarry, 2014).

Though many factors are to blame for the rising suicide rate, technology allows bullies to hide behind the veil of anonymity when committing social and relational acts of aggression. In the past, social and relational tormenting were essentially limited to in-person interactions. Today, however, the internet gives the bully virtually endless opportunities to harm, harass and torment their victims. As a result, the suicide rate for bullying victims has increased in recent years (Hinduja, et al., 2010).

Access to technology is ubiquitous. The millennial generation never lived without virtual communication and global connectivity. We live in a world where even toddlers use Ipads, but children are rarely taught about the dangers of technology. Society focuses on the benefits of technology, yet we seldom consider the negative consequences that arise from a technologically based society.

Until adults begin to educate younger generations about the perils of technology, aggressive behavior on the Internet will likely continue. To eliminate social and relational aggression, children must be warned of the dangers of cyberspace and taught how to use it wisely. Implementing anti-bullying programs in schools and increasing suicide prevention efforts may also lead to a decrease in aggressive behavior and bullying on the Internet and within our communities (Hinduja, et al., 2010).

Victims of cyberbullying experience high levels of emotional trauma and often suffer various mental health problems as a result. The inescapable nature of cyberbullying causes too many of its victims to resort to suicide. By educating current and future generations to use technology responsibly, we can reduce and eventually eliminate social and relational aggression and move one step closer to World Peace.

References

Haythornthwaite, C. (2005). Social networks and Internet connectivity effects. *Information, Community & Society, 8*(2), 125-147.

Hinduja, S. & Patchin, J. W. (2010). Bullying, Cyberbullying, and Suicide. *Archives of Suicide Research, 14*(3), 206-221.

Jhangiani, R., & Tarry, H. (2014). *Principles of Social Psychology-1st International Edition.*

Editors' Discussion Questions

1. What are forms of cyberbullying? Have you or someone you know been a victim of cyber bullying? What should be done to improve the situation?

2. Is cyberbullying a significant problem in your social sphere? Describe.

3. How can social media be used to bring about World Peace?

Chapter 48

Confronting White Supremacy[1]

HALFORD H. FAIRCHILD, PH.D.

Abstract: A group of White Supremacists were arrested before they could execute their plot to kill innocent Black people and start a race war. White Supremacy was the prime mover in Western exploration and conquest. This ideology is supported by a variety of scientific racists. To combat the hate espoused by White Supremacy, we must acknowledge its existence and root it out of our communities and institutions.

The arrest of a group of fanatical skinheads intent on starting a race war in Los Angeles was welcome news. But as shocking as the revelation of the depths of their hatred, the incident provides us with an opportunity to re-examine the nature of race relations in America.

How is it that young Whites can be socialized to hate African people to the extent that they would plot to assassinate African American leaders and indiscriminately kill dozens or hundreds of church parishioners?

It is a mistake to view this case as the machinations of a radical fringe. Instead, we must realize that the Fourth Reich – and groups like it – is the inevitable expression of a social culture that is historically steeped in the ideology of White Supremacy.

The idea of White supremacy is older than the United States of America. It was the prime mover in much of European and American imperialism around the world. The doctrine of "Manifest Destiny" – derived in part from ancient Greek philosophy – was justification for taking control

---

[1] This Chapter was revised from an editorial published in *Psych Discourse*, Volume 24 (9), September 1993. It was in response to a news story in the *Los Angeles Times* that appeared on July 16, 1993. That article described the arrest of eight White Supremacist "skinheads," who had plotted to blow up a prominent Black church in an effort to launch a race war (see Freed, 1993).

of the land, people and resources in Africa, America, Asia and the South Pacific.

In more modern times, the popular belief in inherited racial differences has been strongly supported in the halls of academe. Sir Francis Galton, Charles Darwin's cousin, elaborated upon the theory of natural selection and concluded that intellectual differences among humans were genetically linked. His book, *Hereditary Genius* (published in 1869), set the stage for Arthur Jensen's 1969 essay (published in the *Harvard Educational Review*), that concluded that Whites are superior to Blacks in inherited intellectual potential.

J. Phillippe Rushton, at the University of Western Ontario, reinvigorated the controversy with his "sociobiological" theory of racial differences. Consistent with the generations of racist scholars before him, he concluded that Blacks are a genetically inferior branch of the human family (for a critique, *see* Fairchild, 1991).

Scientific racists such as Jensen and Rushton – along with dozens of others – are well known to the White Supremacy groups, who trumpet their findings as scientific proof for racial intolerance.

At the public policy level, the U.S. Department of Health and Human Services is pursuing the hotly contested "Violence Initiative" that aims its lens of inquiry at inner city Black youth. Many of the studies in the Violence Initiative seek to identify the "biochemical markers" that give rise to violence among Black children, youth and adults. Nowhere in the Violence Initiative is there a mention of the kind of violence that emanates from White Supremacy.

The subjugation of African and other Native People has been nearly complete. The few instances of open opposition to the system of racial stratification have been met with violence and assassinations.

It is no surprise, then, that the leading voices for overturning America's system of racial hatred are the targets of this deadly violence. The names of the targets are, perhaps, an honor role of those individuals and institutions who are truly "doing the right thing" as it relates to American race relations: The Reverend Cecil Murray and First A.M.E. Church, Danny Bakewell, Al Sharpton, Karen Bass, Barack Obama and others.

This endemic problem must be solved first by acknowledging the omnipresence and persistence of racism in America. Malcolm X, the assassinated former leader of the Nation of Islam, said that racial progress is not made 'when the knife in our back is partially removed. It occurs when the wound is fully healed.' The problem, he explained, 'was getting White American to even acknowledge that the knife was there in the first place' (paraphrasing).

The arrest of skinheads in L.A. should serve as a "wake up call" to the brewing problem of racial intolerance in this city, this country, and around the world.

It is good that law enforcement was able to intervene in the outrageous plot to assassinate innocent people in Los Angeles. But it is even more important that we develop concrete solutions for the problems that truly ail us: prejudice re-education and transracial human relations training.

We must tackle White Supremacy and all of its variants as vigilantly as we tackle floods, hurricanes or other disasters. White Supremacy is not a thing of the past; it is a scourge of the present. White Supremacy will remain a part of our future unless we acknowledge its existence and consciously program its elimination.

Reference

Fairchild, H. H. (1991). Scientific Racism: The cloak of objectivity. *Journal of Social Issues, 47*(3), 101-115.

Freed, D. (1993). Skinheads claim FBI 'suckered us in.' *Los Angeles Times*, July 18, 1993. http://articles.latimes.com/1993-07-18/news/mn-14391_1_fourth-reich.

Editors' Discussion Questions

1. What are your experiences with the ideology of White Supremacy? How prevalent is prejudice against other groups?

2. Is it possible to eradicate racism? If yes, how? If no, why not?

Sixth Interlude
Pulling Triggers

DENNIS DAVIS

Pulling Triggers

Pulling triggers won't make wars end
Find one just reason to make amends
Darkened dead end streets and lonely walks
Talk is cheap when the reign won't stop
Pain just mocks the bullet's shock

Thousand pound bombs raining downtown
Nameless faces on the run
Fires fueled by raging war crimes
Blood deposits in the bank
Tragic action video games
No one takes the blame.

We can stop the world ... make a glacier retreat
We can stop the world ... mutate our seed
We can stop the world ... make nations bleed
But are we free ... to make peace?

Part 10
Group Dynamics

*We must be ready to learn from one another, not
claiming that we alone possess all truth and that
somehow we have a corner on God.*

~ Desmond Tutu

Social psychology is concerned with how individuals are affected by
their social environments. Group Dynamics is a large subfield of social
psychology, with many of the early advancements produced at The Research
Center for Group Dynamics at The University of Michigan (Cartwright, 1950;
Cartwright & Zander, 1953).

Understanding Group Dynamics

Groups are ubiquitous in human experience. We are born into an
immediate family – a small group. That family is part of larger group of extended
kin. We live in large and small communities that are part of larger regions and
nation states. We are born into religious, gender and racial groups. We form
groups of friends as children and adults. We move through the world from one
group to another and belong to many groups simultaneously.

Groups may have a finite lifespan and develop healthy or unhealthy
dynamics that affect group outcomes.

Group Lifespan

Memberships in a particular group may be short- or long-term. A study
group may last a few hours, political parties often span generations. Once
formed, groups maintain themselves, set and accomplish goals, and ultimately
end. Groups are comprised of individuals who have shared goals, a "group
identity" or a sense of "entitativity" (Campbell, 1958). Group identities may
apply to very large groups, such as race, gender or national origin (Volkan,
2013).

Groups must recruit motivated members, establish shared norms and objectives, and create a sense of cooperation and inclusion. Lines of communication and leadership issues are paramount in all groups. "Healthy group dynamics" foster a sense of cohesion and collaboration (Burn, 2006).

Bettencourt, Dillmann and Wollman (1996) applied theories of group dynamics to the formation of a grassroots peace organization. In their case study, the group emphasized coordination of efforts, but was less concerned with motivating its members.

Group Performance

Groups often out-perform individuals acting alone (called *process gain*); but group dynamics may also hinder performance (*process loss*). Whether group performance is better than individuals acting alone depends on many factors, including the nature of the group and the nature of the task. Groups may facilitate or inhibit the performance of its members. Some tasks are more divisible and lend themselves to group work.

Groups may offer a level of anonymity or invisibility for some of its members, which may encourage *social loafing*, wherein individuals contribute less than their fair share to the group.

Group Decision Making: The Problem of *Groupthink*

Groups make decisions that are affected by the dynamics of the group. Irving Janis (1972) coined the term, *groupthink*, to describe the flawed decision-making processes that led to several "fiascoes" committed by the executive branch of the U.S. government. Of course, hindsight is always 20:20, yet Janis explored several historical instances – the failure to anticipate the attack on Pearl Harbor in 1941, the invasion of North Korea in 1950, and the escalation of the war in Vietnam in the mid-1960s – of flawed decision-making that resulted from group dynamics.

The Nature of the Group. The groups that made catastrophic decisions were generally: (a) highly cohesive; (b) relatively isolated from outside influences; and (c) had a strong leader who pursued a single-minded objective (Moorhead, 1982).

Symptoms of *Groupthink*. In highly cohesive groups, a strong leader uses moral authority to achieve uniformity of opinion and squelch dissent. This leads to a number of defective decision-making practices: failure to explore competing alternatives, selective review of the available information, and the rejection of expert opinions that are contrary to the leader's objectives.

***Groupthink* and the 2003 Invasion of Iraq.** All indicators of *groupthink* were present in the U.S. decision to invade Iraq in 2003. The closed circle of advisors to U.S. President George W. Bush (Richard "Dick" Cheney, Donald Rumsfeld, Colin Powell, John Ashcroft, Andrew Card, Karl Rove) suffered the group dynamics and flawed decision-making that led to the disastrous invasion of Iraq (Mintz & Wayne, 2014; Rodrigues, Assmar & Jablonski, 2005). The violence wrought by that invasion will be felt for generations.

Chapter Overviews

Chapter 49 (*Climate Change: An Emblem of Political Polarization* by Samuel Martin) explores the politics of global warming. Martin urges greater message elaboration in order to better affect the public's attitudes.

Chapter 50 (A Review of *Ghosts of Abu Ghraib* by Samuel Martin) reviews the documentary film on the abuses of Iraqi prisoners by U.S. soldiers in 2004. Martin suggests that the documentary provides valuable lessons if we are to achieve World Peace.

Chapter 51 (*Abu Ghraib and the Power of the Situation* by Madeleine Glouner) considers the U.S. soldiers' torture of Iraqi prisoners in 2004 as depicted in the documentary, *Ghosts of Abu Ghraib*. Glouner underscores the power of the situation in understanding how good people can do bad things.

Chapter 52 (*Today's America Needs Many Tongues* by Halford H. Fairchild, Ph.D.) decries the politicization of language education in the U.S. Fairchild highlights the many benefits of multi-lingual competencies.

References

Bettencourt, B.A., Dillmann, G., & Wollman, N. (1996). The intragroup dynamics of maintaining a successful grassroots organization: A case study. *Journal of Social Issues, 52* (1), 169-186.

Burn, S. M. (2006). Changing within to bring change outside: Promoting healthy group dynamics. In R. M. MacNair, & R. M. MacNair (Eds.), *Working for peace: A handbook for practical psychology and other tools* (pp. 98-108). Atascadero, CA, US: Impact Publishers.

Campbell, D.T. (1958). Common fate, similarity and other indices of the status of aggregate persons as social entities. *Behavioral Science, 3*, 14-25.

Cartwright, D. (1950). The work of the Research Center for Group Dynamics. *Occupational Psychology, 24*, 245-248.

Cartwright, D., & Zander, A. (Eds.). (1953). *Group dynamics research and theory*. Oxford, England: Row, Peterson.

Janis, I. L. (2007). Groupthink. In R. P. Vecchio, R. P. Vecchio (Eds.), *Leadership: Understanding the dynamics of power and influence in organizations (2nd ed.)* (pp. 157-169). Notre Dame, IN, US: University of Notre Dame Press.

Mintz, A., & Wayne, C. (2016). The polythink syndrome and elite group decision-making. *Political Psychology, 37*(Suppl 1), 3-21. doi:10.1111/pops.12319

Moorhead, G. (1982). Groupthink: Hypothesis in need of testing. *Group & Organization Studies, 7*(4), 429-444. doi:10.1177/105960118200700406

Rodrigues, A., Assmar, E. L., & Jablonski, B. (2005). Social-psychology and the invasion of Iraq. *Revista De Psicología Social, 20*(3), 387-398. doi:10.1174/021347405774277659

Volkan, V. (2013). Large-group-psychology in its own right: Large-group identity and peace-making. *International Journal of Applied Psychoanalytic Studies, 10*(3), 210-246. doi:10.1002/aps.1368

Editors' Discussion Questions

1. What are the significant groups in your life? How do they affect your attitudes and behaviors?

Chapter 49

Climate Change:
An Emblem of Political Polarization

SAMUEL MARTIN

Abstract: Public opinion in America is increasingly divided along partisan lines. This is especially evident in the debate surrounding global warming. Despite overwhelming scientific evidence, much of the U.S. population is skeptical about the causes of climate change and group polarization contributes to the taking of extreme positions. Messages need greater elaboration in order to overcome this barrier to World Peace.

> *There is too much at stake for us to surrender to the politics of polarization.*
>
> ~Brad Henry

Since the mid-20th Century, polarization has pushed those most involved in politics away from the middle and closer to the extremes (Fiorina & Abrams, 2009). This process has divided the public's opinion regarding a variety of hotly debated issues including abortion, LGBTQ rights, affirmative action, the economy, national security and the environment.

Sixteen of the seventeen hottest years ever recorded have occurred since 2000, with 2014 having the highest annual temperature since 1880. Recently, the National Oceanic and Atmospheric Administration (NOAA) confirmed that 2016 was the warmest year on record. And in that year, greenhouse gases[1], sea-surface temperature and the global sea levels reached record highs; while sea ice in Antarctica fell to record lows. That same year, the United States suffered no fewer than 15 weather/climate related disasters, at a cost of more than $46 billion.

---

[1] In 2016, both the World Meteorological Organization and NOAA reported primary greenhouse gases emitted through human activities, reached their highest levels in more than 800,000 years.

According to a peer-reviewed article published by the American Geophysical Union, the likelihood of experiencing three consecutive years (2014-2016) of record breaking temperatures – without the effects of human activity on climate change – is .03 per cent or less.

Currently, 2017 is on pace to become the second hottest year on record.

Although no divide exists amongst climate scientists, the opinion of the American people is split regarding whether climate change even exists and what, if anything, can be done about it. Virtually all climate scientists recognize human activity is the main driver of accelerated climate change; yet a quarter of Americans remain "solidly skeptical" of the idea and only 57% of the populations blame human pollution as the cause of global warming (Xie, 2010).

The divide in the public's attitudes toward climate change is due, in large part, to doubts seeded by politicians who are beholden to the fossil fuel industry. Climate change deniers, fearing financial collapse if fossil fuels were made obsolete, have funded skepticism campaigns that wage war against climate science. These fossil fuel industries oppose stronger environmental regulations and maintain the debate in the public sector (Weber & Stern, 2011). As a result, the media continues to characterize climate change as a theory in dispute (Freudenburg & Muselli, 2013).

The political elites at each end of the spectrum propose different measures to deal with climate-change: the left seeks immediate action, such as investments in alternative energies and a carbon pricing system; while the right favors delayed action and inaction. Politicians have resorted to divisive politics that demonize their opponents, making it almost impossible for opposing sides to find common ground. This *group polarization* makes opinions on issues more extreme (Jhangiani & Tarry, 2014) and hardens ideologies, making eventual compromise more difficult.

To ameliorate the effects of group polarization as it relates to global warming and other environmental concerns; the media must focus on empirically proven facts, and not the arguments and opinions of energy lobbyists.

Greater *message elaboration* on climate change should be expected to increase pro-environmental behavior (Yang, Seo, Rickard & Harris, 2015).

The catastrophic projections by climate scientists require immediate action to abate global warming. With the future of our planet in peril, we must solve the problem of global warming if we are to achieve World Peace.

References

Fiorina, M. P., & Abrams, S. J. (2009). *Disconnect: The Breakdown of Representation in American Politics*. Norman: University of Oklahoma Press.

Freudenburg, William R., & Muselli, Violetta. (2013). Reexamining Climate Change Debates: Scientific Disagreement or Scientific Certainty Argumentation Methods (SCAMs)? *American Behavioral Scientist, 57*(6), 777-795.

Jhangiani, R., & Tarry, H. (2014). *Principles of social psychology – 1st international edition.* Licensed under a Creative Commons Attribution-NonCommerical-ShareAlike 4.0 International License.

Weber, Elke U., & Stern, Paul C. (2011). Public Understanding of Climate Change in the United States. *American Psychologist, 66*(4), 315-328.

Xie, Lei. (2010). *Climate Change in the Changing Climate of News Media: A Comparative Analysis of Mainstream Media and Blog Coverage of Climate Change in the United States and the People's Republic of China, 2005-2008.* ProQuest Information & Learning, US.

Yang, Z. J., Seo, M., Rickard, L. N., & Harrison, T. M. (2015). Information sufficiency and attribution of responsibility: Predicting support for climate change policy and pro-environmental behavior. *Journal of Risk Research, 18*(6), 727-746. doi:10.1080/13669877.2014.910692

Websites : 1. http://climate.nasa.gov/scientific-consensus/

2. http://www.gallup.com/poll/167972/steady-blame-humans-global-warming.aspx

Editors' Discussion Questions

1. Why does a debate about the causes of global warming persist? Who drives this debate? Who benefits from denying the role of human activity in climate change?

2. How does climate change affect you? Discuss your feelings.

Chapter 50

A Review of *Ghosts of Abu Ghraib*

SAMUEL MARTIN

Abstract: The terrorist attack on September 11, 2001 prompted the George W. Bush administration to wage war in Afghanistan and Iraq. During the occupation of Iraq, thousands of Iraqi citizens were arrested and imprisoned. The horrors of war were revealed in graphic photographs depicting prisoner abuse at the Abu Ghraib prison. The documentary, *Ghosts of Abu Ghraib*, illustrates pasts wrongs and assesses the U.S. role in global conflicts.

September 11, 2001.

The date is enough to bring a wince to the faces that recognize its significance. It is the day that nearly 3,000 Americans died – including 400 police officers and firefighters – in the largest loss of life caused by a foreign attack on American soil.

After a period of mourning, the George W. Bush Administration was determined to make clear that the American government would not shy away from a fight.

The U.S. wanted revenge. The U.S. wanted blood.

The Global War on Terrorism would follow, as the U.S. increased military operations dramatically. To further hamper its targets, the American government applied significant economic and political pressures on accused terrorist groups and the countries sheltering them. In October 2001, NATO invaded Afghanistan to topple the Taliban regime and capture al-Qaeda (The Guardian, 2001).[1]

---

[1] **Editor's note:** Since the U.S. invaded Afghanistan on October 7, 2001, the ongoing military conflict has earned the ignominious distinction of the longest foreign war in U.S. history. None of the terrorists who participated in the 9/11 attacks were from Afghanistan or Iraq (the majority were from Saudi Arabia).

In 2003, the war traveled to Iraq when a U.S.-led coalition pursued Saddam Hussein and his purported weapons of mass destruction (WMDs). After the invasion, U.S. forces used the Abu Ghraib prison for holding Iraqi criminals (CNN, 2013). The documentary film, *Ghosts of Abu Ghraib*, examines the prisoner abuse scandal that took place there in the fall of 2003.

This documentary offers viewers firsthand accounts of the transformation of U.S. soldiers – otherwise patriotic and decent human beings – into torturers under a ruthless chain of military command. Similar to Stanley Milgram's *Obedience to Authority* experiment (shown at the beginning and end of the film), the persuasion and demands of authority figures had incredible influence upon the soldiers.

An American military, motivated by revenge, intentionally misled its own soldiers and bypassed the Geneva Conventions' rules of war by labelling prisoners as 'terrorists' unworthy of its protections. The Bush administration changed the rules to permit torture as a means of interrogation.

Meanwhile, American soldiers faced constant provocations and stresses from war – the daily deaths of comrades in a foreign country and a confusing, hostile environment – that took great tolls. War prisoners, the default outgroup, were blamed for the soldiers' pain. When mixed with intense authority demands, spontaneous prejudice was inevitable as prisoners became the soldiers' emotional punching bags (Fiske, Harris & Cuddy, 2004).

The abuses were mental and physical, including sleep deprivation, torture, rape, sodomy, and murder.

Eventually, incriminating photographs forced the U.S. Department of Defense to remove seventeen soldiers and officers from duty, with eleven of them charged with dereliction of duty, maltreatment, aggravated assault, and battery. The commanding officer over all of the detention facilities in Iraq was demoted to colonel. Other military personnel of higher rank avoided consequences, while President Bush and others voiced disgust about the 'few bad apples' perpetrating the dehumanizing acts.

The results of the Stanford prison experiment are eerily similar to the events described above. This study, conducted in order to better understand the psychological effects of becoming a prisoner or prison guard, demonstrated how participants adapted to their assigned roles – guards becoming authoritarians, willing to use psychological torture with impunity and without remorse; and prisoners passively accepting that abuse (Bartels, 2015).

Do these conclusions sound familiar?

Ghosts of Abu Ghraib outlines the lessons we must learn if we are to achieve World Peace. We must learn from our past wrongs; make an unflinchingly honest assessment of our role in global conflicts; and identify and implement those actions that allow us to peacefully co-exist. Only then can we achieve World Peace.

References

Bartels, J. M. (2015). The Stanford prison experiment in introductory psychology textbooks: A content analysis. *Psychology of Learning & Teaching, 14*(1), 36-50.

CNN. (2013). Iraq prison abuse scandal fast facts. http://www.cnn.com/2013/10/30/world/meast/iraq-prison-abuse-scandal-fast-facts/

Fiske, S. T., Harris, L. T., & Cuddy, A. J. C. (2004). Why ordinary people torture enemy prisoners. *Science, 306*(5701), 1482-1483. doi:10.1126/science.1103788

The Guardian. (2001). September 11. http://www.theguardian.com/world/2001/sep/11/september11.usa24

Editors' Discussion Questions

1. Does the "power of the situation" exonerate the guards who committed the abuses at Abu Ghraib? Why or why not?

2. The U.S. invaded a sovereign nation, Iraq, in 2003. As of this writing (July 2017), thousands of U.S. troops remain. Is this antithetical to the idea of American freedom and democracy? How do we reconcile this contradiction between our actions and our ideals?

Chapter 51

Abu Ghraib and the Power of the Situation

MADELEINE GLOUNER

Abstract: The documentary, *Ghosts of Abu Ghraib*, examines the U.S. military's torture and abuse of Iraqi prisoners in 2004. The film, incorporating footage from the Milgram Obedience to Authority Experiment and Zimbardo's Stanford Prison experiment, highlights how the power of the situation can make good people do bad things.

The documentary, *Ghosts of Abu Ghraib*, examines the U.S. military's torture and abuse of Iraqi war prisoners in 2004 (HBO Video, 2007). This film – a compilation of interviews from Abu Ghraib prisoners, troops and political and military experts – explores the circumstances that gave rise to such brutality, and the effects of that extreme physical and emotional stress on the prisoners.

The documentary begins with a scene from the infamous Milgram experiment conducted by psychologist Stanley Milgram in the early 1960s (Milgram, 1961). Milgram measured the level of obedience to authority figures, even when that compliance required subjects to sacrifice their morals. Results from the experiment revealed that a very high percentage of participants obeyed authority figures, albeit reluctantly, even if that compliance meant causing serious injury and distress to an innocent victim.

This notion of blind obedience features prominently in cases where U.S. troops committed atrocities at the behest of superior officers. The abuses committed at Abu Ghraib prove that good people can do bad things.

Abu Ghraib also provides a real-life example of the hypothesis tested in Zimbardo's Stanford Prison Experiment (Haney, Banks & Zimbardo, 1973). Psychologist Phillip Zimbardo created a mock prison in the basement of the Stanford Psychology Department, and randomly selected young men to play the role of *prisoner* or *guard.*

Zimbardo's findings forecasted the atrocities that later occurred at the Abu Ghraib prison. He concluded that "situational forces dominate most of us at various times in our lives." The high stress environment of Abu Ghraib – coupled with lack of supervision, training and anonymity – explained why seemingly ordinary people were capable of doing unimaginable things to another human being.

Anonymity and *diffusion of responsibility* were evident in the dehumanization of prisoners at Abu Ghraib. The "mask" – the uniform – worn by U.S troops allowed them to dissociate from their personal selves. They were no longer individuals; they were members of U.S military forces – *the good guys* – and their Iraqi captives were nothing more than terrorists – *the enemy.*

Interviews of the troops revealed how little training they received before becoming prison guards. Their blind obedience to authority and perception of any Iraqi as an "enemy" transformed these seemingly ordinary people into human rights abusers. Abu Ghraib provides a real-life example of how the power of the situation can supplant individual morality and agency.

References

Dittmann, M. (n.d.). What makes good people do bad things? *PsycEXTRA Dataset.*

Haney, C., Banks, C., & Zimbardo, P. (1973). Interpersonal dynamics in a simulated prison. *International Journal of Criminology & Penology, 1*(1), 69-97.

HBO Video (Firm). (2007). *Ghosts of Abu Ghraib.* United States: HBO Video.

Milgram, S. (1974). Obedience to authority: An experimental view. New York: Harper & Row.

Editors' Discussion Questions

1. The U.S. invaded Iraq in 2003. Tens of thousands of innocent civilians lost their lives. The fighting continues in 2017. Should anyone be held accountable? Why or why not?

2. In what ways is your everyday behavior controlled by "the power of the situation"?

Chapter 52

Today's America Needs Many Tongues[1]

HALFORD H. FAIRCHILD, PH.D.

Abstract: Language is the currency of human exchange. Yet in the U.S., language is politicized and a vehicle for ethnocentrism, xenophobia and racism. Bilingual education programs are given short shrift, and foreign language education is ineffective. Multilingual competencies are the norm in the rest of the world. Resolving the issues in language education promotes democracy in public education, enhances the intellectual and social development of populations, and promotes intercultural sensitivity and understanding.

Language – written and spoken – delimits our species and is the currency of human exchange.

But language is also heavily politicized and a vehicle for enthocentrism, xenophobia and racism. Language too often serves as a barrier to intercultural awareness and understanding.

The United States is a "salad bowl" of nationalities, ethnicities and languages. Within our borders are individuals who represent hundreds of cultures, languages and dialects.

Despite this diversity, bilingual education is given short shrift in our public and private schools. Too often, "linguistic minority" children are confronted with the bewildering task of acquiring the Three R's in a language that they can scarcely understand. Our sink-or-swim teaching methods deny these children an equal educational opportunity, setting them back for the rest of their lives.

---

[1] This Chapter is revised from an op-ed published in the *Los Angeles Times* on December 5, 1990.

In the context of a tight budgetary reality, bilingual education often finds itself last in line. In Los Angeles, several thousand teaching aides – most of them bilingual – are striking for modest working conditions: four-hour minimum work days, sick pay and health benefits.

Our colleges are ill-equipped to train teachers in bilingual education; and most of the available training emphasizes the teaching of English to non-English speakers. This "subtractive bilingualism" is consistent with a value system that degrades languages and dialects other than "standard" English.

Demographic projections point to the increasing heterogeneity of the U.S. population into the 21st Century. But our educational system appears neither willing nor able to provide relevant learning experiences for the increasingly diverse student bodies that attend our schools.

Bilingual education, in the rest of the world, is the norm; not an odious program fraught with political bickering and divisiveness. In most of the world today, the majority of populations are necessarily bilingual or multilingual.

Educational systems in other countries take linguistic diversity into explicit account, where the expectation is that the well-educated person is conversant in two or more languages.

Schools in large metropolitan areas of the U.S. are characterized by linguistic diversity among pupils. These students can act as linguistic role models for native English speakers. Instead, they are segregated in classrooms that retard their academic development in the interest of making them fluent speakers of English. The sad reality is that these students often lose their native language proficiency, while falling behind their English-speaking counterparts in basic academic skills.

Our research indicates that bilingualism is a cognitive asset (Padilla, Fairchild & Valadez, 1991). Bilingualism affords the individual enhanced learning flexibility and a more empathic awareness and understanding of different cultures and world views.

Foreign-language education in the United States typically treats the study of another language as an object of inquiry, rather than as a tool for communication and intercultural understanding. The result is that although the average American college graduate has been exposed to several years of foreign-language instruction, the majority of college graduates cannot engage in meaningful conversation in other than English for more than a few minutes. We may learn to conjugate verbs, but we fail in meaningful communication.

International business and commerce demand a sensitivity to different cultures and language systems. This requires the development of innovative language-education programs that capitalize on the language resources represented in the diversity of students in our schools. It requires a desire and a willingness for most of us to acquire the ability to read, write, speak and understand a language other than English. It requires the recognition that the influx of immigrants into the United States affords an opportunity, not a challenge.

Bilingual and foreign language education reveal fundamental deficiencies in the quality of American schooling.

By attempting to resolve the issues surrounding language education, we also pursue true democracy in public education; the enhancement of the intellectual and social development of our populations; sensitivity to other peoples of the world; and competitiveness in an increasingly international arena of business, science, politics and culture.

Reference

Padilla, A.M., Fairchild, H.H., & Valadez, C.M. (Eds.). (1991). *Bilingual education: Issues and strategies.* Thousand Oaks: Sage Publications.

Editors' Discussion Questions

1. What are the benefits of bilingualism?

2. What are the pros and cons of an "English-only" policy?

3. Why is the U.S. unique in its opposition to a multi-lingual society?

Part 11

Prejudice, Racism and Discrimination

Never hate.
The way of love is a better way.
The way of peace is a better way.
~ Congressman John Lewis (January 16, 2017)

Since the origin of modern social psychology, the study of intergroup attitudes and behavior has been a major focus of theory and research. One of the first measures of intergroup attitudes was the Bogardus Social Distance Scale (Bogardus, 1925), which assessed how accepting individuals were to members of other racial, ethnic and national groups in their more intimate lives.

In the early years of social psychology, researchers focused on attitudes towards people, ideas or things. Questions relevant to that inquiry were: What is the nature of attitudes? How are they formed? How might they be changed? How well do attitudes correlate with actual behavior?

Given the salience of race in American society, the majority of early attitude research explored racial attitudes, stereotypes, prejudice and discrimination (Dinnerstein, 2003; Fairchild & Gurin, 1978; Fiske, Harris, Lee & Russell, 2016).

Key Terms

Attitudes

Attitudes are evaluative ideas that one has about people, places or things. After many decades of research, social psychologists began to focus on the three components of attitudes: beliefs (or cognitions), feelings (or affects or emotions), and behavioral intentions. Attitudes towards African Americans, for example, involve beliefs (stereotypes about intelligence or motivation), feelings (distrust, dislike, hatred or envy), and behavioral intentions (a desire to pursue or avoid interactions).

Stereotypes

Stereotypes are simplified ideas about a class of objects (Brotherton, 2007; MacRae, Bodenhausen, Milne & Jetten, 1994; Stangor, 2016). In the ethnic and racial arena, stereotypes have been propagated about every group imaginable. Perhaps the most widely held stereotypes are those directed towards racial and ethnic minorities. These stereotypes often justify a "blaming the victim" ideology about the life circumstances of some groups (see Chapter 35, *Understanding Poverty*).

Prejudice

Prejudice involves a more nuanced set of ideas about a target group. Prejudice refers to the tendency to "pre-judge," and may be positive or negative. Prejudice is a predisposition to respond, favorably or negatively, in a new or novel situation. Prejudice may be based on race, religion, sexuality, national origin or any other demographic.

Racism

Racism is the belief that one race is inherently superior to others. The problem of racism in world affairs is more accurately described as a problem of *White Supremacy* – the false belief that White people are superior to all others. The corollary to White racist beliefs is that "Black people" (persons of African descent), who represent the antithesis of Whiteness, are inferior. Other "non-White" groups (Asians, Latinos, East Asians, Indigenous persons) are thought to fall somewhere along the continuum between Blacks (the most inferior) and Whites (the most superior).[1]

Racism operates on several levels: (1) individual racism is expressed within the hearts and minds of specific persons; (2) cultural racism is spread throughout the popular culture, for example, in derogating media images of minority groups (Fairchild, 1988a, 1988b); (3) institutional racism occurs when organizational practices have a disparate effect on racial groups (Fairchild, 2017); and (4) scientific racism is the pseudo-science that supports racist thinking (see Fairchild, 1991 for a critique).

---

[1] One scientific racist regarded Asians as equal to or superior to Whites (Rushton, 2010).

Discrimination

Discrimination occurs when racial attitudes are translated into behavior. Discrimination is the unfair treatment of an individual or group based on some aspect of their demography or other immutable characteristics such as gender or skin color. Discrimination in housing occurs when minorities are steered away from or denied rentals in White neighborhoods. Discrimination in education occurs when individuals are denied admission because of racially biased test scores or other criteria (e.g., quality of secondary school) that systematically disadvantage individuals or groups. Discrimination may also occur through misguided government policy, as in the internment of Japanese Americans during WWII (Okamura, 2003).

Research Traditions

Attitude Research

Early research in intergroup relations focused on attitude measurement, beginning with the Bogardus Scale (Bogardus, 1925). Subsequent decades witnessed the development of more multi-dimensional attitude measures, with more nuanced response alternatives.

Racial attitudes are the product of many influences including childhood socialization, parental attitudes, community practices, and the rewards and punishments associated with expressing attitudes consistent with one's social environments.

A very promising assessment tool is the Implicit Attitude Test (IAT), developed by researchers at Harvard University (Nosek, Greenwald & Banaji, 2007). The IAT explores unconscious (or implicit) attitudes using readily available computers and the internet. Since its inception in 1995, Project Implicit has collected data from hundreds of thousands of individuals that have explored attitudes toward a myriad of attitude targets. Interested readers should explore their own implicit attitudes at https://implicit.harvard.edu/implicit/index.jsp.

Surveys of racial attitudes showed a steady improvement of Whites' attitudes towards Blacks from the 1920s through the present.[2] Attitude research in recent decades has expanded to include the multiplicity of racial and ethnic groups that comprise modern society. More recent attitude

---

[2] The inauguration of Donald J. Trump as U.S. President in 2017 has ushered in an era of heightened racial tensions and a resurgence in White Nationalism, anti-Semitism and hate crimes targeting Muslims, African Americans, Jews and sexual minorities.

research has focused on human sexualities. Modern methods use many of the tools of neuroscience (e.g., EEG and brain imaging studies).

Intergroup Antagonism

Groups are easily formed on the basis of sex, race, ethnicity, sexuality or even arbitrary assignments. Once formed, groups generally exhibit in-group favoritism and out-group antagonism (Tajfel, 1970). Attitudes and behaviors are more favorable toward in-group members; and out-group members are viewed more homogeneously or de-individualized. These conditions often give rise to prejudice, discrimination and, in extreme cases, conflict and war.

These intergroup processes were exposed in the "Robbers Cave Experiment" by Muzafir Sherif and colleagues (Sherif, Havey, White, Hood & Sherif, 1961; also see McLeod, 2008). A group of male adolescents at a summer camp were divided into two teams. Within days, the teams developed strong in-group favoritism and out-group antipathies. These hostilities were overcome when Sherif and his colleagues had the teams work together on a common project.

The Attitude-Behavior Relation

In 1934, Richard LaPiere published the results of a modest study that upended social psychology. He traveled throughout the continental United States with a Chinese couple, stopping at numerous inns, motels and restaurants along the way. Afterwards, LaPiere wrote the proprietors of those establishments and inquired, "Do you accept Chinese customers?" LaPiere reported that the majority of proprietors said that they would *not* serve a Chinese couple, despite the fact that they had already done so.

LaPiere's findings cast doubt on the utility of attitude measurement if they did not correspond with behavior. Although LaPiere's study suffered from a number of major methodological flaws (chief among them, the fact that he did not necessarily measure attitudes and behaviors from the same individuals), his study launched a generation of research into the attitude-behavior relation (or A-B relation).

The conclusion reached from research into the A-B relationship is that attitudes predict behaviors for some people, some of the time. The more specific the attitude measurement, the more likely it will predict specific attitude-related behaviors. Attitudes and behaviors are more likely to correspond when measured close together in time.

Self-Fulfilling Prophecies

Rosenthal and Jacobson (1968) pioneered research into the Self-Fulfilling Prophecy: the phenomenon wherein one's expectations led to behaviors that produced the expected outcomes. For example, teachers who were falsely led to believe that certain children were brighter than others, altered their behaviors in subtle ways that obtained superior achievement from those students. Conversely, teachers who believed that certain children would be slow to learn, demanded less, provided less and obtained less. Whether positive or negative, the expectations were fulfilled.

The widespread belief in Black intellectual inferiority translates into lowered expectations – and poor outcomes – for Black students and people. In the U.S., this problem extends to other minority groups – Latin@s and Native Americans, particularly – as well as poor Whites and other persons of color. These lowered expectations become institutionalized in programs of special education, wherein Blacks and other minorities are over-represented (Codrington & Fairchild, 2012; Fairchild, 2017).

Stereotype Threat

Steele and Aronson (1995) launched many hundreds of studies into the concept of *stereotype threat*, the idea that people vulnerable to stereotypes are at risk of confirming the stereotype when confronted with tasks relevant to the stereotype.

A well-known stereotype of African American students is that they are less intelligent or academically gifted than Whites. Steele and Aronson (1995) reported that African American students who took a test performed better when they thought the test was irrelevant to their own intellectual abilities. However, if the test was believed to be a measure of their intelligence – thereby invoking the stereotype threat – then their performance declined.

One critique of stereotype threat research is that it locates the problem of inequality of achievement test outcomes in the heads of the students – they would perform better if they did not have to worry about confirming a negative stereotype. Instead, research should focus on the structural barriers that place Black and Latin@ students at a significant disadvantage when taking tests of academic achievement or intellectual prowess. Those barriers are segregated living conditions, *apartheid* schools, an alienating curriculum, and teachers and administrators who are often hostile to their success.

Consequences of Racism

The contemporary world was shaped, in large part, by racism. It was racism, in concert with theological egotism, that justified the conquest of the Africa, North and South America, the Caribbean, Australia, the Pacific Islands and much of Asia. It was the belief that indigenous people were "savages" (subhuman) that justified the imposition of an alien culture (Christianity) and the taking of their land, lives and resources. Racism was an ideological necessity for the enslavement of tens of millions of African men, women and children; and the murder of millions of Indigenous Americans. Racism, fueled by economic elitism, shaped the living arrangements of people around the world (Fairchild & Tucker, 1982). Indeed, racial segregation remains the prevailing norm around the globe.

Individual Racism. At the individual level, racism has many consequences. When racism is *externalized*, a person treats "racial-others" in biased and/or inhumane ways. However, when the racism is *internalized*, individuals harbor negative attitudes about themselves and their own racial group. Racism – the notion that Whites are superior – though widespread, is a fallacy. As such, adherents to racist ideologies suffer from sub-optimal psychological health.[3]

At the individual level, racism restricts social interactions to similar others, and may interfere with relationships with persons of different racial backgrounds.

Individual racism contributes to apathy about the plight of those seen as racial minorities, who are often blamed for their victimization (Ryan, 1971).

Internalized racism contributes to depression, mimicry of White cultural themes (and appearances) and may be implicated in the appalling rates of suicide, homicide and other self-destructive behaviors in minority communities.

Institutional Racism. Inequality of educational opportunity for racial minorities is the prime mover in creating and maintaining racial hierarchies. From K-12 through the university, barriers to education are omnipresent for many groups. Educational barriers compound for girls and women who, by virtue of their gender, are members of a non-privileged group. Schools may be the pipeline to universities and well-paying careers; or to jails and prisons.

---

[3] **Editors' note:** This erroneous belief in the superiority of Whites affects nearly everyone on the planet, to a greater or lesser degree.

Cultural Racism. The mass media reflects and influences the values and biases of our society. This is most evident in the transmission of racist ideas. The 1915 movie, *Birth of a Nation*, demeaned African Americans and extolled the virtues of the Ku Klux Klan. More than a hundred years later, media images of African Americans, Asian Americans, Indigenous Americans, Muslim Americans, Latin@s and women remain problematic.

Radio, television, motion pictures and the news routinely project stereotyped and racist images. Reality-television is steeped in racist imagery and replete with outlandish minority characters who are the embodiment of negative stereotypes.

Anti-racist portrayals that actively *challenge* racist thinking are rare and difficult to find.

Scientific Racism. The racism in individuals, institutions and popular culture was born in the halls of academia. The original justification for racial conquest emanated from philosophers and theologians. More recently, as noted throughout this text, Darwinian theory has been misused in application to racial groups.

Philosophical origins of racism may be traced to the ancient Greeks who held that peasants, warriors and rulers were fundamentally different types of people. Scientific racism blossomed when Linnaeus, widely considered the father of taxonomy, published his systems for classifying species in 1735, and was given a boost in 1869 with the publication of *Hereditary Genius* by Sir Francis Galton.

Contemporary manifestations of scientific racism abound in the works of J. Philippe Rushton (2010), Arthur Jenson (2013), Richard Lynn (Lynn & Vanhanen, 2006) and Herrnstein and Murray (1994). These pseudo-scientists produce work that policy makers and hate groups espouse to justify disparate treatment for people of color. (For a critique, see Fairchild, 1991.)

Reducing Prejudice, Racism and Discrimination

Eliminating prejudice and racism is a daunting task. To that end, social psychologists have developed a number of strategies for reducing intergroup hostilities.

The Contact Hypothesis

In his seminal book, *The Nature of Prejudice*, Gordon Allport (1954) articulated the tenets of the contact hypothesis: when groups interact cooperatively and harmoniously, intergroup attitudes improve and the prospects for positive future interactions are enhanced. Intergroup contacts that feature individuals with equal status, who work cooperatively and successfully pursue common goals, are optimal for producing positive outcomes.

The benefits of intergroup contact between Arabs and Israelis was reported by Berger, Abu-Raiya and Gelkopf (2015). Such interactions benefit not just those directly involved; but also has a ripple effect, wherein friends of persons who experience positive intergroup contacts also report improved attitudes (Wright, Aron, McLaughlin-Volpe & Ropp, 1997). Even in circumstances where it is not possible to have certain groups interact (due to distance or other barriers), when participants *imagine* having positive interactions, their attitudes improve (Husnu & Crisp, 2010).

The Jigsaw Classroom

Elliot Aronson and his colleagues developed the *Jigsaw Classroom* based on the principles of the contact hypothesis (Aronson, Blaney, Sikes, Stephan & Snapp, 1975; Aronson, Stephan, Sikes, Blaney & Snapp, 1978). Created specifically for the "desegregated" classroom, the jigsaw technique was a pedagogical strategy wherein children learned in cross-ethnic groups. Children from different backgrounds were each given essential parts of the lesson plan. In order to complete the lesson, children had to share knowledge and information with their fellow students. Such interactions placed each child on an equal status and was demonstrated to encourage intergroup friendships, improve attitudes, and enhance academic achievement.

Pro-Social Television

Television is a powerful medium for the transmission of racial attitudes – whether positive or negative. For most of television's history, minority groups were either absent or portrayed in highly stereotypical roles. These portrayals exacerbated the problems of race relations in America and throughout the world (Huston, et al., 1992).

Some television programs – *The Cosby Show* (1984-1992) is a notable example – challenged traditional stereotypical portrayals and contributed to some improvements in racial attitudes and interactions.

A pilot children's television program, *Star Crusaders*, was created to provide viewers with the vicarious experience of positive inter-racial interactions (Fairchild, 1984, 1988a). Its premise was: an inter-ethnic team of space travelers – a Black male, Latino male, Asian female and White male – work cooperatively to solve a problem of inter-group hostilities on a distant planet. Evaluations demonstrated that viewers discerned the pro-social themes, children preferred *Star Crusaders* to a nature program (*Wild*

Kingdom), and racial attitudes were positively affected (Fairchild, 1984, 1988a).

Dissonance Reduction Techniques

Cognitive dissonance has been used as an attitude change strategy for a wide variety of attitude objects. Individuals engage in a counter-attitudinal activity to create dissonance. For example, persons harboring negative racial attitudes might be tasked with writing an essay in favor of affirmative action. According to dissonance theory, counter-attitudinal behavior creates cognitive tension. How does the individual reconcile his or her behavior with their attitudes? This theory predicts that the counter-attitudinal behavior would push the individual's attitudes in the direction of increased tolerance for those they once reviled.

Chapter Overviews

Chapter 53 (*Race Socialization and Stereotype Threat for Mixed Race Individuals* by Earl M. Schultz) examines racial socialization and the master/slave narrative that derogates marginalized groups. Schultz suggests protections against stereotype threat.

Chapter 54 (*Our 'Ostrich Mentality' on Racism* by Halford H. Fairchild, Ph.D.) considers the omnipresent – yet unconscious – manifestations of racism. Fairchild posits that recognition of how racism is deeply embedded in the fabric of American history and culture is prerequisite to its elimination.

Chapter 55 (*The Truth About Islam* by Omar Alireza) challenges misconceptions about the Muslim Faith. Alireza discusses the treatment of women and the contributions that Islam has made to world culture.

Chapter 56 (*Modern-Day Racism Masks Its Ugly Head* by Halford H. Fairchild, Ph.D.) describes the disguised and subtle expressions of racism. Fairchild recounts the history of racism and explores its real world consequences in health and wealth disparities.

Chapter 57 (*Free at Last!* by Halford H. Fairchild, Ph.D.) is a short story, set hundreds of years in the future, that flips the script on racism. Fairchild uses the character of a White slave to bemoan the injustices of enslavement.

Chapter 58 (*The Stigmatization of Homosexuality* by Sasha Forbath) explores the psychology of stereotypes when applied to LGBQT individuals. Forbath calls for a celebration of human diversity as a necessary step toward World Peace.

References

Allport, G. (1954). *The nature of prejudice*. Oxford, England: Addison-Wesley.

Aronson, E., Blaney, N., Sikes, J., Stephan, C., and Snapp, M. (1975). Busing and racial tension: The jigsaw route to learning and liking. *Psychology Today, 8*, 43-59.

Aronson, E., Stephan, C., Sikes, J., Blaney, N., and Snapp, M. (1978). *The Jigsaw Classroom*. Beverly Hills, CA: Sage Publications.

Berger, R., Abu-Raiya, H., & Gelkopf, M. (2015). The art of living together: Reducing stereotyping and prejudicial attitudes through the Arab-Jewish class exchange program (CEP). *Journal of Educational Psychology, 107*(3), 678-688. doi:10.1037/edu0000015

Bogardus, E.S. (1925). Measuring social distances. *Journal of Applied Sociology, 9*, 299-308.

Brotherton, C. (2007). The social psychology of stereotyping, discrimination and prejudice. *Journal of Community & Applied Social Psychology, 17*(2), 159-165. doi:10.1002/casp.890

Codrington, J. & Fairchild, H.H. (2012). *Special education and the mis-education of African American children: A call to action. (A Position Paper of The Association of Black Psychologists)*. Washington, DC: The Association of Black Psychologists. (Available online at www.abpsi.org.)

Dinnerstein, L. (2003). Antisemitism in America. In S. Plous (Ed.), *Understanding prejudice and discrimination* (pp. 294-303). New York, NY, US: McGraw-Hill.

Fairchild, H. H. (1984). Creating, producing, and evaluating pro-social TV. *The Journal of Educational Television, 10*(3), 161-183.

Fairchild, H. H. (1988a). Creating positive television images. Pp. 270-279 in S. Oskamp (Ed.), *Television as a social issue*. (Volume 8 of the Applied Social Psychology Annual). Newbury Park, CA: Sage Publications.

Fairchild, H. H. (1988b). Glorification of things white. *Journal of Black Psychology, 14*(2), 73-74.

Fairchild, H. H. (1991). Scientific Racism: The cloak of objectivity. *Journal of Social Issues, 47*(3), 101-115.

Fairchild, H.H. (February 26, 2001). SAT's 'halo effect' casts a long shadow. *Los Angeles Times*, page B7.

Fairchild, H.H. (2017). Special education is mis-education. In H.H. Fairchild (Ed.), *Black lives matter: Lifespan perspectives* (pp. 125-130). Delhi: Indo American Books.

Fairchild, H. H. & Gurin, P. (1978). Traditions in the social-psychological analysis of race relations. *American Behavioral Scientist, 21*(5), 757-778.

Fairchild, H. H., & Tucker, M. B. (1982). Black residential mobility: Trends and characteristics. *Journal of Social Issues, 38*(3), 51-74.

Fiske, S. T., Harris, L. T., Lee, T. L., & Russell, A. M. (2016). The future of research on prejudice, stereotyping, and discrimination. In T. D. Nelson (Eds), *Handbook of prejudice, stereotyping, and discrimination, 2nd ed.* (pp. 487-498). New York, NY, US: Psychology Press.

Herrnstein, R., & Murray, C. (1994). *The bell curve: Intelligence and class structure in American life.* NY: Free Press.

Husnu, S., & Crisp, R. J. (2010). Imagined intergroup contact: A new technique for encouraging greater inter-ethnic contact in Cyprus. *Peace and Conflict: Journal of Peace Psychology, 16*(1), 97-108. doi:10.1080/10781910903484776

Huston, A. C., Donnerstein, E., Fairchild, H., Feshbach, N., Katz, P., Murray, J., Rubinstein, E., Wilcox, B. & Zuckerman, D. (1992). *Big World/Small Screen: The Role of Television in American Society.* Lincoln, NE: University of Nebraska Press.

Jensen, A.R. (2013). Rushton's contributions to the study of mental ability. *Personality and Individual Differences, 55*(3), 212-217.

LaPiere, R.T. (1934). Attitudes vs. actions. *Social Forces, 13*, 230-237.

Lynn, R., & Vanhanen, T. (2006). *IQ and global inequality.* Augusta, GA: Washington Summit Publishers.

MacRae, C.N., Bodenhausen, G.V., Milne, A.B., & Jetten, J. (1994). Out of mind but back in sight: Stereotypes on the rebound. *Journal of Personality and Social Psychology, 67*(5), 808-817.

McLeod, S. A. (2008). Robbers Cave. Retrieved from www.simplypsychology.org/robbers-cave.html

Nosek, B.A., Greenwald, A.G., & Banaji, M.R. (Eds). (207). *The Implicit Association Test at age 7: A methodological and conceptual review.* New York, NU: Psychology Press.

Okamura, R. Y. (2003). The American concentration camps: A cover-up through euphemistic terminology. In S. Plous (Ed.), *Understanding prejudice and discrimination* (pp. 149-164). New York, NY, US: McGraw-Hill.

Rosenthal, R., & Jacobson, L. (1968). *Pygmalion in the classroom: Teacher expectation and pupils' intellectual development.* New York: Holt, Rinehart & Winston.

Rushton, J.P. (2010). Brain size as an explanation of national differences in IQ, longevity and other life-history variables. *Personality and Individual Differences, 48*(2), 97-99.

Ryan, W. (1971). *Blaming the victim.* NY: Pantheon.

Sherif, M., Harvey, O. J., White, B. J., Hood, W. R., & Sherif, C. W. (1961). *Intergroup conflict and cooperation: The Robbers Cave experiment (Vol. 10).* Norman, OK: University Book Exchange.

Stangor, C. (2016). The study of stereotyping, prejudice, and discrimination within social psychology: A quick history of theory and research. In T. D. Nelson

(Ed.), *Handbook of prejudice, stereotyping, and discrimination*, 2nd ed. (pp. 3-27). New York, NY, US: Psychology Press.

Steele, C.M., & Aronson, J. (1995). Stereotype threat and the intellectual performance of African Americans. *Journal of Personality and Social Psychology, 62*(2), 207-218.

Tajfel, H. (1970). Experiments in intergroup discrimination. *Scientific American, 223*, 96-102.

Wright, S.C., Aron, A., McLaughlin-Volpe, T., & Ropp, S.A. (1997). The extended contact effect: Knowledge of cross-group friendships and prejudice. *Journal of Personality and Social Psychology, 73*(1), 73-90.

Editors' Discussion Questions

1. How have prejudice, racism and/or discrimination impacted or factored into your life? What should be done to lessen these problems?

2. Why is the idea of "exterminating the enemy" not feasible?

3. How should the American Dilemma – professing democracy while bombing innocents – be reconciled?

4. Should the U.S. pay "reparations" to individuals or groups that have been wronged in the past? Why or why not?

Chapter 53

Race Socialization and Stereotype Threat for Mixed Race Individuals

EARL M. SCHULTZ

Abstract: Part of growing up involves racial socialization, which for people of color invokes the *master/slave narrative* that derogates Black people and other marginalized groups. The idea of race is socially constructed, as evidenced by the "one drop rule," and places special demands on mixed-race or multi-race individuals. *Stereotype threat* affects many populations, in and outside of academia. Stereotypes must not define the range of possibilities for ourselves or others.

Too Black for the White kids, and too White for the Blacks

From honor roll to cracking locks up off them bicycle racks.

-*Chum* by Earl Sweatshirt

Introduction

Race socialization is the informal process through which values, beliefs, aesthetics, and other cultural elements are passed from one generation to the next. Cultural knowledge is derived from various sources including family, community, and institutions. The combination of race socialization and cultural knowledge leads to the formation of one's racial identity.

Race socialization is important as it invokes the *master/slave-narrative*, in which negative stereotypes are formed and propagated about Black people and other marginalized groups. These groups are often subjected to prejudice and discrimination.

Stereotypes are the positive or negative beliefs that we associate with characteristics of different social groups. Stereotypes influence our judgements of others and ourselves, and may affect our performance on various tasks. For a mixed-race or multi-race individual, choosing a particular racial identity makes him or her a target or beneficiary of the various stereotypes that are associated with that race.

Stereotype threat occurs when performance is hindered by cultural stereotypes. For example, when a student from a discriminated against minority group takes a test that is presumed to measure "intelligence," he or she may feel anxious about the possibility of confirming the stereotype, and that anxiety may act as a self-fulfilling prophecy (Steele & Aronson, 1995; Steele, 1997).

Race and Freedom

Multi-racial individuals have received different treatment throughout U.S. history. From the 1600s until centuries later, the "one-drop rule" defined one's *Blackness*. According to this rule, having a single Black ancestor – however distant – branded a person as Black (Brown, 2014).

Freedom and privilege were bestowed upon Whites, while slavery and Jim Crow degradations were foisted upon Blacks. Legislators enacted the socially constructed "one-drop rule," which became the law of the land in North America during the antebellum period.

Today, people adhere to a version of the "one-drop rule," wherein the presence of any physical traits of African descent (the color of skin, facial features or hair texture) makes one "Black" regardless of their personal identity. Placement into a racial category necessarily comes with associated stereotypes, prejudices, privileges and penalties.

If one Black ancestor – regardless of how remote – makes a person Black, then why does one White ancestor – however distant – not make a person White? The difficulty in answering this question exposes the socially-constructed nature of race and the ambiguity that arises when people reside on the boundaries of traditional racial categories (Hamilton, Samek, Keyes, Mgue & Iacono, 2015).

Racial categories and their corresponding stereotypes are deeply embedded in our society. Mixed race individuals typically identify with their more marginalized ancestry due, in part, to societal perceptions ascribed by skin color or other physical features (Charles, Kramer, Torres & Brunn-Bevel, 2015).

Stereotype Threat

Social psychological research has identified several instances where stereotype threat influences behavior. Johns, Schmader and Martens (2005) studied the effects of test instructions on female performance in a testing situation. Women performed worse than men when the problems were described as a math test, as the stereotype of women not doing well in math was invoked. By contrast, when the same test questions were framed as a generic problem-solving task (with no existing gender stereotype), men and women performed equally well. These results suggest that awareness of and teaching about stereotype threat may reduce its harmful effects.

The context in which a test is framed affects performance. Alter, Aronson, Darley, Rodriguez and Ruble (2010) observed that students who reported their race *before* taking a mathematics test performed worse than those who reported their race *after* completing the test. Like gender stereotypes, these results suggest that reframing or describing a test as a *challenge* (to avoid stereotype threat) can eliminate racial differences in test performance.

Black identity, the degree that an individual identified with being Black, was related to the negative effects of stereotype threat in a study of mental ability (Hoskins, 2014). The "Blacker" one's identity, the more likely students were to experience performance deficits in tasks involving mental acuity.

Okeke, Howard, Kurtz-Costes, & Rowley (2009) found that minority students with high racial centrality and strong endorsement of traditional race stereotypes had lower self-perceptions of academic competence. This relationship was not evident for those who reported that race was less central to their identities. These findings may be especially relevant for multi-racial individuals who identify as Black.

Stereotype threat has applications beyond academia. White athletes, for example, were affected by stereotype threat when tasks were related to "natural ability," and gave less effort (Stone, 2002).

Conclusion

A *master/slave-narrative*, in which Black students are deemed to be intellectually inferior, is perpetuated by racial stereotypes that are deeply entrenched in the American psyche.

Nasir, Atukpawu, O'Connor, Davis, Wischnia and Tsang (2009) reported that contemporary stereotypes of Blacks included the hoodlum or thug, who listens to rap music and performs poorly in school. These all derive from the *master/slave narrative*.

Racial and cultural stereotypes threaten one's ability to succeed. Multi-racial people struggle with forming racial identifications and are often forced to choose between the privileges or disadvantages that are associated with one race or another. Stereotype threat is a consequence of forming certain racial identities.

To reduce stereotype threat, tests should be reframed as challenges; awareness should be raised about the dangers of stereotypic thinking; and positive characteristics about oneself or one's group should be affirmed.

One's *Blackness*, specifically for multi-racial people, should not limit academic success.

We should celebrate each other's individuality; and never allow stereotypes to define the range of possibilities for ourselves or others.

References

Alter, A. L., Aronson, J., Darley, J. M., Rodriguez, C., & Ruble, D. N. (2010). Rising to the threat: Reducing stereotype threat by reframing the threat as a challenge. *Journal of Experimental Social Psychology, 46*(1), 166-171. doi:10.1016/j.jesp.2009.09.014

Brown, K. D. (2014). The rise and fall of the one-drop rule: How the importance of color came to eclipse race. In K. J. Norwood, K. J. Norwood (Eds.), *Color matters: Skin tone bias and the myth of a postracial America* (pp. 44-94). New York, NY, US: Routledge/Taylor & Francis Group.

Charles, C. Z., Kramer, R. A., Torres, K. C., & Brunn-Bevel, R. J. (2015). Intragroup heterogeneity and blackness: Effects of racial classification, immigrant origins, social class, and social context on the racial identity of elite college students. *Race and Social Problems*, doi:10.1007/s12552-015-9157-2

Hamilton, E., Samek, D. R., Keyes, M., Mgue, M. K., & Iacono, W. G. (2015). Identity development in a transracial environment: Racial/ethnic minority adoptees in Minnesota. *Adoption Quarterly, 18*(3), 217-233. doi:10.1080/10926755.2015.1013593

Hoskins, O.D. (2014). *Relationships between internalized stereotypes, Black identity, race salience, and self-esteem among African American college students*. (2014-99180-277).

Johns, M., Schmader, T., & Martens, A. (2005). Knowing is half the battle: Teaching stereotype threat as a means of improving women's math performance. *Psychological Science, 16*(3), 175-179. doi:10.1111/j.0956-7976.2005.00799.x

Nasir, N. S., Atukpawu, G., O'Connor, K., Davis, M., Wischnia, S., & Tsang, J. (2009). Wrestling with the legacy of stereotypes: Being African American in math class. In D. B. Martin (Ed.), *Mathematics teaching, learning and liberation in the lives of Black children* (pp. 231-248). New York, NY, US: Routledge/Taylor & Francis Group.

Okeke, N. A., Howard, L. C., Kurtz-Costes, B., & Rowley, S. J. (2009). Academic race stereotypes, academic self-concept, and racial centrality in African American youth. *Journal of Black Psychology, 35*(3), 366-387. doi:10.1177/0095798409333615

Steele, C. M. (1997). A threat in the air: How stereotypes shape intellectual identity and performance. *American Psychologist, 52*(6), 613-629. doi:10.1037/0003-066X.52.6.613

Steele, C. M., & Aronson, J. (1995). Stereotype threat and the intellectual test performance of African Americans. *Journal of Personality and Social Psychology, 69*(5), 797-811. doi:10.1037/0022-3514.69.5.797

Stone, J. (2002). Battling doubt by avoiding practice: The effects of stereotype threat on self-handicapping in White athletes. *Personality and Social Psychology Bulletin, 28*(12), 1667-1678. doi:10.1177/014616702237648

Editors' Discussion Questions

1. How do you define "race"? With how many "racial" groups can you identify? Explain.

2. Have you ever suffered the effects of *stereotype threat*? In what circumstances? How did it affect behavior in that situation? Did it alter how you behaved afterwards? Explain.

Chapter 54

Our 'Ostrich Mentality' on Racism[1]

HALFORD H. FAIRCHILD, PH.D.

Abstract: During an interview in the summer of 1987, Los Angeles Dodgers' executive, Al Campanis, made an injudicious comment that Blacks lacked "the necessities" to be baseball managers. The following uproar, his apology and termination revealed certain truisms about racism in America. We pretend it no longer exists; so that on the occasion when someone makes a verbal blunder to reveal an obviously racist sentiment, we react in indignation and outrage. Instead, we should recognize that racism is deeply embedded in the fabric of American history and culture. That recognition is necessary so that we can identify, challenge and eliminate racism.

The recent remarks by Dodger executive Al Campanis about Blacks in baseball, the ensuing public outcry, and his public censure and dismissal offer poignant lessons for understanding contemporary race relations in America.

In his casual comments expressing doubt in Black people's ability to fill managerial positions in baseball, Campanis revealed that he is as much a victim of racism as those he disparaged. The subsequent calls for his firing also demonstrate a failure on the part of civil rights activists to perceive the true significance of public disclosures of prejudicial beliefs.

Campanis' beliefs about the inherent inferiority of Blacks is only a symptom of racial stereotyping that far transcends baseball or professional sports. Indeed, the belief that Blacks are intellectually inferior is, sadly, as American as *Mom and Apple Pie*.

---

[1] This Chapter was revised from an op-ed published in the *Los Angeles Times* on April 12, 1987.

Racism has a long, enduring history in America. This country was founded in a climate of unbridled and unrepentant racism and the belief in the innate inferiority of African (and Indigenous) peoples. The result of hundreds of years of slavery and decades of Jim Crow legislation, segregation and discrimination has been a cultural belief system steeped in racist ideology.

Campanis' remarks demonstrate the "unconscious" nature of racism, and how easily a person in his position can be caught off-guard. They reveal both the depth and the pervasiveness of a racist ideology that courses through the veins of our society.

The demands for Campanis' punishment are also problematic. Termination punishes Campanis for his indiscretion, yet his firing does nothing to redress the racist ideology that permeates our society. It is as if prejudice is tacitly accepted so long as it remains unspoken.

It is incorrect to castigate Campanis for his racist beliefs. To do so is tantamount to "blaming the victim." Like the rest of us, Campanis is a product of his culture and environment. His racist remarks remind us that bigoted belief systems harm us all; and that *bigotry is blind to itself.*

Both phenomena – the inadvertent disclosure of racial prejudice and the public condemnation of it – are reflective of the denial syndrome that cloaks American racism. Most Americans suffer from a condition that might be described as an "ostrich mentality" when it comes to the difficult social issues that confront us: If we do not see the problem, we can pretend that it does not exist; and when we do see it, we posture in outrage and indignation. Such posturing contributes to the denial syndrome as it fails to acknowledge the omnipresence of prejudice and racism.

Professional sports are a microcosm of society. In it we find courage, competitiveness, teamwork, violence, drug abuse – and yes, racial prejudice. Certainly, removing Campanis from baseball will not solve the problem of prejudice in baseball or anywhere else. The true nature of the problem is institutionalized, woven into the social fabric of this country.

Professional sports are also one of the focal points for the fight against drug abuse. Now, it can be a catalyst for the struggle against the tenacity of racial prejudice. The Campanis incident should be used as a vivid example of how prejudicial beliefs can affect the complexion of upper management in baseball, other sports and much of the rest of the working world.

Campanis's apology and resignation were necessary as a symbolic gesture of our intolerance of intolerance. However more important than the apology and resignation, the incident should spur definitive actions to reverse prejudicial beliefs – and their associated actions – that have denied equal opportunities to Blacks and other people of color.

We must acknowledge the reality and pervasiveness of racism in our lives and confront it head on, if we are ever to successfully move toward its elimination. Civil-rights leaders must be vigilant in the public exposure of prejudice, to be sure; but they also must develop more aggressive, proactive agendas for identifying and eradicating racism in the broader social culture.

To demand an apology for racism perpetuates the ostrich mentality that allows racism to flourish. Instead of apologizing and denying that racism continues to exist, Campanis – and all of us – must acknowledge the reality of bigoted belief systems and be willing to take the deliberate steps to eliminate prejudice and discrimination.

Editors' Discussion Questions

1. Is racism pervasive or exceptional? What accounts for differences of opinion regarding the prevalence of racism?

2. What strategies should be undertaken to challenge and eliminate racism?

Chapter 55

The Truth About Islam

OMAR ALIREZA

Abstract: Despite the fact that it is a belief system that seeks peace and harmony, Islam often conjures negative connotations and stereotypes. Islam is a religion of peace that respects women, and encourages education and human progress. It is only when the beliefs of all are accepted and valued that World Peace is possible.

When the topic of Islam is discussed, it conjures negative connotations for many – '*jihad*,' 'terrorism,' 'subjugation of woman,' and 'backwardness.' These stereotypes are the result of ignorance and misinformation. This chapter provides an insider's perspective: Islam is a belief system that seeks peace and harmony.

Jihad is To Struggle

Inspiring fear in many, the term '*jihad*' is erroneously defined as 'holy war' in Western media. However, its true meaning is '*to struggle*'. If one is engaged in '*jihad*', one is engaged in *struggle*.

Two Forms of *Jihad*

"We have returned from the *lesser jihad* to the *greater jihad*." The *lesser jihad* is the physical effort of struggling against oppression or for any cause. It is also undertaking any 'virtuous' action that requires effort and struggle. This includes charity and placing others' needs before one's own. The same applies to other virtuous acts such as being fair and trustworthy.

By contrast, the *greater jihad* is the struggle against one's *lower self*. This encompasses struggling against base desires such as lust, gluttony, hatred, envy and anger. The purpose of this struggle is to control one's desires.

The *Noble Qur'an,* the central religious text of Islam believed to be a revelation from Allah, prohibits the killing and oppression of innocents. One of many examples is as follows:

Because of that, We decreed upon the Children of Israel
that whoever kills a soul unless for a soul or for
corruption [done] in the land – it is as if he had slain
mankind entirely. And whoever saves one – it is as if
he had saved mankind entirely. (Qur'an 5:32).

The Prophet Muhammad (*Peace be upon him*) said, "(t)he best of people are those that bring most benefit to the rest of mankind."

The *Qur'an* and the teachings of Prophet Muhammad (*PBUH*) – the highest sources of Islamic jurisprudence – are antithetical to Western portrayals of Islam.

Women

Many people assume that Muslims oppress women. In reality, Islam has a history of raising the status of women.

According to the Prophet (*PBUH*), "Heaven lies under the feet of our mothers."

Islam abolished practices that devalued daughters (Muslim Women's League, 1995). Indeed, Quranic injunction allowed women to inherit property – a right that has been extended only recently to women in the West (Muslim Women's League, 1995).

The *Qur'an* instructs:

"Men shall have a share in what parents and kinsfolk
leave behind, and women shall have a share in what
parents   and   kinsfolk   leave   behind."
(Qur'an 4:7).

The West also views the *hijab* (veil) as demeaning; yet it is meant to be empowering to Muslim women. When a woman is veiled, men look at her true personality.[1] The *hijab* gives women control over how men perceive them, allowing a woman to declare her personality without obfuscation by physical appearance or sexuality.

Progress

While the West conceives of Islam as a 'backward' religion, history proves otherwise.

Examples of progress due to Islam are plentiful. The Prophet Mohammed (*PBUH*) popularized the first toothbrush in around 600 A.D.

---

[1] Western cultures value women more for their appearance than their intellectual prowess. Hence, women in the West adorn and alter themselves to resemble the feminine cultural ideal.

Using a twig from the Meswak tree, he cleaned his teeth and freshened his breath. Substances similar to Meswak are used in toothpaste today (Sterns, 2010).

Eighth century mathematician, geographer and astronomer Muhammad al-Khwarizmi developed a systematic approach to solving linear and quadratic equations. His work ultimately led to the creation of algebra as its own discipline and to advances in trigonometry (Sterns, 2010).

Hospitals, as we know them today, were originally developed in 9th century Egypt (Sterns, 2010).

Conclusion

Far from the West's (mis)perceptions, Islam is a religion of peace that promotes peace. It commands men to respect women, and encourages education and the positive progress of humanity. We must respect all people and embrace all religions if we are to achieve World Peace.

References

Muslim Women's League. (2016). Women in Pre-Islamic Arabia. *Muslim Women's League*. Web. 26 Apr. 2016.

Sterns, Olivia. (2010). Muslim Inventions That Shaped the Modern World. *CNN*. Cable News Network, 29 Jan. 2010. Web. 14 Apr. 2016.

Other Sources

Jihad in the Hadith. *Jihad in the Hadith*. N.p., Web. 14 Apr. 2016.

Sound Vision Staff Writer. The Quran and Hadith on Mothers. *The Quran and Hadith on Mothers*. N.p., n.d. Web. 14 Apr. 2016.

Steps To Enter Paradise. *The Best Among You (Muslim)*. N.p., n.d. Web. 14 Apr. 2016.

Surat Al-Ma'idah [5:32]. *The Noble Qur'an*. N.p., Web. 14 Apr. 2016.

University, Harvard. The Pluralism Project. *Struggling Against Stereotypes*. The Pluralism Project, n.d. Web. 14 Apr. 2016.

Editors' Discussion Questions

1. The author describes Islam as a religion of peace. Why is Islam portrayed differently in Western media? Do you agree with the former or the latter? Why?

2. If the conflicts in the Middle East – ISIL, ISIS, the Syrian Civil War, Israeli-Palestinian conflict – are not about religion, then what are the sources of these conflicts?

Chapter 56

Modern-Day Racism Masks Its Ugly Head[1]

Halford H. Fairchild, Ph.D.

Abstract: Far from being a relic of the past, racism is alive and well; but its expression is simply more subtle. Racism arose as the justification for racial exploitation (genocide and slavery); it currently manifests in opposition to policies and programs seeking to undo the history of discrimination. Racism has real-world consequences in health and wealth disparities. Racism must be brought "out of the closet" because it is only when all people have equal opportunity that we can have peace around the globe.

There are those in the U.S. who insist that racism is a vestige of the pre-civil rights era and not a contemporary problem. But racism is a current scourge; only its expression is more veiled and nuanced. The insidious nature of racism demands that we intervene.

We can best understand the contemporary reality of racism by delving into the past. In antiquity, knowledge of racial differentiation was not necessarily accompanied by dehumanizing sentiments. The ancient Egyptians' awareness of racial variation did not carry with it the stigma of the dehumanization of those who were superficially different. Similarly, the ancient Greeks and Romans looked upon the ancient Ethiopians with respect and romanticism.

The concept of race acquired the patina of a scientific enterprise in the early to mid-1800s, as part of what is largely known as the European Enlightenment. Scientists at that time, particularly biologists and botanists,

---

[1] This Chapter was revised from an op-ed published in the *Los Angeles Times* on September 11, 2000.

213

were earnest in classifying the diversity of life on Earth, including the human species. Perhaps because of ethnocentrism and cultural chauvinism, the classification of human beings ranked Europeans at the top and Africans at the bottom.

The institution of slavery within the Americas required an intellectual justification for the mistreatment of millions of African men, women and children. *Slavery required racism and was the proximate cause of it.*

Racism became unique in the United States largely because of the efforts to abolish slavery. Abolition intensified slavery's apologists' efforts to justify their "peculiar institution," and they did so by derogating the humanity of African people. Thus, if contemporary racism is a product of American slavery, then slavery has other consequences that are also alive and well today.

Racism in contemporary world affairs is disguised – what some refer to as symbolic racism, modern racism or aversive racism. These new forms of racism eschew the old-fashioned, red-neck ideology of White supremacy and Black inferiority and, instead, espouse equality in human affairs. Yet the concept of equality is discordant with the simultaneous preference for the *status quo* of White privilege.

Aversive racism manifests in opposition to programs and policies that seek to undo White privilege or provide reparations to Blacks on the basis of historical discrimination. Interestingly, current research in social psychology demonstrates that the aversive racist is unaware of his or her racism – much of modern racism is an unconscious process.

In a series of laboratory and real-world experiments, social psychologists have demonstrated unconscious or aversive racism in a number of contexts.

The effects of aversive racism are manifest and impact the quality of life, both physically and psychologically, of Africans and African Americans. The ravages of racism are apparent in the appalling statistics of HIV/AIDS in Africa and among African Americans. We see the life-and-death consequences of old-fashioned and modern racism in the high infant mortality rates that afflict African and African American communities, as well as their much higher rates of preventable deaths from hypertension, heart disease, diabetes, cancer and violence.

Modern racism has widened the economic gulf between White and Black Americans. While the proportions of African Americans in the middle and upper classes have increased, so too has the proportion of African American children reared in poverty. African Americans in the higher echelons of corporate America, government and the military is about *one tenth* of what one would expect given a system of true equal opportunity.

To solve these problems of structured inequality, we must first acknowledge the reality of racism in contemporary world affairs. We can no longer afford to hide from this reality and must thrust unconscious racism to the forefront of our attention. Only then can we develop and propagate social and institutional norms and values that reject racism – conscious and unconscious – and advance true equal opportunity.

Editors' Discussion Questions

1. How is racism manifested in your social world? What can be done to redress the problem of racism?

2. Many African Americans and Latinos live in racially isolated communities that tend to be more impoverished and crime infested. Why?

3. Blacks are under-represented in the higher echelons of academia and corporate America, but over-represented in jails, prisons and professional sports. How do you account for these differences?

Chapter 57
Free at Last![1]

HALFORD H. FAIRCHILD, PH.D.

Abstract: Set hundreds of years in the future, this short story is the suicide note of a White slave who lived his entire life in captivity on the Moon. He seeks "freedom" by taking his own life.

I was born on the Moon 35 years ago. I have lived in *Douglass Dome* all of my life. Because my skin is White, I was born a slave. But on this night, I will take my own life because my soul yearns to be free! Yes, dear diary, this is a suicide note. On what authority does my master deem himself superior to me? Because his skin is brown?

I have learned that a thousand years ago, the situation was reversed. White men and women ruled the Africana people and held *them* as slaves. Oh! Would it only be true today. I can scarcely believe that we Whites once ruled the Earth; our subjugation seems to have existed forever.

But this slavery is an abomination to humanity. Why must I suffer the lash at the whim of my master? Why must my children be stolen from me in the dead of night, tearing my heart asunder in grief and sorrow? This is why many have killed their children, to spare them the indignity of a life of unrelenting servitude.

It was my mistake not to take my children's lives; it was my father's mistake not to take mine; and his father before him and on and on. But tonight I will do what should have been done upon my birth: to end this life of perpetual misery. My plan is simple: I will exit from the South Airlock and cut a hole in my suit. My death will be slow and painful, but no worse than the living death of being a chattel slave to these Africana people.

---

[1] This short story was previously published in *Psych Discourse: NewsJournal of The Association of Black Psychologists*, Volume 33, December, 2002.

My uncle whispered to me the story of when White men ruled the Earth. It was *we* who held the Africana people in subjugation. But somehow the Africana people, made strong by their own struggle for redemption, seized military and political control of the world. It seems, my uncle said, that White people were only too willing to vote an Africana person into political office or to place her in command of the military.

After a thousand years, Thomas Jefferson Baumfree, then President of North and South America, decreed that all persons with at least 51% White blood would be held in captivity for the duration of their lives. And we have now been enslaved for 400 years if my uncle is to be believed.

I, for one, do not believe it. How is it possible for my miserable brethren – illiterate, poor and helpless – to ever have ruled the world?

How could anyone challenge the Africanas, with their hyper-space drives and bombs that can destroy a planet?

My life is pure misery. We toil 15 hours a day, with scarcely a moment's rest, refueling the starships that park in our orbit. The lower gravity doesn't help much when the tankers that we push and pull weigh a million tons. So today, dear diary, I will get my freedom. I will escape to that home in heaven where paradise is to be found.

What kind of life is this where every moment we are made to feel ugly because of the color of our skin and the shapes of our noses? This skin is a wicked veil that marks us from the cradle as inferior. And I will tell you that there are White men and women who are as attractive as the most attractive Africana person. But, then, *beauty is in the eye of the beholder*, according to a saying that goes back to antiquity.

Even our names are ascribed to us. Who was my mother? My father? What is my real name? My master was said, by some, to be my father; but I have no sign of his brown skin in my paleness. Oh! Would that I did! For I would be free. Only those who are half or more White – *the 51% rule* – are deemed the kinds of infidels and barbarians that require our enslavement. They want to tell us that slavery is good for us; that if left to our own devices we would destroy ourselves in an epileptic fit of self-directed violence. But they are wrong, for I want to be free!

> *Oh veil of night*
> *Hear my sorrowful plight*
> *I stand on the edge of eternity*
> *My life over – a certainty ...*

This institution, as peculiar as it is, is bad for the White slaves. But it is also bad for the Africana masters. It has made them cruel. They treat us like animals, branding our backs with their insignia. They deny us an opportunity to learn, keeping us forever ignorant of our wretched condition. We are chastised and despised for not knowing what we have not been taught. We have been sent, all of us, to live on this desolate rock that circles the Earth, so that the Africana people need not experience the revulsion they have for our pale bodies. Their only debate is how to ensure the *free trade* of our enslaved bodies. What a cruel irony! Their men rape our women and claim their mixed children as their property, to be bought and sold at auction. What kind of man would consign his own son or daughter into this hell of existence? How can they claim to be enlightened when they practice such barbarism?

Since when would the color of one's skin mark him a slave for life? Since forever, it seems.

But tonight, I find my freedom in that endless sleep that claims all that live on Earth or in space.

The night, cold
My heart, broken
Our nation state, a mockery
Of Freedom and Justice
My suit, torn
My life, past
Free at last, Lord
I am free at last!

Editors' Discussion Questions

1. Describe your *feelings* about this reading.

2. How is this story pessimistic? Is there anything optimistic in the reading?

Chapter 58

The Stigmatization of Homosexuality

SASHA FORBATH

Abstract: Stereotypes tend to homogenize outgroups and derogate their targets. This is especially true for the LGBQT community, whose members face both homophobia and sexual structural stigma. To achieve World Peace, we must first replace stigmas and stereotypes with an appreciation for and celebration of human diversity—including diversity in sexualities.

Stereotypes that derogate certain demographic groups are an inescapable reality. Prejudices are a set of beliefs toward a target group, whereas stereotypes carry more of an evaluative component to those beliefs (Herek, 1998).

Those who identify as members of the LGBQT community[1] are often targets of prejudices and negative stereotypes. The U.S. has a long history of *homophobia* (an active dislike for sexual orientations that are not heterosexual). In fact, homophobia is so deeply ingrained that psychiatry previously diagnosed homosexuality as a treatable mental illness (Herek, 1998).

Sexual minorities face continuous discrimination and, as a result, many non-heterosexuals develop internalized homophobia (Kaysen, Kulesza, Balsam, Rhew, Blaynew, Lehavot & Hughes, 2014). Individuals who identify as a sexual minority face constant devaluation by society, which may lead to an internalized devaluation of the self.

Unfortunately, the stigmatization and stereotyping of the LGBQT community is not limited to homophobia. *Outgroup homogeneity* – the tendency for in-groups to view members of out-groups as similar – is an equally harmful

---

[1] LGBQT (Lesbian, Gay, Bi-sexual, Queer and Transgender) is an evolving acronym to describe sexual orientations.

prejudice faced by this demographic (Jhangiani & Tarry, 2014). Out-group homogeneity of the LGBQT population is illustrated by the common stereotype that gay men are effeminate and flamboyant and lesbians are masculine or "butch."

In addition to out-group homogeneity, the LGBQT community faces many other stigmas, including *sexual structural stigma,* that disadvantage them in comparison to their heterosexual counterparts (Herek, 2015). Its impact on LGBQT populations is often profound and can negatively affect virtually every aspect of their lives, from employment prospects to housing opportunities. Homophobia and sexual structural stigma work in tandem to marginalize LGBQT populations.

The LGBQT community is one of the many marginalized populations that face stereotypes and stigmatization on a daily basis. Before World Peace can be achieved, society must destigmatize marginalized groups. Stereotypes come in all forms, but share the destructive characteristic of further isolating or "othering" already disenfranchised populations.

A celebration of human diversity – including diversity in sexualities – is a necessary step toward World Peace.

References

Herek, G. M. (1998). *Stigma and sexual orientation: Understanding prejudice against lesbians, gay men, and bisexuals*. Thousand Oaks, CA, US: Sage Publications, Inc.

Herek, G. M. (2015). Beyond 'homophobia': Thinking more clearly about stigma, prejudice, and sexual orientation. *American Journal of Orthopsychiatry, 85*(5, Suppl), S29-S37. doi:10.1037/ort0000092

Jhangiani, R., & Tarry, H. (2014). *Principles of Social Psychology-1st International Edition.*

Kaysen, D. L., Kulesza, M., Balsam, K. F., Rhew, I. C., Blayney, J. A., Lehavot, K., & Hughes, T. L. (2014). Coping as a mediator of internalized homophobia and psychological distress among young adult sexual minority women. *Psychology of Sexual Orientation and Gender Diversity, 1*(3), 225-233. doi:10.1037/sgd0000045

Editors' Discussion Questions

1. What are the stereotypes of the LGBQT community? How do these stereotypes differ for each sexual identity within the LGBQT community? What are the origins of these stereotypes?

2. Why are people homophobic? How does knowing the source of these motivations help to identify ways to change those biases?

Seventh Interlude

MATRE

Artist: Matre & Embassy Live
Song: "Listen"
YouTube: https://youtu.be/GXFnQAAMloM
Verse 1

The United States Department of Defense just sent

Some heavy artillery to the city where I live

And it must be a hell of a monster they're trying to conquer

'Cause they sent an armored vehicle and three grenade launchers

And on top of that they sent like 60 M16s

Y'all think I'm crazy like this some apocalyptic dream

Uh-uh

This is the news

Today's news it's true

And to make it deeper all of this was shipped to our schools

"What?!"

Yup

L.A. Unified School District

Police have just received a whole military shipment

And we already know who gets it

Same neighborhoods where the kids get

Treated like criminals daily 'cause of the color that their skin is

Where metal detectors don't help students feel protected

But instead they send the message

There's a crime and you're suspected
And meanwhile I'm sittin'
On a high school class visit
Wondering why it's so quiet
When I ask about their ambitions.

Chorus

Ey! Ey! Ey! Ey!
I put my hand up and wait to be called
Ey! Ey! Ey! Ey!
But I can't wait here my whole life long
Ey! Ey! Ey! Ey!
They want my hands up my face to the wall
Ey! Ey! Ey! Ey!
But I don't fit in these lines that you draw

Verse 2

Ok, so LAUSD School Police just accepted
An arsenal of military grade assault weapons
Ooh, wait, correction
Breaking news just detected
Apparently they did return the three grenade launchers I mentioned
Hmm, good move
That did seem like a little bit much
But the M16s and the armored truck
They did not give that up
Naw
Know what else they didn't do?
They didn't move
And get it through
To the military
That we're well aware
That it simply isn't true

"What?"

That somehow more weapons at school

Make it more safe

Send us a strategy that actually creates a safer place

Send us ears

Enough to hear

What all our students say

And the courage to stay when their pain makes us wanta' turn away

"Ey"

Let's build our schools around asking them what they know

Instead of telling them what they should know

Until they overflow

With anger that's been pent up

Under all that information

Can we listen?

'Cause without that is it really education?

(Chorus)

Verse 3

So dear L.A.U.S.D.

And L.A. school police

I know the kids that you surround and search with those machines

The ones you're sniffing out with dogs set up in their classrooms

They're friends of mine

So now I feel I have to

Send you this message that they're scared

And they are mad too

They do not trust their schools

'Cause they're not trusted as they pass through

And I should also make it very clear they're not alone

I am standing at the schools where your weapons grow

I am walking with the youth to protect their gold

And I am met by crowds from all around

here to let you know

We're parents, teachers, friends

And we feel this like an injury

We're now demanding that you treat our kids with dignity

Every student, neighborhood, vicinity

We know which youth are viewed like criminals consistently, no mystery

Stop

Young people should not have to fear the cops

Or that the color of their skin could have them shot

You must respect them

No exceptions

Teach them by example and put down your own weapons

And a question

For the young ones

Wanta' hear what you're envisioning

We know you hold the future on your tongues

And we're listening.

(Chorus)

Part 12

Cooperation and Competition

...we can help ourselves only if we help the Other.

~ Dalai Lama

Cooperation and competition are ubiquitous among social animals (Brosnan, 2013). Without cooperation, social organization is impossible.

Cooperation. Cooperation occurs when individuals act in concert for the common good or shared purpose. In cooperative relationships, all participants benefit from their interaction.

Competition. Competition occurs when individuals strive to obtain an unequal share of limited resources – where one gains at another's expense. Extreme competition may lead to aggression, violence and war.

On the Origin of Species

In recent years, evolutionary theory has been resurgent in the behavioral sciences. The study of cooperation and competition affords behavioral scientists another opportunity to invoke – and critique – these deterministic approaches.

The essence of Darwinian theory is that species evolve through competition – *survival of the fittest*. However, the earliest humans were small in number with plentiful resources, making cooperative living much more likely. Despite the plethora of violent conflicts and wars in modern history, the vast majority of humans live peacefully with one another (Fuentes, 2004; Goldman, 1937).

Across species, social animals are remarkably peaceful and cooperative; conflict arises when resources are maldistributed or scarce (Brosnan, 2013).

225

Human nature is peaceful and cooperative. This is also true of our closest relatives – chimpanzees and apes (Brosnan, 2013). Situational factors, largely the maldistribution of resources, cause competition and create conflict (Barker, Barclay & Reeve, 2012; Mead & Maner, 2012; White, Waller & Boose, 2013).

The idea that humans are inherently competitive, aggressive and violent is also contradicted by the existence of dozens of human communities where non-violence is the norm and instances of interpersonal violence *never* occur (Bonta, 1997).

Benefits of Cooperation

Cooperation is the norm in human affairs – from familial units to neighborhoods and local communities, people generally help one another (Tomasello, 2009).

Studies have identified the benefits of cooperative learning, including higher achievement, better student attitudes towards each other and teachers, improved communication skills, and enhanced conflict resolution (Johnson & Johnson, 1979).

Chapter Overviews

Chapter 59 (*Competition: Good or Evil?* by William "Court" Mangum) explores the good and bad consequences of competition. Mangum links competition to aggression and urges the socialization of children to emphasize more cooperative relationships.

Chapter 60 (*Increasing Fairness: A Call for Individual Action* by Casey Chong) reviews literature that suggests that the wealthy adhere to the *just world hypothesis* and are less likely to help others. Chong calls for more altruistic and charitable actions.

Chapter 61 (*Why We Compete* by Halford H. Fairchild, Ph.D.) debunks the idea that competition is "hard-wired" in our genes. Instead, competition is borne from the maldistribution of resources. The solution is to ensure that resources are equitably distributed.

Chapter 62 (*A [Truly] New World Order* by Halford H. Fairchild, Ph.D.) is a fictional piece that describes a *coup d'etat*. Fairchild's global Emperor, Frantz Fanon, uses his unrestrained power to destroy the weapons of war and to redistribute wealth.

References

Barker, J. L., Barclay, P., & Reeve, H. K. (2012). Within-group competition reduces cooperation and payoffs in human groups. *Behavioral Ecology, 23*(4), 735-741. doi:10.1093/beheco/ars020

Bonta, B. D. (1997). Cooperation and competition in peaceful societies. *Psychological Bulletin, 121*(2), 299-320. doi:10.1037/0033-2909.121.2.299

Brosnan, S. F. (2013). Conflicts in cooperative social interactions in nonhuman primates. In D.P. Fry (Ed.), *War, peace and human nature: The convergence of evolutionary and cultural views* (pp. 406-420). New York, NY, US: Oxford University Press. doi:10.1093/ acprof:oso/9780199858996.003.0020

Fuentes, A. (2004). It's not all sex and violence: Integrated anthropology and the role of cooperation and social complexity in human evolution. *American Anthropologist, 106*(4), 710-718. doi:10.1525/aa.2004.106.4.710

Goldman, I. (1937). The Ifugao of the Philippine islands. In M. Mead (Ed.), *Cooperation and competition among primitive peoples* (pp. 153-179). New York, NY, US: McGraw-Hill Book Company. doi:10.1037/13891-005

Johnson, D.W., & Johnson, R.T. (1979). Cooperative learning: The power of positive goal interdependence. In R.E. Clasnoff (Ed.), *Structuring cooperative learning experiences in the classroom: The 1979 handbook.* Minneapolis, MN; Cooperative Network.

Mead, N., & Maner, J. (2012). When me versus you becomes us versus them: How intergroup competition shapes ingroup psychology. *Social and Personality Psychology Compass, 6*(8), 566-574. doi:10.1111/j.1751-9004.2012.00447.x

Tomasello, M. (2009). *Why we cooperate.* Boston: MIT Press.

White, F. J., Waller, M. T., & Boose, K. J. (2013). Evolution of primate peace. In D. P. Fry (Ed), *War, peace and human nature: The convergence of evolutionary and cultural views* (pp. 389-405). New York, NY, US: Oxford University Press. doi:10.1093/acprof:oso/ 9780199858996.003. 0019

Editors' Discussion Questions

1. The editors suggest that the human species is inherently cooperative and harmonious. Why do you agree or disagree with this position?

2. Is anything wrong with 20 individuals in the U.S. having more wealth than one half of the American population combined? Why or why not?

Chapter 59

Competition: Good or Evil?

WILLIAM "COURT" MANGUM

Abstract: Competition can have good and bad consequences: It may lead to advances in medical technologies or mortgage industry meltdowns. Competition may also cause an increase in aggression. Cooperation should be valued and encouraged, beginning with early childhood socialization.

> *Competition has been shown to be useful up to a certain point, but cooperation, which is the thing we must strive for today, begins where competition leaves off.*

> ~ Franklin D. Roosevelt

Many regard competition as the catalyst for innovation and increased productivity. Others caution that unbridled competition leads to a number of negative consequences, including a rise in amoral behavior and unethical business practices. Who is right?

Competition among corporations has led to the discovery of new cancer drugs and other advancements in medical technologies. Competition has also led to catastrophe, such as the mortgage meltdown of 2008.[1]

As a society, our embrace of competition has had unfortunate and, at times, horrendous consequences. Intense pressure in the finance industry led to increased criminal activity, such as insider trading (Lacy, 2001). If one trader's sales fall below that of co-workers, his or her job may be in jeopardy.

How can we expect world peace with so much competition and so little cooperation? Competition brings out some of the best and worst in

---

[1] The intense competition in the mortgage industry led to the creation of sub-prime loans which, in turn, led to the 2008 housing market crash (Steightfeld, 2004).

humanity. While our focus on competition has led to countless innovations and discoveries, it has also caused us to become more aggressive towards others (Balas & Thomas, 2015).

To achieve world peace, we must decrease our emphasis on competition and promote more cooperation. This paradigm shift should be reinforced throughout childhood and adolescence.

Children are the future leaders of all societies. Encouraging cooperative learning in children may lead to a more peaceful world.

References

Balas, B., & Thomas, L. E. (2015). Competition makes observers remember faces as more aggressive. *Journal of Experimental Psychology: General, 144*(4), 711-716.

Lacy, John P. "Illegal Conduct in the Workplace." *Connell Foley.* N.p., 2001. Web. 27 Apr. 2016.

Steightfeld, David. (2004, March 2nd). "No Gain, Know Pain." Los *Angeles Times.*

Editors' Discussion Questions

1. On balance, is competition good or bad? Why?

2. Education in America is inherently competitive. Is there a way to produce high achieving individuals through cooperative learning instead of competition? Is this desirable? Why or why not?

Chapter 60

Increasing Fairness:
A Call for Individual Action

CASEY CHONG

Abstract: Recognizing that a lack of fairness exists is necessary if we want to achieve World Peace. Yet the people who can most readily eradicate inequality – the wealthy – are the least likely to do so. The wealthy adhere to the *just world hypothesis* and applaud themselves for their accomplishments. We must address this problem through our altruism and charitable actions, if we are to achieve World Peace.

The world is not fair. Why?

In a fair world, every person would have equal opportunity, respect and treatment under the law. Yet, this is not the world in which we live. Reminders of global inequality are ever present in our news, scholarly research and even in our interactions with others.

Recognizing this unfairness is necessary to achieve World Peace.

Socioeconomic status has an interesting relationship to altruism and ethics. One researcher found that social class positively predicted *unethical* behavior when that behavior was self-serving (DuBois, Rucker & Galinsky, 2015). Miller, Kahle, and Hastings (2005) reported that children from low and middle income families behaved more altruistically than their wealthier counterparts.

The negative correlation between class and altruistic behavior is obvious.

The people within society's higher socio-economic classes are the ones who can be the most influential in the creation of global equality, given they have the most monetary freedom, education, and access to global networking. Such individuals have the means to contribute to World Peace, yet, they are the *least* likely to help others (Kopp & Finney, 2013).

This phenomenon may be because the world has been "good" or "fair" to those individuals. One has less incentive to better the world around them when the system has worked in their favor. Those who benefit from inequality – the *haves* –are unlikely to support any redistribution of wealth to aid the *have nots*.

According to Jhangiani and Tarry's (2014) *just world hypothesis:*

> If we have high status, we will generally be content with our analysis of the situation because it indicates that we deserve what we got. We are likely to think, 'I must have a good education, a good job, and plenty of money because I worked hard for it and deserve it.' In these cases, the reality supports our desires for self-concern, and there is no psychological dilemma posed (Jhangiani & Tarry, 2014, p. 511).

Sadly, those who benefit from the system often turn a blind eye to those who suffer because of systemic inequalities. Therein lies the problem.

This trend and unwillingness to change the status quo hinders progress toward World Peace and perpetuates the inequality that defines today's society.

So, what is the solution? What can we do?

We must not let gaining and possessing knowledge about global inequality be the only effort we take toward World Peace – we must take action. With privilege comes power – power to be heard, power to influence, power to facilitate change. We must use that power to ensure future generations' ability to enjoy equal opportunity, respect and treatment.

We must encourage everyone, regardless of stature, to exercise their power to uplift their less fortunate neighbors in whatever way possible – donating to a good cause, joining a charity organization, volunteering time and resources, or simply reaching out to someone in need.

We cannot be complacent or content simply *knowing* inequality exists; we must *act* to combat it or be complicit. Through our *actions,* we can make an impact on global inequality.

References

Dubois, D., Rucker, D. D., & Galinsky, A. D. (2015). Social class, power, and selfishness: When and why upper and lower class individuals behave unethically. *Journal of Personality and Social Psychology, 108*(3), 436-449. doi:10.1037/pspi0000008; 10.1037/pspi0000008.supp (Supplemental)

Jhangiani, R., & Tarry, H. (2014). *Principles of social psychology – 1st international edition.* Licensed under a Creative Commons Attribution-NonCommerical-ShareAlike 4.0 International License.

Kopp, J. P., & Finney, S. J. (2013). Linking academic entitlement and student incivility using latent means modeling. *Journal of Experimental Education, 81*(3), 322-336. doi:10.1080/ 00220973.2012.727887

Miller, J. G., Kahle, S., & Hastings, P. D. (2015). Roots and benefits of costly giving: Children who are more altruistic have greater autonomic flexibility and less family wealth. *Psychological Science, 26*(7), 1038-1045. doi:10.1177/ 0956797615578476

Editors' Discussion Questions

1. In a "meritocracy," people are rewarded for their merit, intelligence and hard work. This concept also relates to "Social Darwinism," and the survival of the fittest. Do you agree or disagree? Why?

2. Based upon Chong's analysis, what "actions"are necessary to reduce inequality?

Chapter 61

Why We Compete

Halford H. Fairchild, Ph.D.

Abstract: Competition is caused by the maldistribution of resources and the monopolization of wealth creates conflict between nations. The Banquet Table Metaphor suggests that the Earth has plentiful resources were it not for the hoarding of wealth in the U.S. and Europe.

Individuals and societies differ in their competitiveness. Western societies are notably more competitive than those in Africa, Asia or the Pacific. In the U.S., competition is the norm in schools, sports, business and interpersonal relationships (Garcia, 1984).

Competition occurs when resources are scarce or become monopolized (Barker, Barclay & Reeve, 2012). This finding, confirmed in animal and human studies, is a clue to the prevalence of competition in American society.

The U.S. was founded in the violent confrontation between European settlers and the Indigenous Americans. That confrontation, fueled by the conquest of Africa and the islands of the Caribbean and Pacific, created "a new world order" characterized by massive inequalities in resources.

The monopolization of wealth creates conflict between nations.

The U.S.'s history of genocide, slavery and conquest produced immense wealth and tremendous wealth inequality. The U.S. is the wealthiest nation on Earth, commanding 41.6% of total global wealth (Sherman, 2015). The next richest country, China – with four and a half times the population – claims just 10.5% of total global wealth. Per capita, the U.S. citizen has sixteen times more wealth than his or her Chinese counterpart.

Despite this concentration of wealth, the U.S. also ranks number one in terms of wealth inequality, with wealth concentrated in the hands of comparatively few individuals. According to one report, 20 individuals in the U.S. possess more wealth than one half (1/2) of the entire American population (Holland, 2015). Moreover, nearly 900,000 people die preventable deaths every year in the U.S. because of wealth inequality (Holland, 2014). Frustrated by blunted opportunities for upward mobility, the masses often succumb to drugs, alcohol, or suicide; never realizing that their life circumstances were short circuited by the usurpation of wealth and opportunity by a privileged few.

Worldwide, more than 22,000 children die *every day* because of wealth inequality (DoSomething.Org, 2017).

The maldistribution and hoarding of resources are the basis for the competitive spirit that is emblematic of American society. Virtually every aspect of U.S. culture emphasizes competition (Garcia, 1984); and competition breeds aggression and violence (Bonta, 1997).

A Banquet Table Metaphor

While traveling through Central Africa several years ago, I marveled at the abundance of the natural resources. The forests, savannahs, lakes, rivers and coastal areas were all teeming with life. The land provided more than enough resources for the people who lived there. Yet I learned that the raw resources of Africa (lumber, cattle, fish, oil, minerals, precious metals, etc.) were not shared equally, but *exported* to Europe. The wealth of Africa was enriching European countries in a system of economic neo-colonialism. Raw products in Africa were processed in Europe and then resold to African consumers at highly inflated prices.

It was then that I developed a Banquet Table Metaphor to understand the problems confronting our world:

> The people of the Earth are seated at a large banquet table. The table is filled with fresh fruits, vegetables, meats and fish. There is more than enough for everyone seated at the table. But one visitor comes to the table, pulls out a weapon and says, "Might makes right," and scoops up more than half of the food for himself. This leaves everyone else at the table scrambling for the crumbs left behind.

Competition and conflict are caused by the maldistribution of resources (Levy, 2010). The United Kingdom, European Union and the United States of America are the unwelcome gluttons at the proverbial dinner table, usurping a grossly disproportionate share of the planet's natural and human resources.

The United States, already the richest country on Earth many times over, uses its economic, political and military policies to continue the exploitation of lives and resources for the economic benefit of a relative few.

On the Re-distribution of Wealth

The recent history of the world, for two thousand years or more, has been one of disproportionate wealth accumulation. The disparities in wealth and resources lead to human conflict and war. World Peace requires a redistribution of wealth to ensure the wellbeing of all who inhabit this planet.

One concrete way to accomplish this is to entreat the world's multi-billionaires to give one half or more of their wealth away to the public good. This idea was started by Bill and Melinda Gates and Warren Buffett, in 2010, when they pledged to give away more than one half of their wealth to philanthropic purposes. They have invited other billionaires to join the *Giving Pledge*, and more than 150 individuals have signed on (Clifford, 2017).

But more than philanthropy is needed for global wealth re-distribution. The material, human and cultural wealth of so-called Third World nations (in Africa, South America, Asia and the Pacific) has been stolen for hundreds of years (Fairchild, 2017).

The royal families in Europe and the United Kingdom – and their citizenry – were enriched by the appropriation of land and people in Africa, Asia and the Pacific. This stolen wealth should be accounted for and returned.

References

Barker, J. L., Barclay, P., & Reeve, H. K. (2012). Within-group competition reduces cooperation and payoffs in human groups. *Behavioral Ecology, 23*(4), 735-741. doi:10.1093/beheco/ars020

Bonta, B. D. (1997). Cooperation and competition in peaceful societies. *Psychological Bulletin, 121*(2), 299-320. doi:10.1037/0033-2909.121.2.299

Clifford, C. (2017). These 14 billionaires just promised to give away more than half of their money like Bill Gates and Warren Buffet. *CNBC.com*. (May 31, 2017). https://www.cnbc.com/2017/05/31/14-billionaires-signed-bill-gates-and-warren-buffetts-giving-pledge.html.

DoSomething.Org (2017). 11 facts about global poverty. Retrieved July 27, 2017 from: https:// www.dosomething.org/us/facts/11-facts-about-global-poverty.

Fairchild, H.H. (2017). (Re)Solving violence in America. Chapter 11 in H.H. Fairchild (Ed.), *(Re)Solving violence in America (Second Edition)*. Delhi: Indo American Books.

Garcia, F. (1984). Competition: A cultural script issue in the USA. *Transactional Analysis Journal, 14*(1), 44-47.

Holland, J. (2014). High inequality results in more US deaths than tobacco, car crashes and guns combined. Bill Moyers & Company. Retrieved June 27, 2017. http://billmoyers.com/2014/04/19/high-inequality-results-in-more-us-deaths-than-tobacco-car-crashes-and-guns-combined/

Holland, J. (2015). 20 people now own as much wealth as half of all Americans. *The Nation*. https://www.thenation.com/article/20-people-now-own-as-much-wealth-as-half-of-all-americans/

Levy, S. G. (2010). Cooperation, competition, and conflict. In G. Fink (Ed.), *Stress of war, conflict and disaster* (pp. 833-847). San Diego, CA, US: Elsevier Academic Press.

Sherman, E. (2015). America is the richest, and most unequal, country. http://fortune.com/2015/09/30/america-wealth-inequality/#. Retrieved December 24, 2016

Editor's Discussion Questions

1. The world's wealth is concentrated in the hands of comparatively few people. For many of them, their massive wealth was passed down to them as the result of conquest, slavery and exploitation. Should that wealth be re-distributed?

2. What can be done to reduce wealth inequality between and within nations?

Chapter 62

A (Truly) New World Order[1]

HALFORD H. FAIRCHILD, PH.D.

Abstract: Set hundreds of years in the future, this short story describes how a revolutionary leader accomplished a military *coup d'etat* and used threat of thermonuclear annihilation to end all wars on Earth. Wealth is re-distributed; the *isms* that divide us are challenged; and individual welfare is cherished.

My name is Frantz Fanon. In less than an hour, I will be recognized as *Emperor* of the World. It is a title that I both crave and detest. My task, in the next 30 minutes, is to decide what to say as I address the people of the world, and how to alleviate their anxieties. I am neither worried nor nervous; I have planned for this day for as long as I can remember.

//Λ\\//Λ\\//Λ\\

My story begins with my naming. The name *Frantz Fanon* means nothing to all but a small handful of scholars who have studied the ancient struggles of African people to overcome slavery and colonization. Most within my new dominion can think only of *today*; or, at most, *this life*. And who can blame them? Earth's teeming billions live hand-to-mouth existences where life and death seem to hang in the balance on a daily basis. Who cares about an Algerian psychiatrist that lived more than 500 years ago?

Frantz Fanon was my given name – an unusual name to be sure. It was a name that provoked ridicule among my schoolmates. It was a name for which I learned to feel ashamed. But as I grew, I learned.

My father told me at the tender age of 7 years that I was named after a man who wrote the blueprint for African liberation. He said, simply, *"Be your name."*

---

[1] This paper was originally written September 20, 2000, and revised for the current volume. This short story was also published in *Black Lives Matter: Lifespan Perspectives* (2017, Indo American Books).

"Be your name." The words echoed in my ears and reverberated through my soul. *"Be your name."* Who was *Frantz Fanon*?

After years of deep study, complicated by the fact that the man lived more than half a millennium ago and his writings were contained in only the most obscure repositories of microchips that no one cared about, I developed a burning desire to *"Be my name."*

To *"be"* Frantz Fanon ... was to be a *revolutionary*. And, of course my father, a visionary, planned from my conception to infuse me with this burning desire to 'set afoot a new Black man' as Fanon was known to say. And as a contemporary of Fanon said, *"You cannot liberate the African without liberating everyone else."*

But how?

For more than a thousand years, since 1492 when the Europeans made first contact with the so-called "New World" and claimed it as their God-given property, White people have ruled the Earth. And while there is nothing wrong with White people *per se*, the few who had usurped the power to rule the world have done so quite badly. World Wars in the 20th and 21st centuries, and raging in this century, have wreaked havoc on people and the planet. The aftermath of each war required a hundred years to recover; billions of lives were lost through the senseless violence to satisfy Euro/America's lust for the Earth's resources and world domination.

What the bombs did not destroy, nuclear contamination did.

But White rule also assaulted the Earth in various and sundry ways: fouling the lakes and seas, destroying the rain forests, opening a continent-wide hole in the protective ozone layer. If only the early settlers had recognized and adopted that indigenous proverb of the Americas: *We do not inherit this Earth from our parents, we borrow it from our children.* Instead, the dictates of Manifest Destiny were such that they *stole* the earth from their children.

I should hasten to add that the unbridled greed and avarice does not afflict all White people. The problem is with a small handful of oligarchs and despots, who happened to be White, that usurped power and control of the Earth's resources for their personal and lustful profit. They built storehouses of wealth so that they could live luxurious lives *in perpetuity*. Well, dear reader, *perpetuity ends today*.

My story is a story of a life time. My life time. In naming me, my father imbued me with the unquenchable thirst to *"Be my name"* – to fulfill the revolutionary plan laid out so carefully by my namesake.

And so, I was properly educated about the nature of the world. I was not fooled by the hypocrisy of "freedom" and "democracy" bandied about so recklessly by those who controlled the planet's bountiful resources. I learned that my people have been engaged in struggle, from the slavery of the 1500s to the forced unemployment and homelessness of the 2500s. My father gave me an empathy for the pain and suffering of the masses, even though we were, by any measure, quite well off.

My earliest memory of my ambition was to lead the military of the strongest nation on Earth, the United States of North America. This was a delusion, a fantasy, that somehow became reality.

Anything that can be conceived

Can be achieved

If we only believe

In the power

Of the collectivity

I have no doubt that it was my father who planted this ambition firmly in my consciousness; as I developed the tools of literacy, criticism, and social activism. My resolve to lead our armed forces was emboldened by my early training in the Combat Navy; strengthened in my years of officer training; yet actively suppressed (or should I say, *hidden*) during my 25 years of playing the "good soldier" role for the ruling minority.

Oh yes! Make no mistake! I am a revolutionary! But I had to keep my revolutionary yearnings to myself. To speak of revolution, of a truly new world order, would be to speak of death. My death. And I knew that I had to fulfill my destiny; I had to *"Be my name."*

The plan was simple, even if it did take 30 years to bring to fruition. The hardest part was being appointed Chairman of the Joint Chiefs of Staff, the top officer in the U.S. military. My appointment, not at all coincidentally – in fact, it was by design – was by then President Frederick Douglass Lewis, the second Black president of the U.S. and a direct descendant of a nearly forgotten freedom fighter by the name of John Lewis, who was a near contemporary of my namesake.

Within months of my appointment, the plan was set in motion. For the previous 200 years, Black men had populated the U.S. military. Almost exclusively. And most of these were loyal to the White capitalists that I sought to overthrow. However, by the third year as Chairman, I had enough closet revolutionaries, in the right places, to secure complete control of the

U.S. stock of thermonuclear weapons. And once doing so, it was a rather simple matter to announce, "It is a new day."

The next five years were difficult ... and I begged God to forgive me for the lives that were lost in the violence that ensued. Rebels within the military vowed to fight to the death to overturn this *coup d'etat;* and they did die. Urban and rural militias, long armed for the race war that they knew was coming, also vowed to fight to the death. And they too died. I lament these deaths to this day, and I regret that I do not know their names or numbers. Millions, certainly.

At long last, at this very hour, we have silenced any meaningful opposition to my complete control of the world. They say that you can't mess with Mother Nature, well, you can't mess with thermonuclear weaponry either. With God as my witness, I would have used those weapons if necessary, and I thank God that they were not. It was only by violence, or to put it more correctly, through this threat of violence, that we won our revolutionary struggle. But, then, *power concedes nothing without a demand.*[2]

And now, my time has come to address the world. I need not prepare my text, my life has been preparation enough.

//\\//\\//\\//\\

Ladies and Gentlemen of the press, members of Congress, Parliament, and governments around the world, but most of all, to the citizens of the world, I greet you in peace.

Many of you fear me and fear what the future holds for our planet. As I speak, my representatives are assuming the seats of power in every country on the planet. The insurrections and resistance have been silenced, and I speak to you now as your *Emperor.* Yet *Emperor* is a title that I both crave and resist – for no man should rule another.

Our struggle for this revolution and for this upending of our social, political and economic order, has been motivated by one thing only: *to return the resources of the Earth to the people of the Earth.* Our use of violence was an unavoidable tactic to wrest control from those who have usurped power and resources and the riches of the world to satisfy their own rapacious appetites and overblown egos. After all, it was they who mastered the art of violence in their misguided and morally bankrupt conquest of the world. The predecessors of this monopoly on the world's

---

[2] Frederick Douglass

resources also resorted to the psychological tactic of making animals out of those who were exploited, as if it were better to be a slave than to be free.

To those who have enjoyed fabulous wealth for the past 1000 years or more, I say to you that you are rich no more. Your bank accounts and assets are being seized as I speak, and you will join the rest of humanity in the pursuit of the common good.

To those of you who have suffered from racism, poverty, homelessness, joblessness, ignorance, and death, I say to you that *your suffering has come to an end.* This world is a rich world with abundant resources; there is enough to go around for everyone – more than enough – as long as the few do not consume for the many.

Five percent of the world – those descendants of slave traders, plantation holders, and industrial factories – has controlled 90% of the wealth of the world. As I speak, that statement is past tense. The monopoly of wealth and resources is now over.

This mal-distribution of resources was accomplished only through the use of violence or the threat of violence. That threat no longer exists as only I, and my *Council*, control the mechanisms of violence. And I want to assure you that we will *practice war no more!*

Tonight, as I speak, the rule of the multi-national corporations, whose wealth rose from the blood, sweat and tears of the teeming masses, *is over.* From this day forward, all CEOs, all Presidents and Vice Presidents, all Managers and Executives, all those who are under-worked and overpaid, will be compensated the same as every other person who works and contributes to their family, community and world. You have had your day – your millennium – *but that day is past.*

The world's wealth – and friends, it is inexhaustible – will be distributed equally to all. For those who have toiled your entire lives and suffered from the indifference of the ruling capitalists and socialists, I say to you that your life will improve tomorrow. Epidemic diseases will be vigorously fought, human starvation is to be an anathema to an earlier obsolete age, and we will recognize homelessness and unemployment for what they are: the barbarous consequences of a world devoted to the accumulation of capital for the few.

The nation states, as you have known them, are now dismantled. There will be no national boundaries, no passports, and no restrictions on the freedom of movement of any human being to any place on this planet.

There will be no more violence. Once our revolution has finally ended and our transition complete, we will then mandate the destruction of all weapons, including our own, from the face of the Earth. Every nuclear missile, every submarine, every military satellite, every tank, every rifle, every bomber, every fighter plane, every mine, every handgun, will be destroyed. The factories that have manufactured these weapons of human genocide too will be destroyed. Every citizen who surrenders his weapons will be paid richly for them.

Our mission is to bring peace and prosperity to the world. And where there is no peace, there can be no prosperity. And where there are weapons of mass destruction, or of individual destruction, there can be no peace.

The prison-military-industrial complexes will be converted into institutions for restoring the integrity of our environment, schools, hospitals, and people. We will practice war no more!

We will challenge the many *isms* that divide us: racism, sexism, heterosexism, classism. We accomplish this by recognizing our common fate and our common destiny. The categories we use to divide us are social constructs that have no meaning outside of the collective fictions we have adopted as reality. But these fictions were only the perverse intellectual tools of the oppressors of human kind. We will now re-educate ourselves to the true dignity and worth of every member of our species.

Our priorities are simple: promoting the health, education, safety and welfare of every citizen of the world. This is my hope, this is my dream, this is my pledge:

One Planet, One People, Please!

References

Banks, R. R., & Eberhardt, J. L. (1998). Social psychological processes and the legal bases of racial categorization. In J. L. Eberhardt & S. T. Fiske (Eds.), *Confronting racism: The problem and the response*. Thousand Oaks: Sage Publications.

Fanon, F. (1999). The wretched of the Earth. In M. Bulmer & J. Solomos (Eds.), *Racism* (pp. 116-120). New York: Oxford University Press.

Kiernan, V. (1999). Africa. In M. Bulmer & J. Solomos (Eds.), *Racism* (pp. 97-99). New York: Oxford University Press.

Mason, P. (1999). Patterns of dominance. In M. Bulmer & J. Solomos (Eds.), *Racism* (pp. 106-116). New York: Oxford University Press.

Smith, M. G. (1999). Ethnic and cultural pluralism in the British Caribbean. In M. Bulmer & J. Solomos (Eds.), *Racism* (pp. 99-106). New York: Oxford University Press.

Editors' Discussion Questions

1. Is it possible to bring about the revolution envisioned by the author without resorting to violence? If so, how? If not, why not?

2. The author envisions a certain utopia. With which aspects do you agree or disagree? Why?

Eighth Interlude
Make Love Not War[1]

HALFORD H. FAIRCHILD, PH.D.

"Give War a chance!"
Is what Bush said
Something must be wrong
Up inside his head!

Dropping bombs on
Defenseless people
The war against Iraq
Isn't even legal.

Innocent children's
lives are lost
Just so Bush can say,
"I'm the boss!"

Walking through Iraq
Our Troops are sitting ducks
Gettin' blown away
In transit trucks.

Blood for oil
Is the reason We're there
But with people Like Us
There is Hope in the Air!

---

[1]   This poem was written on the occasion of a "Love In," sponsored by the author's Freshman
Seminar, *War or Peace?* at Pitzer College, Fall 2004.

This war is for profits
Let us not forget
Our demands for Peace
Must get met.

They're addicted to war
And making big money
We should turn to Peace
And hug our honey

Making war
for financial gain
But making Love
Don't cause no pain.

To heal our nation
As we move towards peace
Healing our souls
Must never cease.

Make love not war
Is what I want to say,
Make peace a reality
And make it Stay!

Editors' Discussion Questions

1. Was the invasion of Iraq by the Bush administration a war crime? Why or why not?

2. When is war justified?

Part 13
Invited Chapters

"Everyone should strive to be a world citizen. Boundaries were created by man, not the Creator. There is no such thing as THEM vs. US. There is only 'WE'."

~ Suzy Kassem

As this book was in its final days of compilation, the editors invited several authors to contribute to the volume. These were former students (Calcagnini, Lamar, Sparks), members of The Association of Black Psychologists (Drinkard, Cothran), friends (Cooper, Dorrel, Dorrel, Rampell and the songwriters) and relatives (Choy). These papers focused on biographies of peace scholar-activists and related themes. Also included are two documents placed into the public domain by the U.S. White House in 2016.

Chapter Overviews

Chapter 63 (*Promoting Peace Activism: From Herbert Kelman [2010] to Black Lives Matter* by D. Lisa Cothran, Ph.D.) reviews an autobiographical account of a leading peace activist. Cothran relates elements in Kelman's autobiography to the scholarly activism of Mamie Phipps-Clark and the social activism of the Black Lives Matter movement.

Chapter 64 (*Women's Voices in Peace Psychology: A Review of McKay [1995]* by Haley Sparks) considers McKay's classic article. Sparks describes McKay's program of research and concludes that World Peace requires the eradication of the worldwide subjugation of women.

Chapter 65 (*Meanings and Preconditions of Forgiveness: A Review* by Toni Cooper) reviews Nyarko and Punamaki's (2017) study of forgiveness among a small sample of African refugees. Cooper links Nyarko and Punamaki's (2017) findings to Desmond Tutu's eloquent call for forgiveness.

Chapter 66 (*Ethel Tobach and Peace Psychology* by Elaine Choy) presents the life story of one of the pioneers in Peace Psychology. Choy offers Ethel Tobach as a model for scholar-activists who seek World Peace.

246

Chapter 67 (*Constructive Disobedience: Life Lessons from Gandhi, Mandela and King* by Shawndeeia L. Drinkard) examines a published content analysis of the autobiographies of Gandhi, Mandela and King. Drinkard considers the life experiences of the three men as the source of their commitment to non-violent disobedience.

Chapter 68 (*Warnings from the Past, Regarding the Future: Ending Cycles of Violence* by Addison Calcagnini) reviews Pettigrew's (2003) analysis of human conflict. Calcagnini emphasizes solutions for dispelling the myths that lead to war and developing realistic empathy.

Chapter 69 (*White Gaze Dehumanizes: The Case of Indigenous Americans* by Emily Dorrel) reviews "Gendered Construction of the American Indian" by S. Elizabeth Bird (1999). Dorrel traces the history of the constructed images of Native American men and women that satisfied the prejudicial views of White Americans.

Chapter 70 (*On American Violence* by Demetrius Lamar, Ph.D.) bemoans the prevalence of violence in the United States. Lamar connects this violence to a culture of militarism that is celebrated in the mass media.

Chapter 71 (*Paying the Price for Peace* by Frank Dorrel) promotes a film that chronicles the sacrifices of anti-war activist Brian S. Willson. Dorrel is also publisher of *Addicted to War* by Andreas Jonas.

Chapter 72 (*Profile in Pacific Courage: The Railroading of the Other Brian Willson* by Ed Rampell) provides a review of the film described by Dorrel (Chapter 71). Rampell hails Willson as a hero and reveals how his story is placed within the context of anti-war movements from Vietnam to Central America and the Middle East.

Chapter 73 (*Remarks by President Obama and Prime Minister Abe of Japan at Hiroshima Peace Memorial*) presents the unedited remarks of two world leaders to memorialize the atomic bombing of Hiroshima and Nagasaki. This paper was placed into the public domain by the U.S. White House on May 27, 2016.

Chapter 74 (*Address by President Obama to the 71st Session of the United Nations General Assembly*) provides the unedited remarks of the President. This paper was placed into the public domain by the U.S. White House on September 20, 2016.

Chapter 75 (*What to the Slave is the Fourth of July?* by Frederick Douglass and Halford H. Fairchild, Ph.D.) is a condensed and edited version of one of Frederick Douglass's most famous speeches. Douglass and Fairchild suggest that the U.S. is guilty of crimes that would shame a nation of barbarians.

Chapter 63

Promoting Peace Activism: From Herbert Kelman (2010) to Black Lives Matter

D. LISA COTHRAN, PH.D.
ALABAMA STATE UNIVERSITY

Abstract: Herbert C. Kelman's life's works are a testament to peace activism. His path to activism through hardship parallels others' – from Mamie Phipps-Clark to the founders of the Black Lives Matter Movement.

Introduction

Herbert C. Kelman is the Richard Clarke Cabot Professor Emeritus of Social Ethics, and a Faculty Associate of the Weatherhead Center for International Affairs at Harvard University. As described in his 2010 autobiography, *Looking Back at My Work on Conflict Resolution in the Middle East,* Kelman's life and work evince the power of one person to facilitate peaceful negotiations. His personal and professional experiences influenced his work on interactive problem solving and conflict resolution. Kelman's prescriptions for peace activism are reflected in historical figures (e.g., Mamie Phipps-Clark) and in contemporary civic activism (e.g., #BlackLivesMatter).

Kelman's Biography

Born into a Jewish family in Vienna, Austria, Kelman and his family fled Nazi rule in the late 1930s and eventually settled in the United States. Kelman, throughout his early adult years, participated in groups and organizations that emphasized social advancement and upward mobility.

Due in part to his challenging beginnings, Kelman studied psychology because of its relevance to social justice and related issues. Throughout his life, he actively participated in various protest movements including: the abolition of nuclear weapons, the Civil Rights Movement, and opposition to the Korean and Vietnam Wars. This Yale-trained social psychologist's publications and selfless contributions toward human rights, peace, and the resolution of the Israeli-Palestinian conflict spanned more than 60 years.

Kelman's publications helped to establish the psychological study of international relations and peace research (e.g., Kelman, 1965; Kelman & Hamilton, 1989). His work also led to the drafting of the 1995 Oslo Agreement, which facilitated a more peaceful coexistence between Israel and Palestine.

In addition to his research with the Weatherhead Center, Kelman interacted with many of the world's leaders (e.g., Boutros Boutros-Ghali and Yasser Arafat), thereby influencing international policy and practice. Kelman derived four essential ingredients for successful conflict resolution based on his personal experiences: continuous networking, strategic team building, respectful listening, and active participation in the successful transfer of ideas (Kelman, 2010).

Kelman (2010) also identified five personal qualities essential to his life's successes: developing a healthy sense of humor; maintaining continuity between one's life's work and personal life; persisting earnestly in the pursuit of social justice; maintaining a strong self-concept and healthy level of self-esteem; and empathizing with other people and groups. Kelman needed these qualities while working to resolve the Cypress Conflict (BBC News, 2016) and to alleviate tensions in the Middle East.

Commentary

Privilege is political and Kelman clearly benefited from being wealthy, White and male. As a child, his family purchased visas that afforded their safe escape from Nazi-controlled Austria to Belgium, before eventually settling in the United States.

In his youth, Kelman garnered a criminal arrest record and a reputation as an agitator, protestor and draft resister. And yet, he secured highly regarded and coveted positions at Yale University, Stanford University, Harvard University and The University of Michigan.

As a third-party promoter of peace, he gained the audience of several world leaders, including Yassar Arafat. Kelman's privileges afforded him safety, an international voice and audience, and access to some of the most influential people and institutions in the world.

The experiences that propelled Kelman into peace activism are paralleled in the lives of other social-justice activists such as Ida B. Wells-Barnett, Rosa Parks, Mamie Phipps Clark, Alicia Garza, Patrisse Cullors and Opal Tometi. Like Kelman, these historical figures experienced extreme injustices and, in the face of socio-political turmoil, were able to bolster their self-esteem and self-concept with individual and group activism. Those women worked to improve the living circumstances for themselves and others (African Americans, African American women, American women and all women).

For example, just as Kelman protested and fled Nazi rule, Wells-Barnett escaped and vehemently protested against lynchings and other forms of oppression in the Jim Crow South.[1]

The persecution Kelman witnessed during his formative years cultivated his peace activism; similar to the civil rights activism of the iconic Rosa Parks. The racism and sexism that Parks faced as a young African American woman in Jim Crow Alabama nurtured her tenacious drive for justice and equality.

Mamie Phipps-Clark's work with Black children in a segregated America led her to study Black children's development of poor self-concepts and low self-esteem as a function of their consistent and widespread separate and lesser treatment. Phipps-Clark influenced public attitudes and behaviors at an international level. Her thesis and subsequent research (conducted with her husband, Kenneth Clark) served as the foundation for the 1954 *Brown v. Board of Education Supreme Court* decision (Butler, 2009; Martin, 1994; Fairchild, 2017), which held that segregation in public schools was inconsistent with the 14th Amendment of the U.S. Constitution.

Similar examples of activism borne of life experiences are found in the lives and work of Alicia Garza, Patrisse Cullors and Opal Tometi (see Abdullah, 2017). Their creation of what began as a hashtag campaign entitled "Black Lives Matter" (#BLM) exemplifies Kelman's four most important behaviors for peace activism.

Egregious injustice toward people of color is rife in the American legal system (Cothran, 2011). In response, the #BLM was established in 2012 to "broaden the conversation around state violence to include all of the ways in which Black people are intentionally left powerless at the hands

---

[1] Jim Crow referred to the system of racial segregation imposed in Southern States after Emancipation (1863) through the 1950s. Separate schools, public facilities and living arrangements imposed a strict racial hierarchy between Whites and Blacks.

of the state…(and) the ways in which Black lives are deprived of our basic human rights and dignity" (About the Black Lives Matter Network, 2017).

BLM founders, Garza, Cullors and Tometi formed a global network of like-minded individuals committed to social justice and established diverse and interdisciplinary teams of collaborators to challenge the mistreatment of Blacks in America and around the world. They continue to communicate with the public and their supporters via social media and in person. They exchange ideas within the #BLM movement and with other organizations. The experience and work of Garza and colleagues provide an excellent example of the tenets of effective activism proposed by Kelman.

Conclusion

Herbert C. Kelman's life and work are excellent examples of transforming persecution and discrimination into effective activism. His prescriptions for effective activism are a guide to others engaged in the pursuit of social justice and World Peace.

References

Abdullah, M. (2017). Black lives matter: Past, present and future. Foreword (pp. xxiii to xxix) in H.H. Fairchild (Ed.), *Black Lives Matter: Lifespan Perspectives*. Delhi: Indo American Books.

About the Black Lives Matter Network. Retrieved Jan. 4, 2017 from http://blacklivesmatter.com/about/.

BBC News. (2016). Cypress Country Profile. Retrieved Dec. 19, 2017.

Butler, S. (2009). Mamie Katherine Phipps Clark (1917–1983). *The Encyclopedia of Arkansas History & Culture*. Retrieved Jan. 25, 2012. Retrieved Dec. 23, 2016 from http://www.encyclopediaofarkansas.net/ encyclopedia/entry-detail.aspx?entryID=2938.

Cothran, D.L. (2011). The role of facial affect in race-based threat perception. *Imagination, Cognition and Personality, 30,* 341-355.

Fairchild, H.H. (2017). Glorification of things White. Chapter 32 (pp. 133-135) in H.H. Fairchild (Ed.), *Black Lives Matter: Lifespan Perspectives*. Delhi: Indo American Books.

Kelman, H.C. (2010). Looking back at my work on conflict resolution in the Middle East. *Peace and Conflict, 16,* 361–387.

Kelman, H.C., & Hamilton, V.L. (1989). *Crimes of obedience: Toward a social psychology of authority and responsibility.* New Haven: Yale University Press.

Martin, J. (1994). Clark, Kenneth B. 1914–2009. *Contemporary Black Biography.* Retrieved Dec. 23, 2016. Retrieved Dec. 23, 2016 from http://www.encyclopedia.com/people/social-sciences-and-law/education-biographies/kenneth-bancroft-clark#2870700021.

Editors' Discussion Questions

1. Why does the author describe Kelman as a man of "privilege"? Is this a fair assessment? Why or why not?

2. Is the #Black Lives Matter Movement a part of, or separate from, the Peace Movement? Why or why not? What can be done to integrate these movements?

Chapter 64

Women's Voices in Peace Psychology: A Review of McKay (1995)

HALEY SPARKS

THE UNIVERSITY OF MICHIGAN

Abstract: Susan McKay's "Women's Voices in Peace Psychology: A Feminist Agenda" (1995) explores the marginalization of women's perspectives in peace psychology. She further outlines areas of research that would benefit from a feminist perspective. World Peace requires an end to the subjugation of women.

In "Women's Voices in Peace Psychology: A Feminist Agenda" (1995), Susan McKay examines the marginalization of women's perspectives and the silencing of their voices within peace psychology. She outlines specific areas of research that would benefit from feminist scholarship.

Defining key terms such as women, feminism, androcentric and gender, McKay's analysis focuses on peace psychology in the Western world and the writings of Western, White, middle-class feminists.

She describes instances of marginalization of women in peace activist groups. For example, very few women hold leadership positions and, most often, serve as supporters of men in these organizations. Media coverage of women's roles in peace activism is also negligible. Despite and because of the foregoing, McKay celebrates female peace activists who have been instrumental in illustrating the intersections among sexual, racial, social and economic injustices.

Recognition of feminist perspectives is relatively new within peace psychology. Women's contributions to peace psychology have focused on local mentoring and activism; men's contributions have been in academia and on global issues.

To establish a discipline of international relations that includes both men and women, gender boundaries must be eliminated. McKay calls for increased appreciation of women's contributions in all areas of public and private life.

McKay asserts that the values of peace psychology should embrace feminist consciousness and practical strategies for eliminating the constraints of male-centered thinking. She proposes a number of practical "start up" strategies to combat women's marginalization:

1. Advance feminism and feminist perspectives about sexism and the war system;

2. Describe women's experiences with militarism;

3. Understand the profound problem of sexual violence against women during war;

4. Acknowledge the relation between domestic and political violence;

5. Work for equal representation of women in designing conference proceedings;

6. Use women's (and men's) full names in papers and presentations to render their work more visible;

7. Include books/writings by and about women in peace studies courses;

8. Design pedagogical approaches that emphasize discussion of content and deemphasize lecture or other didactic approaches; and

9. Seek women's involvement in developing peace-related research projects, including the consultation from feminist scholars to include women's perspectives and the study of gender as integral parts of the research process.

McKay proffers specific examples and resources for initiating each of the foregoing "start-up strategies."

McKay encourages dialogue about how feminist inquiry can enrich the knowledge of peace psychology. She highlights common themes in feminist rhetoric – such as power and power relations, security, language, enemy imaging, conflict and conflict resolution – that can advance peace psychology. McKay insists that only when the values inherent in peace psychology and feminism converge will we be able to reduce the effects of inequality and hierarchy.

Susan McKay demands that peace psychology address the inequalities perpetuated as part of its legacy from psychology and international relations – and within the context of patriarchal society. As peace psychology grows in significance, it must be inclusive of the voices of both genders and all races.

Peace psychology, by its nature, has the responsibility to be inclusive of all marginalized, oppressed groups. Although feminist perspectives have gained more acceptance in recent years, mistreatment and marginalization of women remains common across the globe. Peace psychology affords us the unique opportunity to recognize and be at the forefront of redressing this injustice.

Peace psychology must address the egregious injustices that women endure (e.g., Donald Trump's racist and misogynistic campaign rhetoric in the 2016 United States presidential election), and the subtle and more enduring ones (e.g., disregard of women's perspectives and opinions in academia and the broader society; lower wages than their male counterparts).

To ignore these injustices is to be complicit in the violence against women and contribute to their oppression. When more than half of the world's population continues to be subjugated, we can never truly be at peace.

Reference

McKay, Susan. (1995). Women's voices in peace psychology: A feminist agenda. *Peace and Conflict: Journal of Peace Psychology, 1*(1), 67-84.

Editors' Discussion Questions

1. In what ways are women "second class citizens" in the U.S.? Is this the same in other countries or cultures?

2. Why do women have unique roles in the Peace Movement?

Chapter 65

Meanings and Preconditions of Forgiveness: A Review

TONI COOPER

Abstract: Nyarko and Punamaki (2017) interviewed 13 refugees of the Liberian Civil War and identified five themes of forgiveness: religious beliefs, apology and act of contrition, importance of justice, personal choice and influence of revered leaders. Forgiving those who commit atrocities is necessary as we move towards World Peace.

Nyarko and Punamaki's 2017 article, *"Meanings and Preconditions of Forgiveness Among Young Adult War Survivors in African Context: A Qualitative Study,"* addresses two main questions: (1) What are the experiences, memories, and histories of young adults who lived through the Liberian civil war? and (2) How do young adults who grew up in a society in conflict conceptualize forgiveness and what preconditions do they consider to forgive their persecutors?

Methodology

Nyarko and Punamaki (2017) interviewed 13 young adult Liberian refugees at Buduburam camp in Ghana. The sample was nearly evenly divided in gender. The semi-structured interviews were audiotaped, transcribed and coded.

Findings

Each of the study participants survived war atrocities and were displaced multiple times. Many of them recounted the killing and persecution of family members. One female was sexually assaulted, her mother was beaten, and her brother was shot.

Despite the small sample size, Nyarko and Punamaki derived 5 major themes from these interviews.

1. **Religious Beliefs**. Many survivors were willing to forgive as it conformed with their religious and spiritual worldviews. Religious beliefs and participation allowed them to forgive their persecutors and cope with their personal trauma.

2. **Apology and Act of Contrition**. Survivors were more likely to forgive the perpetrators who took responsibility for their heinous actions. Some survivors even sought to understand the perpetrators' behavior from their point of view.

3. **Importance of Justice**. Some of the survivors made their willingness to forgive contingent on the perpetrators' punishment. For those who espouse the law of retaliation or "an eye for an eye," only the imprisonment or punishment of their perpetrators would alleviate their suffering.

4. **Personal Choice**. Forgiveness for two of the survivors was a matter of personal choice. For one, hatred of the perpetrator was harmful to the self; for another, the failure to forgive for something that happened in the past, would damage or negatively impact that survivor's future.

5. **Influence of Revered Leaders**. For one participant, forgiveness was motivated by the example of Nelson Mandela.[1]

Discussion

Nyarko and Punamaki's (2017) study was limited by a small and non-random sample, however its strength was the in-depth interviews of each participant. Future research would benefit from larger samples from various regions.

Interventionists and clinicians might benefit from this research by better understanding when a person is ready to begin the process of forgiveness, noting that the time lapse after trauma may contribute to the willingness to forgive.

This research also has implications for society as a whole. With atrocities committed every day around the world, we must treat its victims with compassion, forgive those who commit those atrocities, and evolve toward a more compassionate and peaceful society.

---

[1] Nelson Mandela (10 May 1994 – 14 June 1999) was a South African anti-apartheid revolutionary, politician and philanthropist who, after 27 years of imprisonment for subversion, served as President of South Africa from 1994 to 1999.

According to Archbishop Desmond Tutu:

> When I talk of forgiveness, I mean the belief that you can come out the other side a better person. A better person than the one being consumed by anger and hatred. Remaining in that state locks you in a state of victimhood, making you almost dependent on the perpetrator. If you can find it in yourself to forgive, then you are no longer chained to the perpetrator. You can move on, and you can even help the perpetrator to become a better person, too.

Hope for the future of our society hinges upon our ability to make Archbishop Desmond Tutu's dream become a reality.

Reference

Nyarko, F. & Punamaki, R.L. (2017). Meanings and preconditions of forgiveness among young adult war survivors in African context: A qualitative study. *Peace and Conflict: Journal of Peace Psychology,* 23,162-173. http://dx.doi.org/10/1037/pac0000245

Editor's Discussion Questions

1. Why is the refugee problem concentrated in certain parts of the world? How does knowing the answer to this question help solve the problem?

2. Under what circumstances have you had to forgive someone? Have you ever made the decision NOT to forgive someone? Why?

3. Is it possible to forgive those who commit atrocities against others? How?

Chapter 66

Ethel Tobach and Peace Psychology

ELAINE CHOY

Abstract: Ethel Tobach was a pioneer in peace psychology. McKay, Roe and Wessells (2008) presented Tobach's life story as a model for scholar-activists pursuing World Peace. Ethel Tobach's life demonstrates that one person *can* make a difference.

This chapter reviews a biography of Ethel Tobach, a "pioneer" in peace psychology (McKay, Roe & Wessells, 2008). Her life story is a model for scholar-activists who seek World Peace.

Ethel Tobach (1921-2015) was born to a socialist Jewish family of modest means in Russia. Fleeing the Soviet persecution of Jews, Tobach's family emigrated to Palestine before permanently relocating to the United States in 1923. Her parents were always engaged in the fight against "war, poverty, and inequality" (McKay, et al., 2008). Tobach learned from her mother that she could do anything, and she was not limited by prescribed gender roles.

Her passion for peace activism emerged during her formative years in the late 1930s. In her senior year of high school, Tobach became involved with a peace movement to ban sales of weapons to the Franco dictatorship in Spain (McKay, et al., 2008). She later joined the American Student's Union and remained active throughout her first year in college.

Yearning to do more, Tobach left college in 1944 and enlisted in the Army (during the Battle of the Bulge). She witnessed the horrors of war first hand as the U.S. dropped two atomic bombs on Japanese cities. After the war ended, she returned to New York to continue her education in physiological and comparative psychology.

During her years of study, Tobach met her husband, Charles Tobach, a co-worker at a labor union. The couple was politically compatible and united in their passion for education, work and activism. They advocated for social responsibility in psychology and other fields, and were signers of the Stockholm Peace Pledge to abolish war.

Tobach earned her Ph.D. in 1957 from New York University and worked as a researcher in comparative psychology at the American Museum of Natural History for the remainder of her career. She authored numerous papers, founded the International Society for Comparative Psychologists, and held offices in New York Academy of Sciences, the Eastern Psychological Association, the Association for the Advancement of Psychology, the American Psychological Association (APA), and the Association of Women in Science.

During the Civil Rights Era, Ethel Tobach and Betty Rosoff co-founded the Genes and Gender Collective which challenged *genetic determinism* and its role in scientific racism. The Collective's diverse membership explored controversial issues and produced seven books as a result (see McKay, et al., 2008).

Tobach's involvement with the Psychologists for Social Action (PSA) encouraged more social responsibility in the American Psychological Association and increased inclusion of minorities, women and LGBT perspectives.

Tobach was elected into the New York Academy of Sciences, and received the Kurt Lewin Award by the Society for the Psychological Study of Social Issues. She was also the recipient of the Award for Lifetime Peace Activity from the Society for the Study of Peace, Conflict and Violence; and the Gold Medal Award for Life Achievement in Psychology in the Public Interest from the American Psychological Foundation.

Tobach attributed her successes to her humble beginnings, and especially to her mother for being a "strong and capable woman" (McKay, et al., 2008). Her lifetime of activism transcended peace psychology to include military abuse, religious intolerance (especially anti-Semitism), poverty in the U.S., and the plight of Native Americans.

Ethel worked tirelessly for social justice and World Peace. Her life story is a lesson for future generations: one person *can* make a difference.

Reference

McKay, S.A., Roe, M.D., & Wessells, M.G. (2008). Pioneers in U.S. peace psychology: Ethel Tobach. *Peace and Conflict, 14*, 1-14. DOI: 10/1080/ 10781910701839643

Editors' Discussion Questions

1. What about Tobach's life do you find inspirational? How does it motivate you?

2. How is *genetic determinism* related to scientific racism? How would you dispute these ideas?

Chapter 67

Constructive Disobedience: Life Lessons from Gandhi, Mandela and King

SHAWNDEEIA L. DRINKARD, M.A.

ALLIANT INTERNATIONAL UNIVERSITY-LOS ANGELES

Abstract: This chapter reviews Morselli and Passini's (2010) content analysis of the autobiographies of Mahatma Gandhi, Nelson Mandela and Martin Luther King, Jr. In addition to their commitment to non-violence, similarities between these men include a strong parental presence during childhood; salient experiences during adolescence; and critical social connections that developed during imprisonment and jailings.

Morselli and Passini (2010) reviewed the autobiographies of Mahatma Gandhi, Nelson Mandela, and Martin Luther King, Jr.,[1] in search for commonalities between the personal accounts of their childhood, adolescence, periods of incarceration and significant interpersonal relationships. They sought to understand how these iconic leaders developed the motivations for engaging in constructive disobedience.

These historic men – Mandela and King were Nobel Peace Prize recipients and Gandhi was nominated five times – were of different eras and geographic locales. Born in India and educated in London, Mahatma Gandhi (1869 – 1948) waged non-violent protest in South Africa and throughout the Indian subcontinent. Nelson Mandela (1918 – 2013), a member of the Xhosa tribe in South Africa, led the African National Congress, and spent 27 years of martyrdom when he was imprisoned for fighting to overturn *Apartheid*. A Baptist preacher from Georgia, Martin Luther King, Jr. (1929 – 1968) led the Civil Rights Movement in the U.S. during the 1950s and 1960s.

---

[1] Martin Luther King, Jr. was assassinated on April 4, 1968, leaving his autobiography unfinished. Morselli and Passini reviewed Clayborne Carson's detailed first-person account of Dr. King's life, based on voluminous archival material including previously unpublished writings, interviews, recordings and correspondence (Carson, 1998).

Morselli and Passini (2010) described how each leader developed alternative ways of thinking, became engaged in activism, and managed to find resolve in the face of persecution.

Gandhi, Mandela, and King internalized events during their adolescence that shaped the rest of their lives. When confronted with racism and discrimination, each developed a lifelong quest for the liberation of their people.

Imprisonment–for acting according to their conscience–is another common theme in these biographical accounts. These men endured multiple jailings with dignity and unwavering commitment to their causes. Indeed, they emerged from confinement energized and even more committed to their struggle. More than a punishment, imprisonment only strengthened their activism and served to validate that their cause was just and their sacrifice was both necessary and noble.

Mahatma Gandhi spent a total of 6 years and 10 months in prison; he was 75 years old during his last imprisonment. Nelson Mandela was imprisoned for 27 years, during which inmate relationships, even those with some of the guards, were integral to the development of his anti-*Apartheid* activism. Martin Luther King, Jr. was arrested and jailed 29 times in his quest for Civil Rights for all Americans. King authored one of his most famous writings, *Letter from Birmingham City Jail*, during one of these arrests.

For each leader, inmate relationships during and after imprisonment were important as they created cohesion and helped them to persevere.

The autobiographies of Mahatma Gandhi, Nelson Mandela, and Martin Luther King, Jr. – activists from different eras and parts of the world – illustrate how life events can inspire a lifetime devoted to activism.

Reference

Carson, C. (1998). *The Autobiography of Martin Luther King, Jr.* New York: Warner Books.

Morselli, D., & Passini, S. (2010). Avoiding crimes of obedience: A comparative study of the autobiographies of M.K. Gandhi, Nelson Mandela, and Martin Luther King, Jr. *Peace and Conflict, 16*, 295-319.

Editors' Discussion Questions

1. Please share what you know about each of these men. What about their lives do you most admire? How is it possible to cultivate those qualities in yourself and others?

2. Who are the heroes and sheroes in your life? Who are the people we should admire that would help lead toward World Peace?

Chapter 68

Warnings from the Past, Regarding the Future: A Review of Pettigrew (2003)

ADDISON CALCAGNINI

Abstract: Since its publication in 2003, Thomas Pettigrew's treatise remains germane for understanding contemporary human conflict. Fear, prejudice and collective threat combine to dehumanize those perceived as 'enemies.' Fear and threat set the stage for authoritarians to rise to power. Solutions include implementing Osgood's GRIT strategy (Osgood, 1962), dispelling the myths that lead to war and developing realistic empathy.

Understanding and Ending Cycles of Violence

Thomas Pettigrew's 2003 article, "Peoples Under Threat: Americans, Arabs, and Israelis," offers relevant insights into intergroup violence and the current global political climate.

Pettigrew describes how people are motivated to act in ways that do not correspond with their deeply held moral principles. He explores why Americans, Arabs, and Israelis often violate their own moral principles and values to wage war on their neighbors.

The cycle of violence involving these three groups is a reaction to extreme collective threat and fear.

Collective Threat and Fear

When we experience threat and fear, our cognitive capacity is diminished. We begin to react rather than respond; and allow emotions, not reason, to govern our actions.

When cognitive capacity is diminished, people rely on group stereotypes and perceive out-groups as more dangerous, threatening,

263

homogenous and extreme. This increased prejudice is accompanied by heightened distrust, suspicion and a narrowed acceptance of different attitudes and beliefs.

Public fears become free-floating anxiety due to the frequency of terrorist attacks, non-specific terror warnings, and government calls for hyper-vigilance in everyday situations.

Collective threat exacerbates these effects by supplying social support to people behaving illogically or immorally. We are much less likely to question our fear and prejudice when those around us appear to share our feelings.

These cognitive effects combine to amplify the dehumanization of groups that are perceived as 'enemies,' which allows us to justify using extreme preemptive violence against these groups. Pettigrew notes that people rarely aggress against others without rationalizing their force as retaliatory. When we view an outgroup as inherently ill-willed, all violence against them can be seen as justifiable.

After the 9/11 terror attacks, Americans felt so vulnerable and fearful that many did not protest when the U.S. government violated its own *Constitution* and *Military Code of Justice* by detaining, torturing and executing thousands of innocent Muslims.

Arabs and Muslims worldwide learned of these actions, thereby perpetuating the cycle of violent retaliation.

Authoritarianism

Pettigrew proffers a foreboding message along with his explanation of the rise of authoritarianism during times of collective threat. A society that is gripped by fear and seeking relief from rising panic, creates a perfect milieu for aggressive rhetoric and action.

The lack of self-reflection and insight, coupled with the punitive nature of authoritarian personalities, serves to further rationalize violence by reinforcing a polarized perception of the world. Dialogue centers around *us* and *them* – the decent people fighting for their security against the faceless, barely-human enemy.

When threat and fear are heightened, people are more likely to accept authoritarians in positions of power. In fact, these tough, 'shoot first, talk later' people who hold significant social, religious, or political power need one another to maintain the public's support. When an authoritarian commits violence against the perceived enemy, it provokes a more violent and destructive response. *Violence begets violence.*

Solutions

Osgood's GRIT

Pettigrew recommends implementing Charles Osgood's GRIT (Graduated and Reciprocated Initiatives in Tension Reduction) method to reduce tensions and resolve conflict (Osgood, 1962). This involves gradually replacing violence and mistrust with cooperation and trust through reciprocal concessions.

Pettigrew highlights the efficacy of the GRIT method in describing Israel's agreement to allow Egypt to reopen the Suez Canal. In return, Egypt allowed Israeli ships to use the canal and tensions dissipated enough to begin further negotiations.

Dispelling Myths

Pettigrew urges the denunciation of three specific myths that contribute to war. The first is *that war is inevitable.* Humans are not inherently violent and aggressive; rather these traits are learned and therefore can be unlearned. We must not forget our long history of altruism and cooperation. Pettigrew powerfully cites Adams (1989): "The same species who invented war is capable of inventing peace."

The second myth is that *one side must win;* that compromise is not possible. When one side refuses to cooperate or concede, the result is perpetual conflict and genocide.

The third harmful myth is that *military action can put an end to terrorism.* History has repeatedly shown that violence as a justification for more violence is not sustainable. Modern armies are not equipped to fight terrorists or guerilla fighters and the elusiveness of the targets has resulted in countless civilian deaths.

Realistic Empathy

In addition to using the GRIT method and unlearning pervasive, harmful myths, Pettigrew recommends developing *realistic empathy* as a means of viewing the conflict through the eyes of our opponents. Such empathy may provide the insights that could lead to the non-violent resolution of conflict and ultimately to World Peace.

Realistic empathy may provide a clue to our opponents' thoughts and feelings so that we may better understand their actions. Furthermore, this practice can remind us that our enemies are human; and that their motives are not necessarily immoral or irrational, nor are ours wholly pure.

Pettigrew does not profess to know whether humanity can end war and live in peace; but he cautions that if we do not believe that it is possible, our prophecy will be fulfilled.

We owe it to ourselves – and to future generations – to reach for World Peace.

References

Adams, D. (1989). The Seville Statement on Violence and why it is important. *Journal of Humanistic Psychology, 29*, 328–337.

Osgood, C. E. (1962). *An alternative to war or surrender*. Urbana: University of Illinois Press.

Pettigrew, T. F. (2003). Peoples under threat: Americans, Arabs, and Israelis. *Peace and Conflict: Journal of Peace Psychology, 9*(1), 69-90. doi:10.1207/s15327949pac0901_03

Editors' Discussion Questions

1. What are the sources of fears and threats in our world today? How do you respond to them?

2. Try to develop a *realistic empathy* with someone who commits a terrorist act, such as running a truck into a crowd. Describe what insights you gain into the perpetrator's motives and how he or she justifies his or her actions.

Chapter 69

White Gaze Dehumanizes: The Case of Indigenous Americans

EMILY DORREL

Abstract: S. Elizabeth Bird (1999) examined the roots of gendered stereotypes toward Indigenous Americans. She explored how images of Native American men and women evolved over time. White cultural hegemony must be dismantled to allow Native Americans to establish authentic and respectful images of their people.

Since the arrival of European colonizers in the 15th century, Native American people have been slaughtered, relocated, discriminated against, stigmatized and stereotyped. The oppressive, domineering power of White society created and promulgated negative, unauthentic, stereotypical representations of Native Americans to further marginalize them.

In her treatise, "Gendered Construction of the American Indian in Popular Media" (Bird, 1999), S. Elizabeth Bird examined how Native Americans remained under colonial domination through the media representations of gender and gender roles. Bird considered the origins and the contemporary implications of these gendered stereotypes.

First projected onto Native Americans in the 15th century, *White Gaze* (the colonialist construction of the "other" for the consumption and convenience of White people) became the means of defining, devaluing and diminishing the existence of Native People. *White Gaze* was a contrived construction of Native men and women, prescribed by the "Indian" identity foisted on them by White patriarchy. Stereotypes of Indigenous Americans as non-cerebral allowed Whites to consider themselves as superior.

In the 18th and 19th centuries, Native men were demonized for their purported "sexual savagery" and "the captivity narrative" – the idea that Native men held White women captive (Bird, 1999, p. 65). The captivity narrative became the prevailing stereotype of Native American males during the 19th century, and remained such until Native people were no longer a threat to White settlements.

The "ignoble savage" was another stereotype perpetuated by the objectifying *White Gaze*. The "ignoble savage" (or "doomed warrior") trope eroticized and exoticized Native American men as objects of fear and desire. While this stereotype in media portrayals persists; its popularity has given way to the tamer, more complaisant "noble savage."

No longer deemed a threat to White settlers, the "noble savage" was admired for his physical beauty (Bird, 1999, p. 66). The obsession over the Native American male body was consistent with an ideology that valued intellect over physicality, and linked the physical body with primitive desires, needs and drives.

White society embraced representations of Native American men and women that reduced them to sexual objects. These negative representations of Native people were juxtaposed against the positive images of White people as intelligent and capable.

Stereotypes of Native American women mirrored those of Native American men. The depiction of the Native American woman as erotic and submissive – the "Indian princess" – was comparable to the male's portrayal as the "noble savage."

Sexual prowess and satisfaction were one of the most notable differences between the princess and squaw stereotypes. The trope of the "gentle, noble, non-threateningly erotic" princess depicted Native women as naively sexual, submissive and easily manipulated (Bird, 1999, p. 72). To make the allure of the "Indian princess" more palatable for the White public, she was often portrayed with White physical features, and was viewed as beautiful, accommodating and previously untouched.

The "squaw,"[1] on the other hand, can best be described as the female equivalent of the "ignoble savage" (Dunbar-Ortiz & Gilio-Whitaker, 2016). Defined through the *White Gaze* as primal, crude and sexually promiscuous, the "squaw" signified the downfall of the "Indian princess." The "squaw" differed from the "princess" in that she embodied a sense of self confidence, sexual desire and satisfaction. Unlike the meek "Indian princess," the "squaw" enjoyed independence from White men. The "squaw" did not exist to serve or pleasure White men; rather, she embraced her sexuality

---

[1] Today, this term is recognized as an epithet.

and crudeness – traits that were antithetical to White, Christian conceptions of womanhood.

The representations of Indigenous women in Western society, for the most part, have been fabricated by White society. In fact, the portrayals of Indigenous women bear little resemblance to the reality of women's roles in many Native American tribes and societies. For example, Cherokee society is matrilineal and its members respect women as spiritual leaders and rely on them to organize the agricultural system (Perdue, 1998).

The creation of stereotyped images of Indigenous women may have been to diminish their actual prominence in American society. White, colonial depictions of Native American women grossly misrepresented, debased and dehumanized them. The stereotypes perpetuated by these representations linger in contemporary popular culture (Boyd, 2015).

Projecting images of Native American families as unstable, Whites sought to separate Native American people from one another and emphasize their purported superiority over them. These socially constructed stereotypes were then used to silence Native American people and limit their access to structural power.

Native American cultures are incredibly heterogeneous, yet these stereotyped images overlook their diversity and undermine their tribal identity.

Native American people were also commodified by the *White Gaze* for the entertainment of the White population (Meyer & Royer, 2001). Even today, representations of Native Americans in the media are oversimplified and clichéd. In movies and television, Whites appropriate Indigenous American culture to arouse nostalgia in White audiences.

More authentic representations of Native American people have begun to emerge, such as Native-directed films and documentaries like *Smoke Signals* (Eyre, 1998) and *Drunktown's Finest* (Freeland, Frazier & Burris, 2014); however stereotypical portrayals can still be found in big budget films like *The Lone Ranger* (Bruckheimer & Verbinski, 2013), wherein A-list White actors play the roles of Native people.

To challenge White cultural imperialism and end the *White Gaze,* Native Americans must have the freedom and opportunity to create authentic and respectful images of their people. It is only when all cultures are valued equally and the Earth's resources are shared, that World Peace is possible.

References

Bird, S. (1999). Gendered construction of the American Indian in popular media. *Journal of Communication, 49* (3), 61-83.

Boyd, Julia. (2015). An Examination of Native Americans in Film and Rise of Native Filmmakers. *Elon Journal of Undergraduate Research in Communications, 6* (1). <http://www.inquiriesjournal.com/a?id=1130>

Bruckheimer, J., & Verbinski, G. (Co-Producers; Directed by G. Verginski). (2013). *The Lone Ranger* (Motion Picture). United States: Walt Disney Pictures.

Dunbar-Ortiz, Roxanne, & Gilio-Whitaker, Dina. (2016). "What's the Problem with Thinking of Indian Women as Princesses or Squaws?" *"All the Real Indians Died Off" and 20 Other Myths About Native Americans*. Boston: Beacon Press, 2016. 137-44. *Bitch Media.* 09 Oct. 2016. Web.

Eyre, C. (Producer/Director). (1998). *Smoke Signals* (Motion Picture). Produced by C. Eyre, S. Alexie, C. Bressler, L. Estes, S. Rosenfelt & D. Skinner. United States: Miramax.

Frazier, M. & Burris, C. (Producers), and Freeland, S. (Director). (2014). *Drunktown's Finest* (Motion Picture). United States: Indion Entertainment Group.

Meyer, Carter Jones, & Royer, Diana. (2001). *Selling the Indian: commercializing & appropriating American Indian cultures*. Tucson: U of Arizona Press.

Perdue, Theda. (1998). Contact. *Cherokee Women: Gender and Culture Change, 1700-1835* (pp. 61-64). Lincoln, NE: U of Nebraska Press.

Editors' Discussion Questions

1. What media images of Native Americans immediately come to mind? In what ways are these images stereotypical or prejudicial?

2. How do media images differ for Native American men and women? How does that compare to the images of men and women of other ethnicities?

Chapter 70

On American Violence

DEMETRIUS LAMAR, PH.D.

UNIVERSITY OF MASSACHUSETTS, LOWELL

Abstract: Violence is especially prevalent in the United States, which has hundreds of millions of guns in circulation, and suffers tens of thousands of gun-related deaths every year. Violence is celebrated in American entertainment media, including children's programming. World Peace requires that we shift priorities from corporate profits to the common good, depict non-violent solutions to conflict; and change American norms on the use of military force.

War is an evil, inasmuch as it produces more wicked men than it takes off.

~ Immanuel Kant

Extreme violence is a grim reality of life in the West, particularly in the United States – where guns outnumber its population by more than 30 million (350 million guns for 320 million people) (Palen, 2012). From 2009 to 2013, gun manufacturers have doubled their annual production of firearms to 10.9 million guns a year (Ingraham, 2015). Relative to other nations, Americans are twice as likely to choose guns to commit suicide (CDC, 2012). The ready accessibility of lethal weapons is embedded in society. The questions we pose are – Why is the United States so steeped in violence? and What can be done to lessen its effects?

The purpose of this essay is not to impugn Americans, but to address the problem of violence in our culture. Western environments are seductive landscapes where good and evil co-exist. America's culture of violence pervades the military, politics, science, business, families and the world of sports. It is reincarnated in technology, children's toys, cinematography and news. Worse still, America's culture of violence is exported around the world.

271

Firearms and their Implication

The U.S. has earned the ignoble distinction as the world leader in death by gun violence. America, in fact, has more homicides each year than all the other Western cultures *combined* (Kirk, 2015; Miedzian, 2013). According to federal statistics, over 40% of murders go unsolved and nearly 70% are gun related (Hargrow, 2015).

With a population of 320 million, the U.S. suffers more than 30,000 handgun related deaths every year (Fairchild, 2016). By comparison, Japan, with a population of 128 million, has few firearms in civilian circulation and almost no gun-related homicides. Similarly, Canada, with its population of 34 million, suffers only 200 homicides each year—lower than the annual murder rate in the State of New York (Palen, 2012). What accounts for these disparities?

The U.S. is the number one manufacturer of firearms. American gun manufacturing had a total economic impact of nearly 50 billion dollars in 2015, with nearly 10 million guns produced (Molde & Thurman, 2016) The leading manufacturers are Ruger, Remington, Smith and Wesson, and Glock (Harkinson, 2016). These American manufacturers also sell firearms to developing countries, thus contributing to their instability.

Societies with firearms use them.

Militarism

The military features prominently in America's culture of violence. Since 1850, the U.S. has intervened militarily around the world no fewer than 150 times, an average of once a year (Kohn, 1988). The U.S. military, federal government and corporate America are inextricably linked to create what Mills calls "The Power Elite" (Mills, 1956). The chief architect of the normalization of violence in the West is the U.S. military.

The U.S. military is America's most sacred, complex and costly institution. In 2013, the U.S. Defense Department reportedly spent over 700 billion dollars researching, developing, perfecting, producing and manufacturing weapons of war (Palmer, 2013). Strongly implicated in the bloated military budget are the titans of corporate America: Raytheon, Lockheed, Boeing, Northrop, General Dynamics, General Electric, Honeywell, United Technologies and others.

The manufacture and export of weapons perpetuates violence. While the U.S. exports war around the globe, it has assumed the role of police, jury and judge over the rest of the world. With the technology to kill *en masse* without reprisal or consequence, the U.S. foreign policy has been driven by a singular mission: to control a surplus of the planet's wealth and natural resources necessary to ensure its absolute military superiority. Societies perish under the U.S. war machine not because they are "diabolical," rather because their land contains the natural resources the US. needs to maintain its military dominance.

With 5 percent of the world's population, the U.S. spends more than 50 percent of the world's total military expenditure.

The United States is the world's leading producer of Weapons of Mass Destruction.

The Role of Mass Communication

Since the advent of motion pictures and television, violence has been omnipresent and treated as legitimate entertainment. Televised warfare – real and imagined – has become a fixture in Western media. How does the media contribute to Americans' willingness to go to war?

In their formative years, children are exposed to violence in television cartoons. Cartoons portray more violence than the evening news (every 3 minutes as compared to every 12 minutes for adult programs). By age 18, young Americans will have witnessed more than 40,000 murders and 200,000 acts of violence on TV (Huston, et al., 1992). Even in the beloved children's film, *The Wizard of Oz*, Dorothy (the lead character) is implicated in the death of two people!

Killing is normalized in American entertainment and news media.

Conclusion

Violence in the United States and the rest of the West is nurtured through a variety of sophisticated environmental structures and cultural institutions. However, the most significant influence on American attitudes towards violence is the U.S. government and its military.

In his warning about the war mindset that contaminates even developing countries, Oscar Arias Sanchez, former President of Costa Rica, cautioned:

> When a country decides to invest in arms, rather than in education, housing, the environment, and health services for its people; it is depriving a whole generation of its right to prosperity and happiness. We have produced one firearm for every ten inhabitants of this planet, and yet we have not

bothered to end hunger when such a feat is well within our reach. Our international regulations allow almost three-quarters of all global arms sales to pour into the developing world with no binding international guidelines whatsoever. Our regulations do not hold countries accountable for what is done with the weapons they sell, even when the probable use of such weapons is obvious (Stubbs, 2015).

The solutions to American violence become manifest once its true causes are identified. We must de-militarize foreign policy and shift priorities from corporate profits to the common good. Mass media can reflect and usher in these changes by providing portrayals that celebrate non-violent solutions to social problems.

We must identify, challenge and eliminate the *isms* that contribute to unnecessary human suffering: militarism, racism, terrorism, nationalism, heterosexism, sexism, among others.

Most importantly, the greatest purveyors of violence – the U.S. military and its allied corporations – must acknowledge their role in creating violence at home and abroad and adopt a foreign policy that promotes the interests of the planet and encourages peaceful resolutions to conflict.

American norms for violent solutions to conflict must change if humanity is to have a chance for World Peace.

References

Bandura, A., Ross, D., & Ross, S. A. (1961). Transmission of aggression through imitation of aggressive models. *Journal of Abnormal and Social Psychology, 63*, 575-582.

Fairchild, H.H. (2016). Gun violence in America. Chapter 2 in H.H. Fairchild (Ed.), *(Re)Solving violence in America* (pp. 17-24). Delhi: Indo American Books.

Harkinson, J. (2016, February 4). Fully loaded: America's ten biggest gun manufacturing firms. Mother Jones. Retrieved from: http://www.motherjones.com/politics/2016/04/fully-loaded-ten-biggest-gun-manufacturers-america.

Huston, A. C., Donnerstein, E., Fairchild, H., Feshbach, N., Katz, P., Murray, J., Rubinstein, E., Wilcox, B. & Zuckerman, D. (1992). *Big World/Small Screen: The Role of Television in American Society.* Lincoln, NE: University of Nebraska Press.

Ingraham, C. (Oct. 10, 2015). There are now more guns than people in the United States. *The Washington Post.*

Kirk, C. (2015, October 2). The U.S. is far more violent than other rich countries. *The slate.*

Kohn, A. (1988). Make love, not war. *Psychology today, 6,* 35-38.

Miedzian, M. (2013, February 25). Why our homicide rates are the highest of any advanced industrialized country: It's not just about guns. *Huffington Post.* Retrieved from http: //www.huffingtonpost.com.

Mills, C. W. (1956). *The power elite.* New York: Oxford University Press.

Molde, J., & Thurman, R. (2016) U.S. firearms industry today 2016.*ShootingIndustry.com.* https://shootingindustry.com/u-s-firearms-industry-today-2016/

Palen, J. (2012). *The Urban World.* (9th ed). Boulder, CO: Paradigm Publishers.

Stubbs, T. (2015). *Ultimate Justice.* London: Troubador. Also, Anonymous. The Global Arms Trade: Strengthening International Regulations. Interview with Oscar Arias Sanchez. Harvard International Review. Date: Tuesday, July 1, 2008. http://www.allbusiness.com/government/ government-bodies-offices/ 11664335-1.html accessed 10 Feb 2010

Editors' Discussion Questions

1. Why do Americans cling so tenaciously to their guns?

2. Enormous wealth is generated by "the war industry." Who profits?

3. Whose interests was the U.S. military protecting, and what were the goals of U.S. involvement in the following conflicts?

   - WWI (1914-1918)
   - WWII (1939-1945)
   - Korean War (1950-1953)
   - Vietnam War (1955-1975)
   - Afghanistan (2001 – 2014)
   - Iraq (2003 – 2011)

Chapter 71
Paying the Price for Peace

FRANK DORREL

Abstract: *Paying the Price for Peace* is a 97-minute documentary that chronicles the life of anti-war peace activist S. Brian Willson, who literally used his body to block a military munitions train. Despite his tremendous sacrifice, Willson's passion for justice and dedication to peace activism has never waned.

PAYING THE PRICE FOR PEACE:

The Story of S. Brian Willson and Voices From The Peace Movement

Produced and Directed by Bo Boudart ~ Narrated by Peter Coyote

~ Associate Producer Frank Dorrel

Featuring:

Daniel Ellsberg, Ron Kovic, Roy Bourgeois, Medea Benjamin, Blase Bonpane, Martin Sheen, Alice Walker, Amy Goodman, Ramsey Clark, Camila Mejia, Phil Donahue, Col. Ann Wright, David Hartsough, David Swanson, Chelsea Manning, Charlie Clements, Charlie Liteky, Duncan Murphy, George Mizo, Jack Ryan, Bruce Gagnon, Daniel Ortega, Miguel d'Escoto, Cindy Sheehan and Ed Ellis.

Music by:

Joan Baez, Jackson Browne, Creedence Clearwater, Barry McGuire and Malcolm Payne.

Synopsis:

On September 1st, 1987, Vietnam veteran S. Brian Willson paid the price for peace when he was run over and nearly killed by a military train during a non-violent protest at The Concord Naval Weapons Station in Northern California. The train was carrying weapons that were to be shipped to Central America and used to kill innocent civilians in Nicaragua, El

Salvador & Guatemala. The train that ran over him amputated both of his lower legs. Since that life changing day, Brian has not stopped calling attention to the U.S. government's defiance of international law through waging endless illegal wars.

"PAYING THE PRICE FOR PEACE" exposes the truth about the United States' addiction to war and the lies it perpetuates in order to wage ongoing violence. Brian's story is very moving, inspirational and educational.

www.payingthepriceforpeace.com

www.brianwillson.com

www.addictedtowar.com

Editors' Discussion Questions

1. What price are you willing to pay for peace?

2. What price does the U.S. need to pay to achieve World Peace?

Chapter 72

Profile in Pacifist Courage: The Railroading of the Other Brian Willson[1]

ED RAMPELL

"In America, if you say 'Brian Wilson,' people think the Beach Boys; but in Nicaragua if you say 'Brian Willson,' people think of the peace activist," said Frank Dorrel, Associate Producer of *Paying The Price For Peace: The Story of S. Brian Willson & Voices From The Peace Movement*.

As Bo Boudart's award-winning documentary recounts, what made the *other* Brian Willson so prominent is this Vietnam veteran's commitment to the cause of peace, culminating in an enormous sacrifice. Yes, as the title indicates, Willson paid an unimaginable price for peace, but this documentary is also about the antiwar movement. Although Boudart's sprawling film focuses on Willson, it is also a compendium of the struggle for peace from the Vietnam War to the bloody U.S. intervention in Central America up to the ongoing armed conflicts in Iraq, Afghanistan and beyond.

In chronicling the U.S. peace movement for the past 50 years, *Paying The Price* is essential viewing for everyone concerned with issues of war and peace.

Today, Willson lives in Nicaragua, where he is rightfully hailed as the hero he is.

Paying The Price For Peace: The Story of S. Brian Willson & Voices From The Peace Movement won the Grand Jury Documentary Feature Award at the 2017 Awareness Film Festival.

---

[1] This Chapter is an excerpt of a film review previously published in 2017 at: http://hollywoodprogressive.com/ other-brian-willson/

Chapter 73

Remarks by President Obama and Prime Minister Abe of Japan at Hiroshima Peace Memorial[1]

Barack H. Obama and Shinzô Abe

Abstract: President Obama recalls the horrors of the atomic bombing of Hiroshima and Nagasaki. He imagines a future without nuclear weapons. He urges that we recognize our connection to one another as members of one human race. Prime Minister Abe offered condolences for the lost American lives in World War II and decried the horrors of the atomic bombing of Nagasaki and Hiroshima. He hopes that Japan and the United States will lead the way for a nuclear free world.

The White House
Office of the Press Secretary
For Immediate Release

May 27, 2016

Hiroshima Peace Memorial
Hiroshima, Japan
5:45 P.M. JST

PRESIDENT OBAMA: Seventy-one years ago, on a bright, cloudless morning, death fell from the sky and the world was changed. A flash of light and a wall of fire destroyed a city and demonstrated that mankind possessed the means to destroy itself.

Why do we come to this place, to Hiroshima? We come to ponder a terrible force unleashed in a not so distant past. We come to mourn the

---

[1] This unedited article was placed into the Public Domain on May 27, 2016 at https://obamawhitehouse.archives.gov/the-press-office/2016/05/27/remarks-president-obama-and-prime-minister-abe-japan-hiroshima-peace.

280

dead, including over 100,000 in Japanese men, women and children; thousands of Koreans; a dozen Americans held prisoner. Their souls speak to us. They ask us to look inward, to take stock of who we are and what we might become.

It is not the fact of war that sets Hiroshima apart. Artifacts tell us that violent conflict appeared with the very first man. Our early ancestors, having learned to make blades from flint and spears from wood, used these tools not just for hunting, but against their own kind. On every continent, the history of civilization is filled with war, whether driven by scarcity of grain or hunger for gold; compelled by nationalist fervor or religious zeal. Empires have risen and fallen. Peoples have been subjugated and liberated. And at each juncture, innocents have suffered, a countless toll, their names forgotten by time.

The World War that reached its brutal end in Hiroshima and Nagasaki was fought among the wealthiest and most powerful of nations. Their civilizations had given the world great cities and magnificent art. Their thinkers had advanced ideas of justice and harmony and truth. And yet, the war grew out of the same base instinct for domination or conquest that had caused conflicts among the simplest tribes; an old pattern amplified by new capabilities and without new constraints. In the span of a few years, some 60 million people would die – men, women, children no different than us, shot, beaten, marched, bombed, jailed, starved, gassed to death.

There are many sites around the world that chronicle this war – memorials that tell stories of courage and heroism; graves and empty camps that echo of unspeakable depravity. Yet in the image of a mushroom cloud that rose into these skies, we are most starkly reminded of humanity's core contradiction; how the very spark that marks us as a species – our thoughts, our imagination, our language, our tool-making, our ability to set ourselves apart from nature and bend it to our will – those very things also give us the capacity for unmatched destruction.

How often does material advancement or social innovation blind us to this truth. How easily we learn to justify violence in the name of some higher cause. Every great religion promises a pathway to love and peace and righteousness, and yet no religion has been spared from believers who have claimed their faith as a license to kill. Nations arise, telling a story that binds people together in sacrifice and cooperation, allowing for remarkable feats, but those same stories have so often been used to oppress and dehumanize those who are different.

Science allows us to communicate across the seas and fly above the clouds; to cure disease and understand the cosmos. But those same discoveries can be turned into ever-more efficient killing machines.

The wars of the modern age teach this truth. Hiroshima teaches this truth. Technological progress without an equivalent progress in human institutions can doom us. The scientific revolution that led to the splitting of an atom requires a moral revolution, as well.

That is why we come to this place. We stand here, in the middle of this city, and force ourselves to imagine the moment the bomb fell. We force ourselves to feel the dread of children confused by what they see. We listen to a silent cry. We remember all the innocents killed across the arc of that terrible war, and the wars that came before, and the wars that would follow.

Mere words cannot give voice to such suffering, but we have a shared responsibility to look directly into the eye of history and ask what we must do differently to curb such suffering again. Someday the voices of the hibakusha[2] will no longer be with us to bear witness. But the memory of the morning of August 6th, 1945 must never fade. That memory allows us to fight complacency. It fuels our moral imagination. It allows us to change.

And since that fateful day, we have made choices that give us hope. The United States and Japan forged not only an alliance, but a friendship that has won far more for our people than we could ever claim through war. The nations of Europe built a Union that replaced battlefields with bonds of commerce and democracy. Oppressed peoples and nations won liberation. An international community established institutions and treaties that worked to avoid war and aspire to restrict and roll back, and ultimately eliminate the existence of nuclear weapons.

Still, every act of aggression between nations; every act of terror and corruption and cruelty and oppression that we see around the world shows our work is never done. We may not be able to eliminate man's capacity to do evil, so nations - and the alliances that we've formed - must possess the means to defend ourselves. But among those nations like my own that hold nuclear stockpiles, we must have the courage to escape the logic of fear, and pursue a world without them.

---

[2] Hibakusha literally means "explosion-affected-people" and refers to the survivors of the 1945 atomic bomb attacks who were exposed to radiation. – The Editors.

We may not realize this goal in my lifetime. But persistent effort can roll back the possibility of catastrophe. We can chart a course that leads to the destruction of these stockpiles. We can stop the spread to new nations, and secure deadly materials from fanatics.

And yet that is not enough. For we see around the world today how even the crudest rifles and barrel bombs can serve up violence on a terrible scale. We must change our mindset about war itself - to prevent conflict through diplomacy, and strive to end conflicts after they've begun; to see our growing interdependence as a cause for peaceful cooperation and not violent competition; to define our nations not by our capacity to destroy, but by what we build.

And perhaps above all, we must reimagine our connection to one another as members of one human race. For this, too, is what makes our species unique. We're not bound by genetic code to repeat the mistakes of the past. We can learn. We can choose. We can tell our children a different story - one that describes a common humanity; one that makes war less likely and cruelty less easily accepted.

We see these stories in the hibakusha - the woman who forgave a pilot who flew the plane that dropped the atomic bomb, because she recognized that what she really hated was war itself; the man who sought out families of Americans killed here, because he believed their loss was equal to his own.

My own nation's story began with simple words: All men are created equal, and endowed by our Creator with certain unalienable rights, including life, liberty and the pursuit of happiness. Realizing that ideal has never been easy, even within our own borders, even among our own citizens.

But staying true to that story is worth the effort. It is an ideal to be strived for; an ideal that extends across continents, and across oceans. The irreducible worth of every person, the insistence that every life is precious; the radical and necessary notion that we are part of a single human family - that is the story that we all must tell.

That is why we come to Hiroshima. So that we might think of people we love – the first smile from our children in the morning; the gentle touch from a spouse over the kitchen table; the comforting embrace of a parent - we can think of those things and know that those same precious moments took place here seventy-one years ago. Those who died - they are like us. Ordinary people understand this, I think. They do not want more war. They would rather that the wonders of science be focused on improving life, and not eliminating it.

When the choices made by nations, when the choices made by leaders reflect this simple wisdom, then the lesson of Hiroshima is done.

The world was forever changed here. But today, the children of this city will go through their day in peace. What a precious thing that is. It is worth protecting, and then extending to every child. That is the future we can choose — a future in which Hiroshima and Nagasaki are known not as the dawn of atomic warfare, but as the start of our own moral awakening. (Applause.)

PRIME MINISTER ABE: (As translated.) Last year, at the 70th anniversary of the end of war, I visited the United States and made a speech as Prime Minister of Japan at a joint meeting of the U.S. Congress. That war deprived many American youngsters of their dreams and futures. Reflecting upon such harsh history, I offered my eternal condolences to all the American souls that were lost during World War II. I expressed gratitude and respect for all the people in both Japan and the United States who have been committed to reconciliation for the past 70 years.

Seventy years later, enemies who fought each other so fiercely have become friends, bonded in spirit, and have become allies, bound in trust and friendship, deep between us. The Japan-U.S. alliance, which came into the world this way, has to be an alliance of hope for the world.

So I appealed in the speech. One year has passed since then. This time, President Obama, for the first time as leader of the United States, paid a visit to Hiroshima, the city which suffered the atomic bombing. U.S. President witnessing the reality of atomic bombings and renewing his determination for a world free of nuclear weapons – this gives great hope to people all around the world who have never given up their hope for a world without nuclear weapons.

I would like to give a whole-hearted welcome to this historic visit, which had been awaited not only by the people of Hiroshima, but also by all the Japanese people. I express my sincere respect to the decision and courage of President Obama. With his decision and courage, we are opening a new chapter to the reconciliation of Japan and the United States, and in our history of trust and friendship.

A few minutes ago, together, I and President Obama offered our deepest condolences for all those who lost their lives during World War II and also by the atomic bombings. Seventy-one years ago in Hiroshima and in Nagasaki, a great number of innocent citizens' lives were cost by a single atomic bomb without mercy. Many children and many citizens perished. Each one of them had his or her life dream and beloved family. When I reflect on this sheer fact, I cannot help but feel painful grief.

Even today, there are victims who are still suffering unbearably from the bombings. Feeling of those who went through unimaginable tragic experiences, indeed, in this city 71 years ago – it is unspeakable. In their minds, various feelings must have come and gone – that of those, this must be in common: That any place in the world this tragedy must not be repeated again.

It is the responsibility of us who live in the present to firmly inherit these deep feelings. We are determined to realize a world free of nuclear weapons. No matter how long and how difficult the road will be, it is the responsibility of us who live in the present to continue to make efforts.

Children who were born on that unforgettable day lit the light believing in permanent peace. To make every effort for the peace and prosperity in the world, vowing for this light – this is the responsibility of us all who live in the present. We will definitely fulfill our responsibility. Together, Japan and the United States will become a light for hope, for the people in the world. Standing in this city, I am firmly determined, together with President Obama. This is the only way to respond to the feelings of the countless spirits – victims of the atomic bombs in Hiroshima and Nagasaki. I am convinced of this. (Applause.)

END

6:05 P.M. JST

Editors' Discussion Questions

1. How can the reconciliation between the U.S. and Japan be a model for other nations in conflict?

2. Are you in favor of global nuclear disarmament? Why or why not?

3. Is global nuclear disarmament possible? Why or why not?

Chapter 74

Address by President Obama to the 71st Session of the United Nations General Assembly[1]

Barack H. Obama

Abstract: President Obama listed many of the successes over the past eight years: averting financial crisis, the Iran nuclear deal, opening relations with Cuba, etc.). The world may choose between global cooperation or the continuation of conflict. A world in which one percent of humanity controls as much as the other 99 percent will never be stable. We must reject racism and embrace the tolerance that results from respect of all human beings.

The White House
Office of the Press Secretary
For Immediate Release

September 20, 2016

The United Nations
New York, New York

10:29 A.M. EDT

PRESIDENT OBAMA: Mr. President; Mr. Secretary General; fellow delegates; ladies and gentlemen: As I address this hall as President for the final time, let me recount the progress that we've made these last eight years.

From the depths of the greatest financial crisis of our time, we coordinated our response to avoid further catastrophe and return the global economy to growth. We've taken away terrorist safe havens, strengthened

---

[1] This unedited article was placed into the Public Domain on September 20, 2016, at https://www.whitehouse.gov/the-press-office/2016/09/20/address-president-obama-71st-session-united-nations-general-assembly

the nonproliferation regime, resolved the Iranian nuclear issue through diplomacy. We opened relations with Cuba, helped Colombia end Latin America's longest warm, and we welcome a democratically elected leader of Myanmar to this Assembly. Our assistance is helping people feed themselves, care for the sick, power communities across Africa, and promote models of development rather than dependence. And we have made international institutions like the World Bank and the International Monetary Fund more representative, while establishing a framework to protect our planet from the ravages of climate change.

This is important work. It has made a real difference in the lives of our people. And it could not have happened had we not worked together. And yet, around the globe we are seeing the same forces of global integration that have made us interdependent also expose deep fault lines in the existing international order.

We see it in the headlines every day. Around the world, refugees flow across borders in flight from brutal conflict. Financial disruptions continue to weigh upon our workers and entire communities. Across vast swaths of the Middle East, basic security, basic order has broken down. We see too many governments muzzling journalists, and quashing dissent, and censoring the flow of information. Terrorist networks use social media to prey upon the minds of our youth, endangering open societies and spurring anger against innocent immigrants and Muslims. Powerful nations contest the constraints placed on them by international law.

This is the paradox that defines our world today. A quarter century after the end of the Cold War, the world is by many measures less violent and more prosperous than ever before, and yet our societies are filled with uncertainty, and unease, and strife. Despite enormous progress, as people lose trust in institutions, governing becomes more difficult and tensions between nations become more quick to surface.

And so I believe that at this moment we all face a choice. We can choose to press forward with a better model of cooperation and integration. Or we can retreat into a world sharply divided, and ultimately in conflict, along age-old lines of nation and tribe and race and religion.

I want to suggest to you today that we must go forward, and not backward. I believe that as imperfect as they are, the principles of open markets and accountable governance, of democracy and human rights and international law that we have forged remain the firmest foundation for human progress in this century. I make this argument not based on theory or ideology, but on facts – facts that all too often, we forget in the immediacy of current events.

Here's the most important fact: The integration of our global economy has made life better for billions of men, women and children. Over the last 25 years, the number of people living in extreme poverty has been cut from nearly 40 percent of humanity to under 10 percent. That's unprecedented. And it's not an abstraction. It means children have enough to eat; mothers don't die in childbirth.

Meanwhile, cracking the genetic code promises to cure diseases that have plagued us for centuries. The Internet can deliver the entirety of human knowledge to a young girl in a remote village on a single hand-held device. In medicine and in manufacturing, in education and communications, we're experiencing a transformation of how human beings live on a scale that recalls the revolutions in agriculture and industry. And as a result, a person born today is more likely to be healthy, to live longer, and to have access to opportunity than at any time in human history.

Moreover, the collapse of colonialism and communism has allowed more people than ever before to live with the freedom to choose their leaders. Despite the real and troubling areas where freedom appears in retreat, the fact remains that the number of democracies around the world has nearly doubled in the last 25 years.

In remote corners of the world, citizens are demanding respect for the dignity of all people no matter their gender, or race, or religion, or disability, or sexual orientation, and those who deny others dignity are subject to public reproach. An explosion of social media has given ordinary people more ways to express themselves, and has raised people's expectations for those of us in power. Indeed, our international order has been so successful that we take it as a given that great powers no longer fight world wars; that the end of the Cold War lifted the shadow of nuclear Armageddon; that the battlefields of Europe have been replaced by peaceful union; that China and India remain on a path of remarkable growth.

I say all this not to whitewash the challenges we face, or to suggest complacency. Rather, I believe that we need to acknowledge these achievements in order to summon the confidence to carry this progress forward and to make sure that we do not abandon those very things that have delivered this progress.

In order to move forward, though, we do have to acknowledge that the existing path to global integration requires a course correction. As too often, those trumpeting the benefits of globalization have ignored inequality within and among nations; have ignored the enduring appeal of ethnic and sectarian identities; have left international institutions ill-equipped, underfunded, under-resourced, in order to handle transnational challenges.

And as these real problems have been neglected, alternative visions of the world have pressed forward both in the wealthiest countries and in the poorest: Religious fundamentalism; the politics of ethnicity, or tribe, or sect; aggressive nationalism; a crude populism – sometimes from the far left, but more often from the far right – which seeks to restore what they believe was a better, simpler age free of outside contamination.

We cannot dismiss these visions. They are powerful. They reflect dissatisfaction among too many of our citizens. I do not believe those visions can deliver security or prosperity over the long term, but I do believe that these visions fail to recognize, at a very basic level, our common humanity. Moreover, I believe that the acceleration of travel and technology and telecommunications – together with a global economy that depends on a global supply chain – makes it self-defeating ultimately for those who seek to reverse this progress. Today, a nation ringed by walls would only imprison itself.

So the answer cannot be a simple rejection of global integration. Instead, we must work together to make sure the benefits of such integration are broadly shared, and that the disruptions – economic, political, and cultural – that are caused by integration are squarely addressed. This is not the place for a detailed policy blueprint, but let me offer in broad strokes those areas where I believe we must do better together.

It starts with making the global economy work better for all people and not just for those at the top. While open markets, capitalism have raised standards of living around the globe, globalization combined with rapid progress and technology has also weakened the position of workers and their ability to secure a decent wage. In advanced economies like my own, unions have been undermined, and many manufacturing jobs have disappeared. Often, those who benefit most from globalization have used their political power to further undermine the position of workers.

In developing countries, labor organizations have often been suppressed, and the growth of the middle class has been held back by corruption and underinvestment. Mercantilist policies pursued by governments with export-driven models threaten to undermine the consensus that underpins global trade. And meanwhile, global capital is too often unaccountable – nearly $8 trillion stashed away in tax havens, a shadow banking system that grows beyond the reach of effective oversight.

A world in which one percent of humanity controls as much wealth as the other 99 percent will never be stable. I understand that the gaps between rich and poor are not new, but just as the child in a slum today can see the skyscraper nearby, technology now allows any person with a smartphone to see how the most privileged among us live and the contrast between their own lives and others. Expectations rise, then, faster than governments can deliver, and a pervasive sense of injustice undermine people's faith in the system.

So how do we fix this imbalance? We cannot unwind integration any more than we can stuff technology back into a box. Nor can we look to failed models of the past. If we start resorting to trade wars, market distorting subsidies, beggar thy neighbor policies, an overreliance on natural resources instead of innovation – these approaches will make us poorer, collectively, and they are more like to lead to conflict. And the stark contrast between, say, the success of the Republic of Korea and the wasteland of North Korea shows that central, planned control of the economy is a dead end.

But I do believe there's another path – one that fuels growth and innovation, and offers the clearest route to individual opportunity and national success. It does not require succumbing to a soulless capitalism that benefits only the few, but rather recognizes that economies are more successful when we close the gap between rich and poor, and growth is broadly based. And that means respecting the rights of workers so they can organize into independent unions and earn a living wage. It means investing in our people – their skills, their education, their capacity to take an idea and turn it into a business. It means strengthening the safety net that protects our people from hardship and allows them to take more risks – to look for a new job, or start a new venture.

These are the policies that I've pursued here in the United States, and with clear results. American businesses have created now 15 million new jobs. After the recession, the top one percent of Americans were capturing more than 90 percent of income growth. But today, that's down to about half. Last year, poverty in this country fell at the fastest rate in nearly 50 years. And with further investment in infrastructure and early childhood education and basic research, I'm confident that such progress will continue.

So just as I've pursued these measures here at home, so has the United States worked with many nations to curb the excesses of capitalism – not to punish wealth, but to prevent repeated crises that can destroy it. That's why we've worked with other nations to create higher and clearer standards for banking and taxation – because a society that asks less of oligarchs than ordinary citizens will rot from within. That's why we've pushed for transparency and cooperation in rooting out corruption, and tracking illicit dollars, because markets create more jobs when they're fueled by hard work, and not the capacity to extort a bribe. That's why we've worked to reach trade agreements that raise labor standards and raise environmental standards, as we've done with the Trans-Pacific Partnership, so that the benefits are more broadly shared.

And just as we benefit by combatting inequality within our countries, I believe advanced economies still need to do more to close the gap between rich and poor nations around the globe. This is difficult politically. It's difficult to spend on foreign assistance. But I do not believe this is charity. For the small fraction of what we spent at war in Iraq we could support institutions so that fragile states don't collapse in the first place, and invest in emerging economies that become markets for our goods. It's not just the right thing to do, it's the smart thing to do.

And that's why we need to follow through on our efforts to combat climate change. If we don't act boldly, the bill that could come due will be mass migrations, and cities submerged and nations displaced, and food supplies decimated, and conflicts born of despair. The Paris Agreement gives us a framework to act, but only if we scale up our ambition. And there must be a sense of urgency about bringing the agreement into force, and helping poorer countries leapfrog destructive forms of energy.

So, for the wealthiest countries, a Green Climate Fund should only be the beginning. We need to invest in research and provide market incentives to develop new technologies, and then make these technologies accessible and affordable for poorer countries. And only then can we continue lifting all people up from poverty without condemning our children to a planet beyond their capacity to repair.

So we need new models for the global marketplace, models that are inclusive and sustainable. And in the same way, we need models of governance that are inclusive and accountable to ordinary people.

I recognize not every country in this hall is going to follow the same model of governance. I do not think that America can – or should – impose our system of government on other countries. But there appears to be growing contest between authoritarianism and liberalism right now. And I want everybody to understand, I am not neutral in that contest. I believe in a liberal political order – an order built not just through elections and representative government, but also through respect for human rights and civil society, and independent judiciaries and the rule of law.

I know that some countries, which now recognize the power of free markets, still reject the model of free societies. And perhaps those of us who have been promoting democracy feel somewhat discouraged since the end of the Cold War, because we've learned that liberal democracy will not just wash across the globe in a single wave. It turns out building accountable institutions is hard work – the work of generations. The gains are often fragile. Sometimes we take one step forward and then two steps back. In countries held together by borders drawn by colonial powers, with ethnic enclaves and tribal divisions, politics and elections can sometimes appear to be a zero-sum game. And so, given the difficulty in forging true democracy in the face of these pressures, it's no surprise that some argue the future favors the strongman, a top-down model, rather than strong, democratic institutions.

But I believe this thinking is wrong. I believe the road of true democracy remains the better path. I believe that in the 21st century, economies can only grow to a certain point until they need to open up – because entrepreneurs need to access information in order to invent; young people need a global education in order to thrive; independent media needs to check the abuses of power. Without this evolution, ultimately expectations of people will not be met; suppression and stagnation will set in. And history shows that strongmen are then left with two paths – permanent crackdown, which sparks strife at home, or scapegoating enemies abroad, which can lead to war.

Now, I will admit, my belief that governments serve the individual, and not the other way around, is shaped by America's story. Our nation began with a promise of freedom that applied only to the few. But because of our democratic Constitution, because of our Bill of Rights, because of our ideals, ordinary people were able to organize, and march, and protest, and ultimately, those ideals won out – opened doors for women and minorities and workers in ways that made our economy more productive and turned our diversity into a strength; that gave innovators the chance to transform every area of human endeavor; that made it possible for someone like me to be elected President of the United States.

So, yes, my views are shaped by the specific experiences of America, but I do not think this story is unique to America. Look at the transformation that's taken place in countries as different as Japan and Chile, Indonesia, Botswana. The countries that have succeeded are ones in which people feel they have a stake.

In Europe, the progress of those countries in the former Soviet bloc that embraced democracy stand in clear contrast to those that did not. After all, the people of Ukraine did not take to the streets because of some plot imposed from abroad. They took to the streets because their leadership was for sale and they had no recourse. They demanded change because they saw life get better for people in the Baltics and in Poland, societies that were more liberal, and democratic, and open than their own.

So those of us who believe in democracy, we need to speak out forcefully, because both the facts and history, I believe, are on our side. That doesn't mean democracies are without flaws. It does mean that the cure for what ails our democracies is greater engagement by our citizens – not less.

Yes, in America, there is too much money in politics; too much entrenched partisanship; too little participation by citizens, in part because of a patchwork of laws that makes it harder to vote. In Europe, a well-intentioned Brussels often became too isolated from the normal push and pull of national politics. Too often, in capitals, decision-makers have forgotten that democracy needs to be driven by civic engagement from the bottom up, not governance by experts from the top down. And so these are real problems, and as leaders of democratic governments make the case for democracy abroad, we better strive harder to set a better example at home.

Moreover, every country will organize its government informed by centuries of history, and the circumstances of geography, and the deeply held beliefs of its people. So I recognize a traditional society may value unity and cohesion more than a diverse country like my own, which was founded upon what, at the time, was a radical idea – the idea of the liberty of individual human beings endowed with certain God-given rights. But that does not mean that ordinary people in Asia, or Africa, or the Middle East somehow prefer arbitrary rule that denies them a voice in the decisions that can shape their lives. I believe that spirit is universal. And if any of you doubt the universality of that desire, listen to the voices of young people everywhere who call out for freedom, and dignity, and the opportunity to control their own lives.

This leads me to the third thing we need to do: We must reject any forms of fundamentalism, or racism, or a belief in ethnic superiority that makes our traditional identities irreconcilable with modernity. Instead we need to embrace the tolerance that results from respect of all human beings.

It's a truism that global integration has led to a collision of cultures; trade, migration, the Internet, all these things can challenge and unsettle our most cherished identities. We see liberal societies express opposition when women choose to cover themselves. We see protests responding to Western newspaper cartoons that caricature the Prophet Muhammad. In a world that left the age of empire behind, we see Russia attempting to recover lost glory through force. Asian powers debate competing claims of history. And in Europe and the United States, you see people wrestle with concerns about immigration and changing demographics, and suggesting that somehow people who look different are corrupting the character of our countries.

Now, there's no easy answer for resolving all these social forces, and we must respect the meaning that people draw from their own traditions – from their religion, from their ethnicity, from their sense of nationhood. But I do not believe progress is possible if our desire to preserve our identities gives way to an impulse to dehumanize or dominate another group. If our religion leads us to persecute those of another faith, if we jail or beat people who are gay, if our traditions lead us to prevent girls from going to school, if we discriminate on the basis of race or tribe or ethnicity, then the fragile bonds of civilization will fray. The world is too small, we are too packed together, for us to be able to resort to those old ways of thinking.

We see this mindset in too many parts of the Middle East. There, so much of the collapse in order has been fueled because leaders sought legitimacy not because of policies or programs but by resorting to persecuting political opposition, or demonizing other religious sects, by narrowing the public space to the mosque, where in too many places perversions of a great faith were tolerated. These forces built up for years, and are now at work helping to fuel both Syria's tragic civil war and the mindless, medieval menace of ISIL.

The mindset of sectarianism, and extremism, and bloodletting, and retribution that has been taking place will not be quickly reversed. And if we are honest, we understand that no external power is going to be able to force different religious communities or ethnic communities to co-exist for long. But I do believe we have to be honest about the nature of these conflicts, and our international community must continue to work with those who seek to build rather than to destroy.

And there is a military component to that. It means being united and relentless in destroying networks like ISIL, which show no respect for human life. But it also means that in a place like Syria, where there's no ultimate military victory to be won, we're going to have to pursue the hard work of diplomacy that aims to stop the violence, and deliver aid to those in need, and support those who pursue a political settlement and can see those who are not like themselves as worthy of dignity and respect.

Across the region's conflicts, we have to insist that all parties recognize a common humanity and that nations end proxy wars that fuel disorder. Because until basic questions are answered about how communities co-exist, the embers of extremism will continue to burn, countless human beings will suffer – most of all in that region – but extremism will continue to be exported overseas. And the world is too small for us to simply be able to build a wall and prevent it from affecting our own societies.

And what is true in the Middle East is true for all of us. Surely, religious traditions can be honored and upheld while teaching young people science and math, rather than intolerance. Surely, we can sustain our unique traditions while giving women their full and rightful role in the politics and economics of a nation. Surely, we can rally our nations to solidarity while recognizing equal treatment for all communities – whether it's a religious minority in Myanmar, or an ethnic minority in Burundi, or a racial minority right here in the United States. And surely, Israelis and Palestinians will be better off if Palestinians reject incitement and recognize the legitimacy of Israel, but Israel recognizes that it cannot permanently occupy and settle Palestinian land. We all have to do better as leaders in tamping down, rather than encouraging, a notion of identity that leads us to diminish others.

And this leads me to the fourth and final thing we need to do, and that is sustain our commitment to international cooperation rooted in the rights and responsibilities of nations.

As President of the United States, I know that for most of human history, power has not been unipolar. The end of the Cold War may have led too many to forget this truth. I've noticed as President that at times, both America's adversaries and some of our allies believe that all problems were either caused by Washington or could be solved by Washington – and perhaps too many in Washington believed that as well. (Laughter.) But I believe America has been a rare superpower in human history insofar as it has been willing to think beyond narrow self-interest; that while we've made our share of mistakes over these last 25 years – and I've acknowledged some – we have strived, sometimes at great sacrifice, to align better our actions with our ideals. And as a consequence, I believe we have been a force for good.

We have secured allies. We've acted to protect the vulnerable. We supported human rights and welcomed scrutiny of our own actions. We've bound our power to international laws and institutions. When we've made mistakes, we've tried to acknowledge them. We have worked to roll back poverty and hunger and disease beyond our borders, not just within our borders.

I'm proud of that. But I also know that we can't do this alone. And I believe that if we're to meet the challenges of this century, we are all going to have to do more to build up international capacity. We cannot escape the prospect of nuclear war unless we all commit to stopping the spread of nuclear weapons and pursuing a world without them.

When Iran agrees to accept constraints on its nuclear program that enhances global security and enhances Iran's ability to work with other nations. On the other hand, when North Korea tests a bomb that endangers all of us. And any country that breaks this basic bargain must face consequences. And those nations with these weapons, like the United States, have a unique responsibility to pursue the path of reducing our stockpiles, and reaffirming basic norms like the commitment to never test them again.

We can't combat a disease like Zika that recognizes no borders – mosquitos don't respect walls – unless we make permanent the same urgency that we brought to bear against Ebola – by strengthening our own systems of public health, by investing in cures and rolling back the root causes of disease, and helping poorer countries develop a public health infrastructure.

We can only eliminate extreme poverty if the sustainable development goals that we have set are more than words on paper. Human ingenuity now gives us the capacity to feed the hungry and give all of our children – including our girls – the education that is the foundation for opportunity in our world. But we have to put our money where our mouths are.

And we can only realize the promise of this institution's founding – to replace the ravages of war with cooperation – if powerful nations like my own accept constraints. Sometimes I'm criticized in my own country for professing a belief in international norms and multilateral institutions. But I am convinced that in the long run, giving up some freedom of action – not giving up our ability to protect ourselves or pursue our core interests, but binding ourselves to international rules over the long term – enhances our security. And I think that's not just true for us.

If Russia continues to interfere in the affairs of its neighbors, it may be popular at home, it may fuel nationalist fervor for a time, but over time it is also going to diminish its stature and make its borders less secure.

In the South China Sea, a peaceful resolution of disputes offered by law will mean far greater stability than the militarization of a few rocks and reefs.

We are all stakeholders in this international system, and it calls upon all of us to invest in the success of institutions to which we belong. And the good news is, is that many nations have shown what kind of progress is possible when we make those commitments. Consider what we've accomplished here over the past few years.

Together, we mobilized some 50,000 additional troops for U.N. peacekeeping, making them nimble, better equipped, better prepared to deal with emergencies. Together, we established an Open Government Partnership so that, increasingly, transparency empowers more and more people around the globe. And together, now, we have to open our hearts and do more to help refugees who are desperate for a home.

We should all welcome the pledges of increased assistance that have been made at this General Assembly gathering. I'll be discussing that more this afternoon. But we have to follow through, even when the politics are hard. Because in the eyes of innocent men and women and children who, through no fault of their own, have had to flee everything that they know, everything that they love, we have to have the empathy to see ourselves. We have to imagine what it would be like for our family, for our children, if the unspeakable happened to us. And we should all understand that, ultimately, our world will be more secure if we are prepared to help those in need and the nations who are carrying the largest burden with respect to accommodating these refugees.

There are a lot of nations right now that are doing the right thing. But many nations – particularly those blessed with wealth and the benefits of geography – that can do more to offer a hand, even if they also insist that refugees who come to our countries have to do more to adapt to the customs and conventions of the communities that are now providing them a home.

Let me conclude by saying that I recognize history tells a different story than the one that I've talked about here today. There's a much darker and more cynical view of history that we can adopt. Human beings are too often motivated by greed and by power. Big countries for most of history have pushed smaller ones around. Tribes and ethnic groups and nation states have very often found it most convenient to define themselves by what they hate and not just those ideas that bind them together.

Time and again, human beings have believed that they finally arrived at a period of enlightenment only to repeat, then, cycles of conflict and suffering. Perhaps that's our fate. We have to remember that the choices of individual human beings led to repeated world war. But we also have to remember that the choices of individual human beings created a United Nations, so that a war like that would never happen again. Each of us as leaders, each nation can choose to reject those who appeal to our worst impulses and embrace those who appeal to our best. For we have shown that we can choose a better history.

Sitting in a prison cell, a young Martin Luther King, Jr. wrote that, "Human progress never rolls on the wheels of inevitability; it comes through the tireless efforts of men willing to be co-workers with God." And during the course of these eight years, as I've traveled to many of your nations, I have seen that spirit in our young people, who are more educated and more tolerant, and more inclusive and more diverse, and more creative than our generation; who are more empathetic and compassionate towards their fellow human beings than previous generations. And, yes, some of that comes with the idealism of youth. But it also comes with young people's access to information about other peoples and places – an understanding unique in human history that their future is bound with the fates of other human beings on the other side of the world.

I think of the thousands of health care workers from around the world who volunteered to fight Ebola. I remember the young entrepreneurs I met who are now starting new businesses in Cuba, the parliamentarians who used to be just a few years ago political prisoners in Myanmar. I think of the girls who have braved taunts or violence just to go to school in Afghanistan, and the university students who started programs online to reject the extremism of organizations like ISIL. I draw strength from the young Americans – entrepreneurs, activists, soldiers, new citizens – who are remaking our nation once again, who are unconstrained by old habits and old conventions, and unencumbered by what is, but are instead ready to seize what ought to be.

My own family is a made up of the flesh and blood and traditions and cultures and faiths from a lot of different parts of the world – just as America has been built by immigrants from every shore. And in my own life, in this country, and as President, I have learned that our identities do not have to be defined by putting someone else down, but can be enhanced by lifting somebody else up. They don't have to be defined in opposition to others, but rather by a belief in liberty and equality and justice and fairness.

And the embrace of these principles as universal doesn't weaken my particular pride, my particular love for America – it strengthens it. My belief that these ideals apply everywhere doesn't lessen my commitment to help those who look like me, or pray as I do, or pledge allegiance to my flag. But my faith in those principles does force me to expand my moral imagination and to recognize that I can best serve my own people, I can best look after my own daughters, by making sure that my actions seek what is right for all people and all children, and your daughters and your sons.

This is what I believe: that all of us can be co-workers with God. And our leadership, and our governments, and this United Nations should reflect this irreducible truth.

Thank you very much. (Applause.)

END

11:17 A.M. EDT

Editors' Discussion Questions

1. President Obama's accomplishments cannot be denied. Why was he vilified for so many years? Why would his successor, Donald J. Trump, say that Obama was "stupid," "incompetent," and the "worst president in history"?

2. President Obama suggests that everyone has a role in reaching for World Peace. What is your role? What should it be?

Chapter 75

What Is the Fourth of July to the Enslaved and Their Descendants?[1]

FREDERICK DOUGLASS AND HALFORD H. FAIRCHILD, PH.D.

My Fellow Citizens:

This is the 4th of July. It is the birthday of America's National Independence, and of *your* political freedom.

What do I, or those I represent, have to do with your national independence? Are the great principles of political freedom that are embodied in the *Declaration of Independence* extended to us? Am I asked to express gratitude for *your* independence, while *my people* are enslaved?

I and my people are *not* included within this glorious anniversary! Your celebration of independence only reveals the immeasurable distance, the chasm, between us.

The rich inheritance of justice, liberty, prosperity and independence, bequeathed by your fathers, is shared by you, not by me. The sunlight that brought life and healing to you, has brought pain, deprivation and death to me. Make no mistake: this Fourth of July is *yours*, not *mine*. *You* may rejoice, *I* must mourn.

Above your national, rapturous joy, I hear the sorrowful wail of millions whose chains, heavy and grievous, are rendered that much more intolerable by your celebration of a freedom that they have never known.

My subject is AMERICAN SLAVERY.

The character and conduct of this nation has never looked more bleak than on this 4th of July! Whether we turn to the declarations of the

---

[1] This chapter is an edited abridgement of a speech, *What to the slave is the 4th of July?*, given by Frederick Douglass to New York abolitionists on July 5, 1852. The original text was 10,420 words. The current version is reduced to 1144 words.

past, or to the professions of the present, the conduct of this nation is equally hideous and revolting. America is false to the past, false to the present, and solemnly binds herself to be false to the future. Standing with God and the crushed and bleeding slave, I denounce, with every fiber of my soul, everything that serves to perpetuate slavery — the great sin and shame of America!

What is it about slavery in America that the people of this country do not understand?

Must I prove to you that the slave is a man? That point is already conceded. The manhood of the slave is acknowledged in the enactment of laws; laws to punish his disobedience.

There are seventy-two crimes in the State of Virginia, which, if committed by a Black man, subject him to the punishment of death; while only two of the very same crimes will subject a White man to the same punishment. Does this not proclaim that the slave is a moral, intellectual and responsible being? The manhood of the slave is conceded in the fact that Southern laws forbid, under severe fines and penalties, the teaching of the slave to read or to write. When you can point to any such laws for the beasts of the field, then I might reconsider debating whether the slave is a man.

The equal manhood of the Negro race is affirmed. Is it not astonishing that, while we are ploughing, planting and reaping, using all kinds of mechanical tools; erecting houses, constructing bridges, building ships, working in metals of brass, iron, copper, silver and gold; that, while we are reading, writing and cyphering; working as clerks, merchants and architects; having among us lawyers, doctors, ministers, poets, authors, editors, orators and teachers; that, while we are engaged in all manner of enterprises common to other men: digging gold in California, capturing the whale in the Pacific, feeding sheep and cattle on the hill-side; living, moving, acting, thinking, planning, living in families as husbands, wives and children; and, above all, confessing and worshipping the Christian's God, and looking hopefully for life and immortality beyond the grave. And yet, after all that, we are called upon to prove that we are men!

Would you have me argue that man is entitled to liberty? That he is the rightful owner of his own body? Must I argue the wrongfulness of slavery? How would I look if I were to argue that men have a natural right to freedom? To do so would insult your intelligence. There is not a man beneath the canopy of heaven, that does not know that slavery is wrong *for him.*

What, then, remains to be argued? Is it that slavery is ordained by God? There is blasphemy in the thought. That which is inhumane, cannot be divine!

What, to the American slave, and his descendants, is your 4th of July? I answer: a day that reveals to us, more than all the other days in the year, the gross injustice and cruelty to which we are the constant victim. To us, your celebration is a sham; your boasted liberty, an illusion; your national greatness, swelling vanity; your sounds of rejoicing are empty and heartless; your denunciations of tyrants, brass fronted impudence; your shouts of liberty and equality, hollow mockery; your prayers and hymns, your sermons and thanksgivings, with all your religious trappings and solemnities, are, to us, mere bombast, fraud, deception, impiety, and hypocrisy — a thinly veiled attempt to cover up crimes that would disgrace a nation of savages. There is not a nation on Earth guilty of practices, more shocking and bloody, than are the people of these United States.

Go where you may, search where you will, roam through all the monarchies and despotisms of the Old World, travel through the New World, search out every abuse; and when you have found the last, lay your facts next to the everyday practices of this nation, and you will say with me: When it comes to revolting barbarity and shameless hypocrisy, *America reigns supreme*.

Fast forward to today, 2018. Two million Black and Brown men are locked in cages, like animals, working for White masters for pennies an hour. The descendants of enslaved Africans who worked the sugar cane plantations in the Caribbean are *still* working those plantations.

The vicious cycle of apartheid schools, draconian drug laws and stop-and-frisk policing results in one-third of Black and Brown bodies under the jurisdiction of law enforcement. Hundreds of unarmed men and women are killed by modern day slave catchers—police who are supposed to serve and protect—who then go unpunished in a criminal justice system that reeks of favoritism and hypocrisy.

When we say Black Lives Matter, we are saying that All Lives Matter. And until Black and Brown lives—and Yellow lives and Red lives—matter as much as White lives, we will continue our active efforts to dismantle unjust systems.

This country, the United States of America, has exercised its military muscle throughout the world in the protection of corporate profits. Since the second world war, the United States has waged war in Korea, Vietnam,

Afghanistan, Iraq, Yemen and the Sudan. These one-sided wars have killed hundreds of thousands of innocents, and for what?

Wars for profits are immoral and never justified. Spending trillions on war, while millions starve to death, is antithetical to what this country says it stands for. It is time to wage war on war, and to promise to practice war no more.

Silence is the voice of complicity!

Agitate! Agitate! Agitate!

Source

Foner, P.S. (1999). *Frederick Douglass: Selected Speeches and Writings.* (pp. 188-206). Chicago: Lawrence Hill.

Editors' Discussion Questions

1. How would Frederick Douglass critique the current domestic and foreign policy of the United States?

2. What will it take for the U.S. to live up to its ideals of freedom and opportunity for all?

Ninth Interlude
War is Not the Way

ANDY MANOFF

War is Not the Way

There's a war in Yugoslavia.
Last week it was Kuwait
And we taught peace in Panama
With guns and blood and hate

Now they say the war is over.
I say war's a shame.
Cause they're spending cash, reloading fast.
They must think it's a game

Chorus:
We can teach them
       That killing's not the answer
We can show them the way
       Hate's not the road to hate
We can help them
       If we all stand together
But before we stand a chance, we must believe
       That war is not the way

There's a war between religions
A war between the races
A war on every channel
And we just turn our faces

A war between the young and old
A war between the masses
If we don't put an end to war
We're blowing our last chances (*Chorus*)

Now there's a war in every one of us
That we don't understand
So we close our eyes and make believe
The pain will surely end

But eyes that never see the light
Will never see the day
That we can walk in harmony
And find a better way (*Final Chorus*)

© 1991. Words and Music by Andy Manoff

Afterword

A Reach for World Peace

Halford H. Fairchild and Heather F. Fairchild

The possibility of cataclysmic nuclear war, imperiling the planet and claiming billions of lives, is ever-present.

We hold the optimistic view that World Peace is possible. Yet we do not envision a world at peace within our lifetime or even within the next few hundred years. Our reasoning for this time frame is tied directly to the enormity of the task: changing a host of long-ingrained ideological, cultural and institutional practices that make violence and war all but inevitable.

Changing Ideologies

Social Dawinism and "Survival of the Fittest"

As noted throughout this text, evolutionary psychology has been ascendant in recent years. Jhangiani and Tarry (2014), the open access textbook that we used to provide background to *Social Psychology and World Peace: A Primer*, relied extensively on evolutionary theory. Consequently, much of the current text debunks the mis-applications of Darwinian theory to account for social phenomena ranging from interpersonal attraction to violence and aggression.

The notion that certain groups are superior to others is at the heart of colonial conquest and the conflict between races and nations. The European "Age of Discovery" coincided with its conquest of continents whose indigenous populations were deemed savage and inferior. Social Darwinism was used to justify this conquest and gave rise to the ideology of White Supremacy.

Sexism/Masculinism

The "Survival of the Fittest" ideology has also justified gender inequality throughout the world. In virtually every modern society, men rule families, communities and nations. They do so on false premises derived, in part, from Darwinian thinking.

This belief in male supremacy – and the cultural and institutional practices that derive therefrom – is the root cause of many of the problems of the world: racial and ethnic conflict, wealth inequality, poverty, global warming, violence and war.

But male dominance is not hard wired into our genes. Rather, it is an imposed condition that is at the heart of all other conflicts, from within families to between nations. Male dominance is not universal and, therefore, cannot be part of the natural order of things. Indeed, male dominance imposes an unnatural order on human relationships that catalyze the problems enumerated above.

Gender relations that elevate men in superordinate positions over women must be challenged and made egalitarian. This applies to relationships and marriages, the workplace, commerce, politics and religion. Gendered hierarchies in organized religions are especially problematic and should be dismantled (Fairchild, 2016b).

Truly egalitarian societies do exist. They are based on communal and cooperative living, where children engage in non-competitive games and acts of interpersonal violence are non-existent (Boyette, 2016; Grøntvedt, & Kennair, 2013; Leach, 2002; Lepowsky, 1994, 1999). Although fewer in number, matriarchal societies – in which women control decision making and resources – exist throughout the world; and generally live in peace (Mattison, 2011; Sudha, 2004).

American Exceptionalism

The United States is fond of claiming "exceptionalism" in world affairs. The U.S. purports to be "different and better" than other nations. But the notion of American exceptionalism is a fraud.

The "Founding Fathers" of the United States ratified a *Constitution* that barred women from voting or inheriting property, and counted African Americans as three-fifths of a person. American "freedom" was defined in a way that permitted slavery and wars against the indigenous populations. American "democracy" was limited to a small segment of the population –

White, male, and propertied. The anti-democratic nature of American democratic systems was starkly revealed in the 2016 presidential elections.[1]

What actually makes the U.S. "exceptional" is its military dominance and its willingness to use intimidation and force to bludgeon weaker countries.

We must reject the notion of "American exceptionalism" and instead make reparations to nations and people that have been exploited by American power.

Militarism

The U.S. boasts the most powerful military on Earth, with annual expenditures in excess of $600 million (in 2017) – more than the next 8 nations combined. And yet, American political elites promote the fiction that the military is "depleted" and in need of even more funding. The U.S. too often succumbs to the "Law of the Hammer": *if we have the weapons, we must find a reason to use them.* Notable examples of the foregoing were the bombings of Hiroshima and Nagasaki in 1945; and more recently, the "Mother of All Bombs" dropped in Afghanistan on April 13, 2017.[2] The U.S. is responsible for more than 20 million deaths in 37 different countries since WWII (Lucas, 2015). The U.S. is the world leader in selling military weaponry to other countries, often giveaways in the form of "foreign aid."

Militarism contradicts every democratic and religious ideal that its proponents profess to cherish. The taking of human life is contradictory to an empathic and psychologically healthy way of interacting with others.

Changing Cultural Practices

Media

Mass media must eschew portrayals of interpersonal violence in favor of pro-social ones. Children's television programming should be non-

---

[1] If "democracy" connotes "one person, one vote," then the U.S. electoral process is systematically anti-democratic. The electoral college was created as a concession to slave states during the writing of the *Constitution*, granting them—and other small states—disproportionate representation. Gerrymandering at the local level maintains a two-party system that disenfranchises people of color and the poor.

[2] On April 13, 2017, the U.S. struck an area of Afghanistan with the $16 million dollar GBU-43/B, commonly known as the Mother of All Bombs – a bomb with the destructive power of over 11 tons of TNT and a blast radius of more than one mile. According to one source, 36 Islamic State terrorists were killed (Fox News, 2017). The number of civilian casualties was undisclosed.

violent and encourage non-violent resolution to conflict. Those who create and produce media content must self-censor to ensure that their works have positive effects on viewers and society at large. Images of human killing and mayhem ought to be morally "off limits" for creators, artists, producers and consumers alike. The visual and aural arts must forego productions that glorify war and violence, and instead advance visions that lead to social harmony and World Peace.

Sports

The ideologies that give rise to war – Social Darwinism, masculinism and militarism – are embodied in many competitive sports, particularly American style football, ice hockey, boxing and mixed martial arts. These sports celebrate aggression, violence and injury. They are emblematic of a society that has misplaced values. As argued elsewhere, we advocate for the abolition of ostentatiously violent sports that lead to serious life-threatening injury and death (Fairchild, 2016b).

Guns

The U.S.'s preoccupation with guns must be challenged and dismantled. Whereas the U.S. reports more than 30,000 gun-related deaths every year, Japan recorded 12 gun-related deaths in all of 2013 (Aleem, 2015).

Even in the aftermath of horrific news, such as the October 1, 2017 mass shooting in Las Vegas that claimed 59 lives and injured more than 500 others, the immediate and vociferous response in the U.S. is to defend the Second Amendment and to buy even more guns.

Guns permeate American culture – from entertainment media to children's toys. It could be that the nation's fascination with guns is a carry-over of the way in which the nation was founded: through the killing of Indigenous Americans and the forced enslavement of millions of Africans and their descendants.

Changing Institutional Practices

Improving Social Environments and Eradicating Poverty

African American and Latin@ men and women are more likely to be imprisoned in America because they have been corralled in an intergenerational cycle of failing schools, informal economies, petty crimes and involvement in the criminal justice system (Fairchild & Fairchild, 2017).

Native American Nations remain out-of-sight and out-of-mind on Indian "reservations"[3] and live predictable lives of not so quiet desperation.

The solution is to transform urban environments (and Indian "reservations") from enclaves of despair to lands of hope and opportunity. Fundamental changes in national priorities – from militarism to human development – can make these utopian visions a reality (Fairchild & Fairchild, 2017). The long over-due revitalization of urban areas and Indian reservations would provide full employment for its residents. Schools must be adequately resourced and held accountable to produce citizens equipped to participate and thrive in a highly technological society.

Abolition of Prisons

The criminal justice system was first established to catch runaway slaves (Abdullah, 2017). Today, the U.S. imprisons more of its population than any other industrialized nation; indeed, more than many third world countries (Fairchild, 2016a). African American men, per capita, are six times more likely to be incarcerated than White men. The chains of slavery have been transformed into the bars of today's jails and prisons.

The practice of placing men and women in cages and treating them as objects of scorn – punishment without rehabilitation – is contrary to what it means to be human. Prisons must be replaced with humane rehabilitation practices.

Exploring Alternatives to War

As of this writing (December 2017), wars are raging all over the globe. In a study of 162 countries, only 11 were free of violent conflict (Withnall, 2014).[4] Hundreds of thousands of innocent civilians – perhaps millions – have been killed in just the past two decades. World leaders seem to suffer from a universal *groupthink* wherein non-violent resolutions to conflict are rarely considered or even mentioned.

We call for the abolition of war. If violent conflict is ruled out as a means of intergroup negotiation, then only non-violent solutions remain.

What is needed is a paradigm shift – from war to peace. The U.S., the self-proclaimed world's only superpower and the world's greatest

---

[3] Indian "reservations" exist throughout the Americas. A more apt term might be "resettlement ghettoes.

[4] The 11 conflict-free nations were Switzerland, Japan, Qatar, Mauritius, Uruguay, Chile, Botswana, Costa Rica, Vietnam, Panama and Brazil.

purveyor of violence, must renounce its history of regime change and bombing populations, and replace it with a compassionate altruism that brings peace and prosperity at home and abroad. Instead of increased investments in the military, we must push societies toward de-militarization (cf. Glaser, 2016). Such a paradigm shift will come only if the public demands it.

It is incumbent upon the citizens of the world to envision and demand World Peace.

Budgeting for Peace

The pursuit of peace requires a budget (Fairchild, 2016b). To parallel the Department of Defense (more aptly named the Department of War), we can create a Department of Peace that provides funding for comprehensive research programs, human relations retreats, and investments in the eradication of poverty and the mal-distribution of resources that provide the catalysts for conflict and war.

Conclusion

World Peace is achievable once it is made desirable. We must change social norms to encourage the non-violent resolution of conflict.

Inter-group schisms are a product of hundreds of years of history. The histories of European and American exploitation have created tremendous wealth inequalities between individuals, races, nations and continents. Economic systems perpetuate these inequalities and contribute to the conditions that give rise to war. At the very least, the exploitation should be acknowledged and halted, and reparations made wherever possible. A return of stolen wealth would be the ultimate expression of justice.

Instead of increased military spending and arms sales; the objective should be, ultimately, disarmament and the cessation of war.

At the individual level, children should be socialized to counter the divisive influences in their social environment. Children must be given an opportunity for inter-cultural contacts, and exposed to media images that promote peaceful social relationships.

Institutions must ensure equal opportunities, equal access, and equal outcomes in well-being. The vast wealth of Earth must be equitably shared. The health and wellness of every human being is a necessary condition for World Peace.

References

Abdullah, M. (2017). Black lives matter: Past, present and future. Foreword (pp. xxiii to xxix) in H.H. Fairchild (Ed.), *Black Lives Matter: Lifespan Perspectives*. Delhi: Indo American Books.

Aleem, Z. (2015). Japan is showing the rest of the world how to deal with gun violence. Mic (October 16, 2015). https://mic.com/articles/126573/japan-has-shown-the-rest-of-the-world-how-to-eliminate-shooting-deaths#.RosMYmVtO

Boyette, A. H. (2016). Children's play and culture learning in an egalitarian foraging society. *Child Development, 87*(3), 759-769. doi:10.1111/cdev.12496

Fairchild, H.H. (Ed.) (2016a). *(Re)Solving violence in America*. Delhi: Indo American Books.

Fairchild, H.H. (2016b). (Re)Solving violence in America. Chapter 11 (pp. 87-96) in H.H. Fairchild (Ed.), *(Re)Solving violence in America*. Delhi: Indo American Books.

Fairchild, H.H., & Fairchild, H.F. (2017). Reflections on Black Lives Matter. Afterword (pp. 307-316 in H.H. Fairchild (Ed.), *Black lives matter: Lifespan perspectives*. Delhi: Indo American Books.

Fox News (2017). Mother of all bombs kills 36 Islamic State terrorists. http://www.foxnews.com/world/2017/04/14/mother-all-bombs-kills-36-islamic-state-militants-afghanistan-officials-say.html

Glaser, J. (2016). Why we should close America's overseas military bases. Time.com (October 7, 2016). http://time.com/4511744/american-military-bases-overseas/

Grøntvedt, T. V., & Kennair, L. E. O. (2013). Age preferences in a gender egalitarian society. *Journal of Social, Evolutionary, and Cultural Psychology, 7*(3), 239-249. doi:10.1037/h0099199

Jhangiani, R., & Tarry, H. (2014). *Principles of social psychology – 1ˢᵗ international edition*. Licensed under a Creative Commons Attribution-NonCommerical-ShareAlike 4.0 International License.

Leach, C. W. (2002). Democracy's dilemma: Explaining racial inequality in egalitarian societies. *Sociological Forum, 17*(4), 681-696. doi:10.1023/A:1021033608845

Lepowsky, M. (1994). Women, men, and aggression in an egalitarian society. *Sex Roles, 30*(3-4), 199-211. doi:10.1007/BF01420990

Lepowsky, M. (1999). Women, men, and aggression in an egalitarian society. In L.A. Peplau, S.C. DeBro, R.C. Veniegas, P.L. Taylor (Eds.), *Gender, culture and ethnicity: Current research about women and men*. (pp. 284-290). Mountain View, CA, US: Mayfield Publishing Co.

Lucas, J.A. (2015). The U.S. has killed more than 20 million people in 37 nations since WWII. https://popularresistance.org/us-has-killed-more-than-20-million-in-37-nations-since-wwii/.

Mattison, S. M. (2011). *Demystifying the mosuo: The behavioral ecology of kinship and reproduction in china's 'last matriarchal' society.* (2011-99110-185).

Sudha, S. (2004). Review of women at the center: Life in a modern matriarchy. *Journal of Marriage and Family, 66*(5), 1339-1350. doi:10.1111/j.0022-2445.2004.00br6.x

Withnall, A. (2014). World peace? These are the only 11 countries in the world that are actually free from conflict. *Independent* (August 11).

Social Psychology and World Peace: A Primer

Artwork by Alannah Forman and Kara Miller-Radest

About the Contributors

Shinzô Abe is the Prime Minister of Japan.

Nicholas S. Abreu is a pre-med student majoring in science and management. He plans on attending medical school to become an orthopedic surgeon. His hometown is Minden, Nevada.

Omar Alireza, an international student at Pitzer College from Saudi Arabia, is on a mission to make the world a better place.

Ross Altman is a singer, song writer and peace activist in Los Angeles.

Paris D. Atwater is a student at Pitzer College. He is majoring in economic and organization studies. He is co-founder of TSB and lives in Maryland.

Justin Darnell Blankson-Phipps is a student at Pitzer College. He graduated from The Peddie School of New Jersey in 2015 as class president. He currently resides in Loganville, Georgia.

Blase Bonpane is Director of the Office of Americas.

Theresa Bonpane is a peace activist and founder of the Office of Americas.

Therese Boter is pursuing a Bachelors of Arts in Economics, with a minor in English, at Pitzer College (Class of 2019). Originally from Honolulu, Hawaii, her passion is for social justice at home and abroad.

Alicia M. Breyer is a recent graduate of Psychology from Scripps College. She lives and plays bridge in Burlingame, CA.

Addison Calcagnini is an artist and educator who strongly believes in the necessity and possibility of positive social change. She graduated from Pitzer College in 2016.

Carla Casares earned her Bachelors of Arts in Organizational Sciences and Economics from Pitzer College in 2017. She is an advocate in the local food movement and hopes to pursue a career in consulting.

Austin Caviness attends Pitzer College (2018-2019) and is a student of social justice.

Tianze Cheng was raised in Dubai, UAE, is currently a student at Pitzer College who is interested in topics along world peace and disarmament. He would like to pursue a career in science.

Casey Chong is a junior at Pitzer College, majoring in sociology. Born and raised in Hilo, Hawaii, she plans to work tirelessly for world peace.

Elaine Choy graduated from Florida Institute of Technology with a B.A. in psychology (2015). She is pursuing a Master's of Science in Human Factors at Embry-Riddle Aeronautical University.

Toni Cooper is a graduate of Azusa Pacific University who dedicates her life to reducing stigma associated with homelessness. She desires to live a life of mercy, justice and humility.

D. Lisa Cothran, a social psychologist, is an Associate Professor of Psychology at Alabama State University.

Erick Cruz Grave is a human biology major at Pitzer College (Class of 2019). He plans to attend medical school and pursue a specialty in gastroenterology.

Kassidy Cuccia-Aguirre is a student at Pitzer College (Class of 2018), where she double majors in political studies and organizational studies. She has been involved in campus leadership programs including the Student Senate. She currently lives in San Dimas, California.

Dennis Davis is a musical artist, songwriter and producer. He produced the documentary, "Women at War: Forgotten Voices of Female Gulf War Veterans" (www.womenatwarmovie.com).

Max Davis is a student at Pitzer College, majoring in economics. American born, he has lived in Indonesia, Papua New Guinea, Australia, Argentina, Nigeria and, most recently, Thailand.

Emily Dorrel is a graduate of Rhetoric and MEDIA Studies from Lewis & Clark College in Portland, OR. She currently attends graduate school in California.

Frank Dorrel is publisher of *Addicted to War* and a leading peace activist in Southern California.

Shawndeeia Drinkard is a fourth year PhD candidate in Clinical Psychology at Alliant International University-Los Angeles, and an active advocate for social change.

Halford H. Fairchild, Ph.D. is Professor Emeritus at Pitzer College in Psychology and Africana Studies. He lives, writes and plays poker in Culver City, CA.

Heather Feiga Fairchild, Esq., is a retired attorney and co-owner of Fairchild Tax Service in Los Angeles. She lives, writes and plays poker in Culver City, CA.

Sasha Forbath is a sophomore at Pitzer College, majoring in organizational studies with a minor in sociology. In 2017, she plans to study abroad in Australia and Nepal. She has no idea what the future may hold, but hopes that it features world travel.

Alannah Forman is a sophomore at Pitzer College. Her current interests include organizational studies, economics and media studies.

Madeleine Glouner is an undergraduate student at Scripps College, majoring in psychology with a focus on human desire.

Aidan Hall is a student at Pitzer College (Class of 2019), majoring in Neuroscience with a Neuropsychology focus. He grew up in Tokyo, Japan, and thinks this work will help unite the world in understanding and peace.

Ed Rampell is a freelance writer who lives in Southern California.

Gillian Hsieh Ratliff is a human biology major at Pitzer College (Class of 2017). She hopes to work in global health. She believes this book not only highlights current obstacles to world peace, but provides a workable solution.

Demetrius Lamar Ph.D., is an Adjunct Professor at University of Massachusetts, Lowell where he teaches Principles of Sociology, Urban Sociology, and Cultures of the World.

Yiran Li (Krystal) is a student at Pitzer College (Class of 2019), majoring in media studies and considering a minor in psychology. She intends to pursue a career in entertainment, specifically video editing.

William "Court" Mangum was born and raised just outside of Boston, Massachusetts, and is a student at Pitzer College. He majors in economics and plans to embark on a career in alternative energy.

Andy Manoff is a peace activist, singer/songwriter who lives in Culver City, CA. Andymanoff@myspace.com.

Samuel Andrew Benjamin Martin is a student at Pitzer College (Class of 2019), majoring in environmental science. Born in San Diego, California, he is a graduate of The Preuss School UCSD (2015).

Matre is an accomplished hip-hop artist, songwriter and educator. Inspired by the transformative power of hip-hop culture and the arts, he tours internationally, performing, speaking, and hosting dialogues, with a focus on community empowerment and social justice.

Taylor Mensik is a student at Pitzer College, majoring in business. The Pacific Palisades, California resident hopes to earn his MBA.

Kara Miller-Radest hails from Chatham, New Jersey, and is a student at Pitzer College. She is a member of the Pomona-Pitzer swim team and enjoys drawing and painting.

Barack H. Obama was the 44th President of the United States (2009-2017).

Brandon O'Neal is a graduate of Claremont McKenna College. He currently lives in Taiwan where he started his brand Blasiantw filming short skits.

Haley Sparks is a psychology doctoral student at The University of Michigan advocating for the empowerment, advancement and wellness of Black women in all aspects of their lives.

Earl M Schultz is a Chicago native and student-athlete at Pitzer College (Class of 2018) majoring in human biology with a minor in dance. He plans to pursue a career in physical therapy.

Acknowledgements

Thanks are due to Vijay Sharma and Agnel Henry, of Indo American Books – and their staff and co-workers – for their faith in this project and expertise in bringing it to fruition.

We are grateful to the countless activists who have embraced movements for peace and social justice. They have put their lives on the line for the benefit of us all.

1. Madeleine Glouner
2. Earl M. Shultz
3. Carla Casares
4. Kassidy Cuccia-Aguirre
5. Taylor Mensik
6. Casey Chong
7. William "Court" Mangum
8. Nick Abreu
9. Erick Cruz-Grave
10. Gillian Hsieh-Ratliff
11. Sasha Forbath
12. Heather Feigá Fairchild
13. Sam Martin
14. Kara Miller-Radest

15. Alicia Breyer
16. Therese Boter
17. Halford H. Fairchild
18. Alannah Forman
19. Tarik Alireza
20. Tianze Cheng
21. Justin Blankson-Phipps
22. Max Davis
23. Austin Caviness
24. Branden O'Neal
25. Yiran "Krystal" Li
26. Aidan Hall
27. Paris Atwater